# DUNCOMBE'S FREE BANKING

# DUNCOMBE'S
# FREE BANKING

AN ESSAY ON

BANKING, CURRENCY, FINANCE, EXCHANGES

AND

POLITICAL ECONOMY

BY

CHARLES DUNCOMBE

[ 1841 ]

REPRINTS OF ECONOMIC CLASSICS

AUGUSTUS M. KELLEY · PUBLISHERS
NEW YORK 1969

First Edition 1841

(Cleveland: Printed by Sanford & Co., 1841)


Reprinted 1969 by

Augustus M. Kelley • Publishers

*New York New York 10010*


SBN 678 00530 3

---

Library of Congress Catalogue Card Number

68–27852

---

PRINTED IN THE UNITED STATES OF AMERICA
*by* SENTRY PRESS, NEW YORK, N. Y. 10019

# MEMORIAL TO CONGRESS

## UPON THE SUBJECT OF

# REPUBLICAN FREE BANKING.

*To the Honorable the Senate, and*
*House of Representatives, in Congress assembled :*

Your memorialists, feeling the importance of a sound currency to a nation desirous of maintaining their political independence, and financial and commercial prosperity, and having observed the zealous, though unsuccessful exertions for years past, of the Congress of the United States and the several State Legislatures, through the agency of incorporated banking companies, to make bank paper and gold silver at all times interchangeable for each other, and current throughout the Union; and having witnessed, with painful anxiety, the various operations of the present chartered bank system of furnishing paper to circulate as money, and finding it to be extremely defective, and occasioning the public much inconvenience, as the bank notes issued under it are not uniformly current throughout the Union, thereby making the rates of exchanges high between distant parts of the United States, expensive and inconvenient in remitting funds from place to place, and in defraying travelling expenses. And also, having seen the frequent expansions, contractions and various fluctuations of the circulating medium furnished under this system, by which the value of property is rendered uncertain, and money looses its peculiar business properties, that of being a medial commodity, passing freely from one person to another, and as an exact, uniform, and unchangeable a measure of values, for past, present and future times, as standard weights and measures are of quantities, and precisely the same throughout the Union.

Your memorialists, therefore, are of the opinion, that there must be something radically wrong in the elementary principles of the present system of banking, as conducted by incorporated companies, to produce such a discrepancy in its working in unison with the other fundamental political machinery of our government; and would respectfully repr esent, that the spirit of the Declaration of Independence, and of the Constitution, gives the people the right to expect the same free control of the currency that they have of the other elementary principles of the government, consequently there should be no more legislation upon that subject than upon the form of our government, our religion or literature.

In the hope of transmitting to the latest posterity, pure, entire and unimpaired, those great and glorious principles of human happiness, of national and individual prosperity, centered in our government by its patriotic founders; and with a view to a radical renovation of our monetary affairs, we beg leave to call the attention of your honorable body to the following plan for Republican Free Banking, in the expectation that your collective wisdom may adopt it, or devise some permanent and efficient system of banking better adapted to the genius of our government, the character of our institutions, and the state of existing contracts, than that of our present incorporated banking companies.

The following plan, based upon the principles of the Declaration of Independence, and of the Constitution, centralizes the government of the currency; thereby furnishing us with all the national advantages of a United States bank, while it avoids its apprehended, financial and political evils by a divided administration, and escapes the vexed question of its constitutionality. It obviates the danger of over-expansions and contractions of the currency, by removing the *influence of private interest, of credit, and of politics.* The first is effected, by giving the people the election of the directors of the Banks, both of Issue and of Discount. The second, by separating the Bank of Issue from the Banks of Discount, and limiting its circulation to not more than three times the amount of specie actually in its vaults at the time of the issue; and confining the Banks of Discount to the discounting of actual business paper, having but short periods to run, and in which no director has any interest. The third, by removing the necessity for future legislation upon the subjects of banks and currency.

This plan is the organization of the people, by Congress, throughout the Union for financial purposes, with power to regulate the pa-

per portion of the currency as they are at present organized to regulate their township adminstrations. Empowering the electors of
the Union to elect the directors of the United States Bank—the
Bank of Issue ; the electors of each State the directors of their respective State Banks ; and the electors of each place, where a Bank
of Discount is located, the directors of such banks respectively;
as they elect the most numerous branches of their legislatures.

The directors of the United States Bank—the Bank of Issue—
should be elected for the same length of time as are the Senators of
the United States, and so that only one-sixth part of them should
vacate their seats annually, for the purpose of giving permanency
and stability to the currency ; while the directors of all the other
Banks should be elected annually to secure their frequent and perfect accountability to the people.

The management of the currency will then, like the other elementary principles of our government, be purely republican.

The duties of the directors of the U. States Bank of Issue shall be,
to ascertain the amount of currency necessary for the permanent
prosperity of the country ; to cause plates to be engraved and bills to
be printed, in the best manner, to avoid counterfeits, and that there
may be a uniformity in their appearance ; and cause to be signed,
registered and numbered so many bills of such denominations as
shall be necessary for the convenient interchange of commodities,
and issue the same to the directors of the several State Banks, according to their demands, together with their respective proportions
of specie.

The duties of the directors of the several State Banks shall be, to
cause to be re-signed and re-registered the bills issued to them respectively by the United States Bank of Issue, and to apportion the
same among their several local Banks according to their demands
for the same, together with their respective proportions of specie,
and to take a general supervision of the same.

The duties of the directors of the several local Banks—the
Banks of Discount—(after giving good security for the faithful discharge of their duties, and the prompt payment over to their successors, when their terms of office shall expire, of all monies or property of the bank in their hands,) shall be, to execute the bills furnished them by their respective State Banks, by signing them, and making them payable in specie on demand, at their several counters,

and loan the same, by discounting actual business paper, having but short periods to rnn, and in which no bank director has any interest, either directly or indirectly.

The directors of the local Banks should not loan large sums to speculators, when their doing so will deprive them of the means of discounting the regular business paper of the place; although such speculators can afford to make the loan much more profitable to the stockholders than their ordinary business, by making their notes due in a distant city, to which they export their purchases, and where the rate of exchange is high against the place where the bank is located, on which place, in addition to the lawful interest, the bankers can sell their drafts for a large premium on the exchange. The election of the directors by the people interested in the dis- counts, will obviate this; since one hundred fair traders, who re- quire a credit at the bank of one thousand dollars each, will exercise far more influence at the election of directors, than one speculator with one hundred thousand dollars. American manufactures will thus be encouraged—inland commerce facilitated—the farming in- terests promoted—and paper money be made strictly convertible, uniform in its value, and as easily to be obtained as other commod- ities, without interfering with existing banking institutions.

The insiduous encroachments upon society, through chartered banking companies, of dishonest principles in our business transac- tions, of a depravity of moral sentiment, and disregard of moral honor and honesty in the conduct of our monetary affairs, will be effectually checked by the adoption of the proposed system of Re- publican Free Banking. The evasion of a law, is but one step short of its open violation. And the passage of bank notes at par, which are one, five or ten per cent. below par, is but one step from paying out a parcel of bills, in which there is known to the payer to be one, five or ten dollars of counterfeit money.

This system of Republican Free Banking, that your memorialists propose to your honorable body for adoption, is designed to give the paper portion of the currency a metalic character; with all the ad- vantages to the bill-holders and stockholders that could be obtained by a chartered United States bank and branches, without the dangers and inconveniences of the centralized administration of such an im- mense financial and political power as the latter must possess, and from the laws of its situation would be likely to exercise. It centralizes the government of the currency and divides its administration. Giving to the United States Bank—the Bank of Issue—the centralized control of the capital stock, the specie received for the sale of the stock, the issue and apportionment of the bills and specie among the several State Banks the profits, the safety fund, the dividends, the forms of business, and of making returns for publication. While it completely separates the administration of the currency from the general U. States or several State Banks of Issue, and divides it among the people, by giving to the electors of the several places where local Banks—the Banks of Discount—are situated, the election of the directors of the same respectively; and confines these banks to the discounting of only actual business paper, having but short periods to run, and in which no director has an interest, either directly or indirectly, and to the ordinary business of a bank of discount. This will render the administration of the currency as divided and independent of its government, as are the election of the officers and administration of the affairs of the townships separate and independent of the government of the Union.

Your memorialists trust, that the stock of an United States Bank, founded upon the principles of republican free banking, will be as saleable and productive as any stocks in America; while it will constitute a bond of union between the citizens and government of this country upon the all-powerful principle of self-interest, equal to that which supports the government of Great Britain in the bond of private interest caused by its national debt, without any of its concomitant evils. This stock would probably constitute the most profitable, safe and permanent investment of capital in the United States, if not in the world: being cash in hand when capital is required, money at interest at all times, and convertible into specie the same as the funded debts of America or England. The bill-holder would be secure from the failure of banks, or the depreciation of their notes; and the public from the expansions and ruinous consecutive contractions of the currency.

Your memorialists, therefore, respectfully pray, that your honorable body will be pleased to take the subject of the banks and currency into your serious consideration; and to authorise the people to provide themselves with a republican currency, that shall be free from the influence of private interest, credit, or politics—strictly convertible, uniformly current throughout the Union, and as easily to be

obtained as other commodities; or in such manner as your honorable body may deem meet, provide for the formation of a sound currency, that shall be current throughout the Union. And your peti-
tioners, as in duty bound, will ever pray, &c.

☞This Memorial has been forwarded by mail to above
four hundred Editors of news-papers, without distinction
of party, with a request for them to publish it, and an offer
of one copy of this book (price One Dollar,) on their send-
ing a paper containing the same to the Author.

# A LETTER

## TO THE

## THE HON. THE SECRETARY OF STATE,

———

CLEVELAND, OHIO, JUNE, 1841.

To THE HON. DANIEL WEBSTER,

SECRETARY OF STATE, &c. &c. WASHINGTON.

HON. SIR:—

I see by the newspapers, that there is a proposition before Congress for an United States Bank; and believing that it is not only the privilege, but the duty of every American citizen, frankly to communicate to the government whatever may appear to him to be important, and having spent much time and attention for several years past upon the subject of Banks, Currency and Exchanges, I take the liberty of forwarding to you briefly my views upon the subject.

The plan I propose is an United States Bank of Issue, with a centralized government, and local Banks of Discount, with divided and independent administrations. This would render currency as republican as the other elementary principles of the government; separate it from POLITICS, from CREDIT, and from the influence of PRIVATE INTEREST; and make bank notes always perfectly interchangeable for gold and silver, equally current throughout the Union, and as easily to be obtained as any other commodities.

I find but few men of either of the great political parties, of any profession, trade or business, who do not believe with me, that the enterprising "go ahead" spirit of Americans, the present state of contracts both at home and abroad, public and private, as well as the inflated credit currencies of Great Britain, and most other countries with which our foreign commerce is carried on, require a larger circulating medium than the quantity of the precious metals that could at present be brought into circulation constitute.

To whom then of right belongs the regulation of the material, that is to a certain extent to supply their place and make up the deficiency? I answer to the sovereign power—that is, to the whole people. In a monarchy, a government of force and fear, the Sovereign should regulate the currency, directly by his own officers, or indirectly through chartered companies exercising their powers at his pleasure.

I conceive the unconstitutionality of chartering companies, to consist in the representative disposing of the trusts delegated to him for a longer period than he had been elected, to companies whose private rights supervene and preclude his successor in office from disannulling his acts, however dissatisfactory to his constituents they may have become; whereby the representative is unable to return into the hands of his constituents ALL the powers that had been entrusted to him. This is equally applicable to States as to United States charters.

I view the evils of a chartered United States bank, with branches, to consist in the concentration of the wealth and money of the country, which, from the laws of its situation, must constitute a powerful financial and political engine; always accumulative and directed to the promotion of its own ends, and the advancement of its own friends. With such an engine at its disposal, a corrupt administration might perpetuate itself as long as it chose to support the bank.

If it be said, that we have had United States banks, with branches, that did not perpetuate themselves, nor the administrations that supported them; to this I reply, the banking business of the country was not then concentrated in one institution—state chartered banks were not only sometimes actually arrayed against the United States Bank, but they accommodated great portions of the community with their credit, rendering them independent of that bank; besides, we may never have had an administration sufficiently corrupt to unite itself to the bank, and through its agency, to bribe the press and thus control legislation; therefore, I by no means view this circumstance as at all conclusive that such an event could not happen.

The object sought to be obtained by the legislature in authorising the issue and circulation of bank paper as money, is to furnish a portion of the circulating medium sufficient to supply the deficiency of the precious metals, occasioned by their exportation, possessing metalic financial properties; being equally current throughout the Union, always strictly convertible at the counter where it was put in circulation, and not liable to be over-issued.

Chartered banking companies, whether incorporated by Congress or state legis-latures, have all failed in their efforts to accomplish this object; and they must continue to fail sooner or later, however carefully their charters are guarded, while they have the whole control of the currency. The laws of their situation compel them to make as much money out of the people and out of the government as they legally can.

Some of the defects of state chartered banks arise from a want of a centralized government of their issues. The currency they produce wants in uniformity in its metalic character; in uniformity in its quantity of circulation; in uniformity in its currency throughout the Union; and it wants in public confidence from its occa-sional defective interchangeability.

A chartered United States Bank, with branches, would remedy some of the exist-ing evils of the currency; but the directors, (like those of all other chartered in-stitutions,) being interested in its business and dividends, must, according to the laws of their situation, make as much money as they can by their charter.

They might be induced to deal in exchanges, as did the old United States Bank, which, by its power of expanding the currency temporarily at points where it wish-ed to purchase, and contracting it at points where it wished to sell, (which it could do at will, to an almost unlimited extent,) kept the currency and exchanges in a constant state of fluctuation and uncertainty, while those who sold bills got less, and those who bought paid more for them, than they would have done had the busi-ness been left to private competition, as it is in other parts of the world; or they might directly themselves, or indirectly, through the agencies of brokers and spec-ulators, engage in commerce and speculations, as did the United States Bank of Pennsylvania—when a similar fate must, sooner or later, overtake them; or, by dis-counting fictitious notes and acceptances, payable at distant places advantageous to themselves, give their credit to speculators to large amounts, to the exclusion of the fair trader, the injury of commerce, and the over-expansions and consecutive con-tractions of the currency.

The proposed plan, by centralizing the government of the currency, possesses all the advantages of an United States Bank and branches, both to the public and to HONEST stockholders, and divides the administration of the currency, thereby whol-ly, entirely and perfectly removing the justly to be apprehended evils of the con-centration of such an immense monied power.

I know of no sound political or financial reason, why the paper portion of the currency should be entrusted to the regulation and control of one or more interested private companies, any more than should be the control of the mint, or the regulation of weights and measures. Money, being the measure of all values, should be as immutable and permanently established as either of these are. Nor can I fancy any good reason, besides the exploded one of expediency, why a few individuals should be allowed to make a profit upon the circulation of paper to make up the deficiency of the precious metals ; or why they should be allowed any more to interfere with its regulation on account of their being stockholders, than would be the holders of States or of United States funds, or than are the holders of the funds of Great Britain, or of any other country. No one will doubt the inexpediency and impolicy of allowing one or more private companies the control and regulation of the public debts.

All these exigencies may, however, be provided for by giving the people the election of the directors of the banks, in the same manner as they elect the most numerous branches of their legislatures, (instead of leaving it to stockholders, who have uniformly exclusively enjoyed it ;) and separating the Bank of Issue from the Banks of Discount ; centralizing the government of the former, and rendering the administration of the latter divided and independent. This may be done by the passage of a law by Congress, authorising the electors throughout the Union to elect directors of the United States Bank, the Bank of Issue ; the electors in each State to elect directors of State Banks, of secondary issue and supervision ; the electors of cities, towns and districts, where Banks of Discount are located, the election of the directors of the same. The directors of Banks of Discount should give good security for the monies passing through their hands ; be restricted in their discounts to not issue more paper than three times the amount of specie in the vaults of the bank at the time of the discount ; and to discounting only actual business paper, having but short periods to run, and in which no director has any interest. They would be limited to the amount of bills furnished them by the Bank of Issue. This would give the people the same control of the currency that they have of their politics.

The centralization of the paper portion of the currency, by giving the United States Bank of Issue the regulation and control of the stock, the specie received for the sale of the stock, the issue of bills to circulate as money, their apportionment (together with the specie necessary for a basis,) between the several States according to their respective demands for a circulating medium, the apportionment of the dividends of the Banks between the stockholders, the reservation of a safety fund, and its application when necessary to relieve any temporary casual embar-

rassments of a Bank or Banks of Discount, and the publication of regular periodical statements of the institution, with every other power necessary to the perfect
government of the currency, that would not interfere with its independent administration by the Banks of Discount. This would give this institution and the country all the benefits of an United States Bank and branches, without its dangerous
concentration of power and influence ; while dividing the administration of the
Banks of Discount between the several cities, towns, and districts, where they are
located, and by whose electors the directors are elected, would complete its independence.

The friends of republican institutions may safely rely for support upon the democracy of numbers possessing virtue and intelligence, unless the power and influence of the aristocracy of wealth should, through the aid of the interest of chartered companies, suborn the press and thereby bandage the people's eyes.

To prevent this, the proposed plan provides this profitable Bank Stock for the investment of capital, to unite the private interests of capitalists in support of republican institutions ; becoming a bond of union between the wealth and wealthy of
the country and our government, upon the all-powerful principle of SELF-INTEREST,
similar to that which unites the monied men of Great Britain in support of their
government.

With an anxious desire for the promotion of the peace, prosperity and good government of these United States, and with high respect for yourself,

I have the honor to subscribe myself,

Your most obedient servant,

CHARLES DUNCOMBE.

# DUNCOMBE'S FREE BANKING:

## AN ESSAY

ON

## BANKING, CURRENCY, FINANCE, EXCHANGES,

AND

## POLITICAL ECONOMY.

BY CHARLES DUNCOMBE,

A NATIVE AMERICAN.

Late Chairman of the Committee on Finance, Chairman of the Committee on Currency and Banking, Acting Commissioner for obtaining information during the recess of Parliament in 1835, upon the subjects of Schools and Colleges, Lunatic Asylums, Finance, Currency, Banking, and other subjects of Public Economy, and Author of a Report upon Education, in the Parliament of Upper Canada.

CLEVELAND:

PRINTED BY SANFORD & CO.

1841.

# CONTENTS.

Page

## CHAPTER VIII.

## CHAPTER XXXIII.

## CHAPTER XXXIV.

## CHAPTER XXXV.

## CHAPTER XXXVI.

## CHAPTER XXXVII.

## CHAPTER XXXVIII.

## CHAPTER XXXIX.

# DEDICATION.

---

In dedicating to you this " Republican Free Banking System," the Author feels the same pleasure that an honest faithful servant feels when he presents his master with a grain of valuable choice seed, which he has cultivated, and with which he hopes to see his master's grounds occupied, and his master thereby permanently enriched.

He dedicates to you, young men, because you are strong, and appointed under Heaven ere long to guide the destinies of the innumerable millions that are to occupy the largest continent on the globe.

He honestly believes that he herewith presents you with a grain of pure republicanism, which may be made a staple product of America if cultivated with your care and industry, and reared under your vigilant superintendance.

Anti-republican, aristocratic, incorporated banking companies have rendered currency a *calcareous* stone in the granite arch of the republican edifice.

If you desire to perpetuate republican institutions in the United States ; if you have studied the political history of our country, and become thoroughly acquainted with the

elementary principles of our government ; and if you have
made yourselves familiar with political and public economy,
after you have read, thoroughly investigated, pondered and
reflected in your own minds upon the republican free banking system herewith dedicated to you, the author may rely
with implicit confidence upon your rendering a verdict in its
favor.

He is proud to subscribe himself,

Young Men,

Your most obedient servant,

THE AUTHOR.

# PREFACE.

The present state of the monetary affairs of the United States—the contraction of liabilities in a foreign country—the sale of State Bonds and various public stocks in the English market—the withdrawal of specie from circulation—the advance of the price of exchanges on London—the high rate of domestic exchanges between the different parts of the Union—the increasing importations of foreign merchandize upon credit, without the prospect of corresponding exportations—the frequent expansions and contractions of the issues of chartered banks, and their repeated suspensions of specie payments, their dependence upon legislative enactments for relief, for new charters, and for an increase of bank capital stock—the substitution of bank paper for capital—the inundation of the country with small unauthorized bills, circulating as money—the increasing action and extension of an unlimited credit system—and the instability of public opinion upon the subject of currency, by which laws for the suppression of small bills, or for preventing bank suspensions, loudly called for by the people at one time, at another time becoming inoperative ; each and all of these causes, having separately and conjointly occasionally produced fluctuations in money—commercial embarrassments—instability in business—as well as a propensity to gambling in stocks, in money, in commodi-

ties, and in lands ; also, political excitement at the election
of the Chief Magistrate—a depravity of moral sentiment
and feeling—an absence of moral honor and honesty in the
conduct of the monetary and financial affairs of the country, must have attracted the attention of all Americans with
well constituted minds, who are not interested in the con-
tinuation of the present defective currency and its abuses—
convincing them that there must be something radically
wrong in the elementary principles of the paper portion of
the currency, as at present furnished by chartered banking
companies, to admit of such repeated expansions and consecutive contractions of the currency, and to induce them to
cast about in their mind's eye for some new system of currency better adapted to the genius of the American people,
as well as to existing values and contracts both at home and
abroad.

Reflections upon this condition of our financial currency
and public economy, and an anxious desire to promote the
peace, prosperity and good government of the Union, have
induced the author to take advantage of the present tran-
quility of the country, while it is free from external alarm,
or impending domestic political excitement, to offer to republican America, a crude undigested system of currency,
composed in part of the precious metals, and in part of
large bills, mutually, perfectly interchangeable for each
other, giving each person the kind of currency he desires,
by the preference that each class of society will have for
that kind of currency least desirable to the other.

The mechanic and laborer will prefer the precious metals to bank notes, from their greater convenience in making
small payments, as well as from their less perishable character by fire, or by time, and especially from their lessened danger of depreciation from political or financial chang-

es; while the commercial man and large dealer will prefer bank paper equally current throughout the United
States, perfectly convertible into specie at the counter
where it was issued, to the precious metals, from its less
labor of counting and less expense of transportation from
market to market.

The author has recommended a *centralized* government
of the currency, to obtain the benefits to the currency of a
United States Bank, and a profitable, permanent investment of capital, with a perfectly *divided* and *independent*
*administration* of the currency, like the administration of
townships, safely to guard against the justly apprehended
danger of the concentration of such an immense monetary
power in the hands of a few interested individuals, whether foreigners or Americans—

That every section of the country may be accommodated with all the facilities of bank convenience, and each individual enjoy his just share in the regulation of the paper
portion of the currency, in the same manner that he enjoys
the right of regulating common schools, as well as to have
it convenient to use, at par at all times, the kind of currency
he prefers, whether it be gold and silver, or current convertible bank paper;

To prevent the inconvertibility of bank paper, he recommends the separation of the bank of issue from banks
of discount and deposit;

To remove private interest from influencing the directors of the banks of discount, either in their discounts, loans
or dividends, they are to be precluded from discounting any
note or acceptance in which a director of a bank may be
interested;

To guard against over-expansions, discounts are to be
confined to actual business paper, having but short periods

to run, to the amount of bills issued by the bank of issue, and never to exceed three times the amount of specie actually in the vaults of the bank at the time of the discount;

Removing credit from currency, by not allowing the issue of paper to circulate as money upon public bonds, notes of other banks, or other public or private evidences of debt, or foreign or domestic exchanges, or aught save a due proportion of gold and silver ;

Removing the influence of politics from the currency, by superceding the necessity of legislative interference in the incorporation of new banks, or the extension of powers and privileges to old ones ;

Rendering the currency republican, by the free election of the directors of the banks by those persons immediately and directly interested in the currency of the place, in the same manner as they elect the most numerous branch of their legislatures.

This plan of a currency, next to its being always convertible and uniformly current throughout the Union, is most valuable as being calculated to encourage domestic manufactures, and prevent the over-importation of foreign merchandize.

This must appear evident from the fact, that every man wishes to have money plenty in his own place, and will have it so whenever it is left entirely to his own choice. Consequently, the interests of the directors will be the same.

If the West imports less foreign merchandize from the East, the East will import less from Europe.

Banks will loan their money to the manufacturer and fair trader of the place, as well for the common interest of the place, as because these men can exercise an influence upon the election of directors ; who, having no direct interest in the dividends, will no longer lend large sums to foreign speculators to obtain the repayment in a foreign place, to enhance the profits of the bank, because a loan of $50,000 to a speculator lessens their means of lending to one hundred men $500 each, while the votes and influence of these one hundred men at the next election must out number that of one speculator.

This would soon reduce our imports to the par exchange of our exports; facilitate the payment of our foreign, commercial, state stock, and bank stock debts; aid in the completion of the immense works of internal improvement that have already commenced without the means of their completion; giving new life and activity to business, and additional stimulus to laudable American enterprise.

# NOTICE OF THE PLAN OF CURRENCY.

The Author proposes to render the paper portion of the currency republican; always perfectly convertible at sight at the counter where it was put in circulation; equally current throughout the Union, and as easily to be obtained as any other commodity.

To accomplish this, he proposes removing from the currency the influence of *private interest*, of *credit*, and of *politics*—centralizing the government of the currency, dividing its administration, and making each bank of discount independent—separating the bank of issue from the banks of discount—limiting the discounts to *not more* than three times the amount of specie actually in the vaults of the bank at the time of the discount, and to the amount of bills furnished in blank to the banks of discount by the bank of issue—confining the supply to the actual demand for currency, by restricting the discounts to actual business paper, having but short periods to run—allowing the free exportation of specie as the only effectual means of preventing over-trading and over-importing—issuing no small bills, that all the small channels of circulation may be filled with the precious metals, as well as to furnish small dealers with the metalic currency of their choice, and large dealers with large current convertible bills for their convenience, by the preference of each class of community for that kind of currency least desirable to the other.

To separate currency from politics. Let Congress organize the people throughout the Union for financial purposes, as they are at present organized for township and
for state political purposes; authorizing them to elect the
directors of all the banks, both of issue and of discount, in
the same manner as they elect the most numerous branch of
the legislature.

Let the people throughout the Union elect directors of a
United States Bank : whose duty it shall be to ascertain
the amount of specie in the country, and the amount of currency required for the permanent prosperity of the country ; to issue blank bank bills upon so much of the specie as
shall appear to be necessary to increase the amount of currency to the actual demand for the convenient interchange
of the commodities of the country; and to apportion the
specie and bills between the several states, in proportion to
their several demands for the same.

Let the electors of each state elect directors of state
banks, to apportion the specie and bills furnished by the
United States Bank of issue, to such parts of each state as
require banks of discount located in them, and to take a
general supervision of the same.

Let the electors of the several cities, towns and districts,
where a bank of discount is required to be located, elect directors of the same, who shall give good security for the
faithful discharge of their duties, and who shall only discount actual business paper, having but short periods to run,
and in which discount *no director has any interest.*

The people being thus organized ; the directors accountable for their conduct, and precluded from any interest in
the discounts—their hope of re-election, their salaries, and
their securities' bonds, will make it their private as well as
public interest, to promote the public good only—there

would be no longer any occasion for legislative interference with banks and currency. Thus currency may be *separated from private interest*, and from politics; rendered strictly convertible, uniformly current throughout the Union, and as republican as our religion or literature.

The centralization of the government of the currency, will render the bills as current throughout the Union as would be the notes of an incorporated United States Bank and branches; while the *divided and independent administration* of the currency removes the financial and political evils of the *centralized administration*, that must by the laws of its situation, attend an incorporated United States Bank.

The government—the capital stock—the specie received for the sale of stock—the issue and apportionment of the specie and bills—the profits—the safety fund—the dividends—the forms of business—of keeping accounts and of making returns for publication, are to be centralized; while the election of the directors of the banks of discount—their sureties for the faithful discharge of their duties—the discount of notes and acceptances—the collection of their debts—the publication of their monthly reports—and all the ordinary business of a bank of discount, must be as divided and independent of the government of currency, as the election of the officers and administration of the affairs of the townships are separate and distinct from the government of the Union.

The election of the directors of banks by the persons interested in the loans and business of the bank and the soundness of the currency, will change the character and business of the banks, by giving the loans of the bank equally to the fair traders of the place, instead of being loaned in large sums exclusively to a few speculators—as the fair traders of the place will exercise the most influence in the election of directors. This will retain the money in the place, and most effectually lessen over-trading; institute a bond of union between the citizens and government of this country upon the all-powerful principle of self-interest, equal to that which supports the government of Great Britain in the bond of private interest found in the national debt, without any of its concomitant evils.

The stock would be the most profitable, safe and permanent investment in the United States, if not in the world ; being cash in hand when capital is required, and money at interest at all times, by its being always saleable in the money market, as are the funded debts of England and America. The bill holder would be perfectly secure from loss from failures of banks, or the depreciation of the currency ; nor would the public be subjected to the evils attendant upon their expansions and contractions ; the convertibility of the notes certain beyond doubt, and the bank paper portion of the currency equally current throughout the Union. In short, this system of banking must place the paper portion of the currency, (being based exclusively upon the precious metals,) upon an equality with gold and silver.

A judicious modification of the usury laws, and appropriate bankrupt laws, must make money as easily to be obtained as any other commodity ; reduce our imports to the par exchange of our exports, and render the currency of the country the key-stone of the arch of this republic.

# INTRODUCTION.

THE author, while chairman of the committee of Finance in the Parliament of Upper Canada, in 1835, was deputed by a resolution of the House of Assembly, to travel in the United States and elsewhere, during the recess of Parliament, to obtain information upon various subjects of public economy, and to report to the House the result of his research at the next meeting of Parliament.

Among the subjects of his enquiry were exchanges, finance, currency and banking.

While in the United States, he was very politely furnished with every facility necessary to the accomplishment of the object of his mission, by political economists, financiers, bankers and merchants; by the members of the administration, as well as by those out of office, and opposed to the administration of the day.

The result of his enquiry upon the subject of banking was, a thorough conviction of the anti-republican tendency of incorporated banking companies, and a confirmation of his opinion, previously expressed in a report made to the House of Assembly during the previous session, by a committee of eleven members appointed upon the subject of currency and banking, of which he was chairman. The object of that committee was, to ascertain whether any better system of furnishing paper to circulate as money, to supply the deficiency of the precious metals, than that

afforded by the chartered bank system, could be devised.
The committee reported in favor of giving the people the
divided administration of the currency, and centralizing the
government of the paper intended to circulate as money,
with the view of separating currency from politics, and removing from the control of the administration of the government the administration of the currency; preventing its
centralized monopoly in commercial transactions and its
political aristocratic tendency. The dissolution of Parliament by Sir Francis Bond Head, the official influence, bribery, corruption, and cunning trickery, with the force and
violence of organized bands of Orangemen, had recourse
to by the executive government at the subsequent election,
to obtain the return of a tory Parliament, induced the re-
formers of Upper Canada to depute the author to London,
to lay before His Majesty's government and the Imperial
Parliament, the manner in which the executive government
of the Province had destroyed the elective franchise in that
Province, and rendered the House of Assembly the mere
tools of the executive government, a mere shield to their
nefarious and ruinous measures : believing that if His Majesty's government was fully and correctly informed of the
grievances of the country, and the manner in which the
people had been unjustly defrauded of their constitutional
rights and privileges, that His Majesty would order a new
election of the House of Assembly, free from the exercise
of bribery and corruption, or of intimidation on the part of
the executive government of the Province ; or direct the
administration of the government of the Province to be
conducted according to the constitutional act of the Province, making the Executive Council responsible to the people through the House of Assembly, after the manner in

which His Majesty's Ministers of the Crown in England are responsible to the House of Commons.

The insurrection near Toronto, under Mr. McKenzie, with which the author was totally ignorant until after the defeat of the Patriots—the order of the government for his arrest and execution—the collection around him of his friends, and their offer to defend him—their voluntary separation upon his advice and recommendation, and his return to his native country, the United States, prevented him from completing and publishing the plan of currency and banking herewith presented to the people of the United States.

His experience for the last few years, and observations of the defective workings of the chartered bank paper currency of the United States, has more than ever confirmed him in the belief, that there is something radically wrong in the fundamental principles of the currency, produced by the issues of incorporated banking companies, whether they be incorporated by the Congress of the United States, or by the legislatures of the several States.

The repeated suspensions of specie payments by the incorporated State banks of the United States—the fluctuations of the currency, and frequent inconvertibility of bank notes—the expense and inconvenience attending the making remittances from one part of the Union to another—as well as the high rate of exchanges with commercial Europe against the United States, are beginning to attract great attention in Europe as well as in the United States.

The thinking portion of the American people with well constituted minds, who are not interested in the present system of incorporated banks, and not influenced by political party prejudices, but who are honestly desirous, by every means in their power, of promoting the peace, pros-

perity and good government of the United States, are beginning to feel and understand that there must be something radically wrong in the elementary principles of currency and banking, as practiced and conducted in the United States, to admit of such frequently repeated, wild and
delusive expansions of the currency and its ruinous consecutive contractions.

If the fundamental principles of the currency were correct, the sagacity and cunning ingenuity of "Yankee speculators would have invented" a remedy for its defective operations.

Changes in the currency have frequently been attempted
by the Congress of the United States, as well as by the
Legislatures of the different States—sometimes with a view
to its permanent uniform perfect convertibility—sometimes
with the intention of rendering it generally current throughout the Union; but more frequently with the hope of increasing the quantity of the circulating medium, without
the expense and difficulty of increasing the amount of the
precious metals, upon which alone a permanent increase of
the money currency can ever be rationally expected to be
effected. But all these changes have failed in converting
credit into cash.

Small banking companies have been formed in the hope
of supplying villages and inland towns with money, when
the inhabitants were unable to obtain loans from the banks
of the large cities. Banks have been incorporated with
large capitals, in the expectation that the credit of an immense banking capital would be a safe-guard against panics,
and enable the institution to support its business against the
most unfavorable currents of trade. But the discounting
fictitious paper, that is, any paper not actual business paper
having but short periods to run, soon exhausted their funds,

and compelled the contractions of their issues, with its usual disastrous consequences ; and, although each of these plans may have succeeded for a time, yet, as they extended their issues beyond their specie basis, the large as well as the small banks, ultimately disappointed the expectations of their adherents.

The projectors of these institutions appear to have lost sight of the first and all-powerful elementary principles of political economy, by which currency and banking are uniformly governed : That the demand and supply always regulate the value of gold and silver, as well as of all other commodities; that the free exportation of specie is the only certain mode of effectually preventing over-trading and over-importing; that credits, whether large or small, and whether made by many small institutions, or by one large one, must be paid sooner or later ; that bank paper is no more capital, than the shoe-maker's promises to *make* your shoes, are shoes ; that, at best, it is but the representative of coin, and cannot perform *all* the functions of coin ; that they who borrow money, and spend more than their incomes, must become impoverished, while they who earn more than they spend, must accumulate wealth ; that the party who lends money safely, and receives the interest thereof, becomes rich, while he who borrows money and pays interest, becomes poor, all other things being equal.

Over issues of bank paper, with the unerring certainty of fate, will sooner or later bring about corresponding contractions, with their ruinous and disastrous consequences. The banks fill the channels of circulation to overflowing: the natural effects of which is the exportation of the surplus. Bank notes not being exportable, they are returned upon the banks for specie for exportation.

Over issues of bank paper produce advanced prices for

foreign merchandize; this leads to increased importations and the exportation of specie. With this diminution of specie, generally occurs a diminution of public confidence : with the diminution of its credit and its specie means, are lessened its ability to discount paper, and lend money, with an increased necessity for calling upon its debtors for pay- ment. This produces a general pressure for money. High rates of interest are demanded by the few who have money to lend. Brokers are making splendid fortunes; bankers are sharing in the spoils of their usurious extortions, while universal ruin pervades the land. Bankruptcies, failures, suspensions of specie payments by the banks, and suspen- sions of business by the commercial community, follow in their train.

The enriching of the few, and the ruin of the many, are the usual and universal consequences of over issues.

## HISTORY OF THE FIRST BANKS.

The first bank established in the United States, was chartered by Congress on the 31st day of December, 1781, with a capital of $10,000,000, without limitation of dura- tion. This charter was confirmed by the legislature of Pennsylvania in 1782; and in 1785, its excesses and ruin- ous effects upon business had become so apparent, that the legislature revoked its state charter. The bank, however, had already become too strong for public opinion. Disre- garding the revocation of its charter by the State of Penn- sylvania, it prosecuted its business under its United States charter until 1787, when it was re-chartered by the State of Pennsylvania, its capital limited to $2,000,000, and *time* limited to 14 years.

## ROBERT MORRIS.

The Chicago Democrat says, " Robert Morris, the man

to whose financial operations our country in the revolution-
ary struggle is said to owe as much as to the negotiations
of Franklin, or the arms of Washington, passed the latter
years of his life in prison, confined for debt,—a victim to
the banking system, which he was among the first to establish in America. Rich in early life, he embarked in a
series of speculations, which rendered him hopelessly insolvent. In 1780, he established a bank by subscription,
in which his share was £10,000, for the express purpose of
supplying the army with 3,000,000 rations and 300 hogs-
heads of rum.

" The following year, the bank of North America superceded this bank, and eventually led its stockholders into
speculations, which proved their ruin, and great detriment
to the country at large."

## THE HISTORY OF BANK SUSPENSIONS.

The first suspension of specie payment by the banks of
the United States, was in 1814, (all previous suspensions
had been called failures.) This occurred soon after the
capture of Washington, the Capitol of the United States,
by the British. The battle of Bladensburg was on the 24th
of August, and on the 27th of the same month, the banks
of Baltimore suspended specie payment, which was followed by the banks of Philadelphia on the 30th, and those of
New York on the 1st September following. This suspension, however, had for apology the exigencies of the times.
It occurred during a great National struggle, in which the
defenders of the American flag and of the National honor,
had to contend with a powerful foreign foe, and the hostile,
secretly growing, aristocratic chartered banking companies
of the several States.

After the resumption of specie payments by the banks in

1817, the public mind began to repose with implicit confidence in the efficiency of incorporated banks; hoping, that
under the vigilance of legislative supervision, with salutary
restrictions, they might serve to furnish the public with
paper to circulate as money to meet the deficiency produced in the circulating medium by the exportation of the
precious metals.

But the second suspension, which commenced in New
York on the 10th May, 1837, and which extended east and
west with the rapidity of " wild fire," for it was followed
by the suspension of the banks of Philadelphia on the 11th,
and by the banks at Boston and Baltimore on the 12th, and
with but few exceptions by all the banks in the Union,
with telegraphic succession. This suspension shocked the
cautious, and nearly overturned the confidence of the most
faithful bankites, for it had not the apology of the dangers
of an external foe, that surrounded them in 1814.

This suspension occurred in a time of profound peace
and unprecedented general prosperity ; at a time too,
when the public Treasury had just been lavishly pouring its
millions of yellow ore into the laps of flourishing wealthy
states; when commerce, agriculture, and internal improvements, were making rapid strides to an unlimited extension ; when banks were vieing with each other in their liberality of discounts, and glorying in the amount of their dividends, bonuses, and bank profits, until bank notes were
more plenty than any other commodity professing to possess value.  At this joyous moment, the tocsin wrung the
knell of departed prosperity in sounds that stunned the ear,
and spoke in words that congealed the blood of those who
heard them: THE BANKS HAVE SUSPENDED SPECIE PAYMENT.

This suspension gave American credit an alarming shock,
both at home and abroad : all was consternation and dis-

may in the money market; yet, the buoyancy of Americans, their enterprising resistless "go ahead" character, and their confiding dispositions, added to their cupidity, inspired them with fresh confidence in new and better bank promises.

The legislatures of the states incorporated new banks, and increased the amount of the capitals of the old ones, " with new and important salutary restrictions, checks and balances." But hope had hardly become confidence, before the public mind was a second time exasperated at the alarming report, that the banks of Philadelphia had suspended specie payments again. This occurred on the 9th of October, 1839. The legislature of Pennsylvania authorised their suspension and continuance of business until the 15th of January, 1841; at which time they were required to resume specie payments or forfeit their charters.

The banks in the several states have been so long and so often indulged by legislative interference in their favor, and have obtained such strong hold upon American credit, and American business, that, like a spoiled child, they have very little to fear from the indignation of indulgent parents, who have already transferred to them their domicils from Maine to Georgia.

Many of the southern and western states, through the agency of their banks, have registered their mortgages in trans-atlantic cities, by the sale of public bonds and debts of their respective states, in foreign markets.

*Credit has assumed the character of capital,* and extended its dominion over the valley of the Mississippi, a country of immense wealth and importance, until their bank paper (with the exception of that of Missouri,) is far below par.

Is it at all surprising that men should loose confidence in institutions that are unable or unwilling to redeem their promises to pay, in times of peace and plenty ? Yet few will deny, that chartered bank paper no longer commands public confidence.

I am aware of the dislike that most men have to hearing the truth, when it interferes with their interests or inclinations. The prophets of truth were formerly frequently stoned to death, while flatterers, false prophets, liars and deceivers, were richly rewarded.

Legislatures, to suit all their constituents, find it necessary to pass almost as many amendatory as original laws. Their having once exceeded the true business of legisla- ting, that of *providing for the protection of persons and prop- erty*, has laid the foundation for much injurious, local, spe- cial and private legislation. We have by far too much le- gislation—affirmative, contradictory and explanatory ; and upon no subject, perhaps, has this been more severely felt than upon that of banking.

Currency being an instrument for the transfer and ex- change of commodities from man to man, passing freely from hand to hand, should be equally adapted to the use and convenience of all. While it is confined to its legiti- mate objects, a large portion of it may as well be composed of paper, at all times perfectly convertible, and uniformly current, as of gold and silver. In some situations, such paper money possesses advantages over the precious met- als, on account of its fitness for remittances in large sums, as well as a saving in expense of material and manufacture for circulation. But the moment currency, whether com- posed of the precious metals or of promises to pay, assumes any other character than that of a medial commodity and a measure of values, it looses its usefulness, and produces deleterious effects upon commerce and exchanges.

If currency assumes to be capital, and unites with credit to augment its powers, the currency becomes first inflated and then depreciated in value ; the channels of circulation become surcharged, and consequently the exportation of the precious metals must ensue, while this variable state of the currency renders it unfit for the measure of all values.

To obviate all these evils, organize the people to transact their own business of money making ; their money will then be composed of such materials as the majority of the people require, and of such denominations as best suit the convenience of either, and all.

Legislatures should no more interfere with currency than with religion. The people, being the sovereign power, should be so organized by the congress of the United States, as to be able to regulate the paper portion of the currency of the country, as the directors of the Mint are to manage the coinage of the precious metals ; and as independently of any legal enactment, beyond that of their organization by the Congress of the United States, as the inhabitants of the townships are, who elect their town officers to transact the whole business of the township, independent of the Provincial legislatures, or of the Congress of the United States, beyond the laws of their organization. Or, in other words, the administration of the currency should be as perfectly isolated and independent of the government of the currency, as is the administration of the townships independent of the Provincial or General governments ; while the government of the currency should be an unit as perfectly centralized as the government of the mint, or the general government of the United States.

The author has endeavored to show that money, banking, finance, currency, and exchanges, are all subjects easily to be understood, when stript of the mystery with which they are intentionally involved by the persons interested in the secrecy of the trade. That, for this purpose, a little plain common sense is all that is necessary to the understanding of the science of money, if the subject be clearly described. No argument is necessary to convince any man who has an American eagle, or an American dollar in his hand, that he holds money.

The author has endeavored to familiarize the subject to the most common understanding, by illustrations plain and easily to be comprehended, as the following description of exchanges and balances of trade will show.

It requires very little learning to comprehend, that if a man sells commodities to an amount greater than the amount for which he purchases merchandize, he will have a balance due to him, which he may take home with him in specie, or he may give any other person an order to receive the money. For the sake of illustrating the subject, we will call this order a bill of exchange. Now if a man sells less commodities in the market than the amount of the merchandize he purchases, he will owe a balance in the market. This he must remit money to pay, or he must purchase an order from some man who has a balance due to him in that market. This order then, is better for the man who has the remittance to make to pay the balance of his overtrading than the money; because the expense of transportation, insurance, &c. to the place where the business has been transacted, is a less expensive, as well as a more certain remittance; while the cash in hand is better to the man who has a balance due to him from a foreign market, when he wants to use the money at the place where he is, by the amount of the expense of freight, risk, and use during the time that must elapse before he could receive it, should he order its immediate shipment for the place where he is.

The merchant in New York, therefore, is willing to receive one ounce of pure silver, or one ounce of pure gold, or their equivalents in standard gold and silver, for a draft on his agent in London for an ounce of pure gold or an ounce of pure silver, or their equivalents in standard gold and silver, in London, or in the place where his money is due ; while the buyer of the bill will willingly give him in hand an ounce of pure gold, or an ounce of pure silver, or their equivalents in standard gold and silver, for the same amount in London, or the country where he owes the debt; since the bill of exchange will save him the expenses attendant upon the exportation of specie to pay his foreign debt. This is the state when the balance of trade is equal, and the exchange at par : both the buyer and seller of the bill of exchange, make one or more per cent. in the saving of the expense of the two transhipments, that is, one transhipment each. But should two men purchase a similar amount above the amount of their sales, they would each one of them leave a balance due against himself, equal to the amount that was due in the market to the man who had sold more than he had bought. It is plain that only one of these men could buy a bill of exchange to the amount of his indebtedness in London, as that was the whole amount due to any person in the United States ; and consequently the other debtor must export specie to meet the demand against him. As each debtor would desire to purchase this bill of exchange, the price of bills of exchange would rise to nearly, or perhaps quite the expense of exporting specie ; that, as there could not be bought what did not exist, there would not be bills of exchange in market to but half the amount of indebtedness of them both : hence it is clear, that the balance of trade will be readily indicated by the rate of exchange, when that is not interfered with by banks or other artificial causes.

The author has also endeavored to show, that so long as the precious metals are interchangeable for paper money, the inflation of the currency by bank paper, reduces the value of the precious metals equally with that of the paper money ; this, however, only becomes sensible when the paper ceases to be convertible, at which time the depreciation appears upon the paper only. The gold bill, (however expedient its passage might have been,) by which the quantity of pure gold in an eagle was lessened, while the legal value continued the same ; although it apparently raised the value of gold to the value of silver, yet, in fact, it reduced the value of silver just as much as it appeared to have raised the value of gold. This also is indicated by the exchanges.

The author has endeavored to show, that state chartered bank paper wants some of the essential requisites of a money currency. That of being invariably convertible into specie at sight; that of a uniform current circulation throughout the Union, and an entire independence of legislation : while the circulation of small bank bills drives the specie out of circulation, from its natural tendency to withdraw from domestic circulation and to become exported. These evils he professes to have traced to the connection of currency with private interest, with credit, and with politics. To remove these evils, he has recommended the organization of the people by congress, in such a manner as to enable them to elect the directors of the bank as independently as they elect their township officers. Precluding these directors from any interest in the loans or dividends of banks, and requiring them to give good security for the faithful discharge of well defined duties ; separating the bank of issue from the banks of discount, and restricting their discounts to actual business paper, having but short periods to run, and to three times the amount of specie actually in the vaults of the bank at the time of the discount; centralizing the government of the bank, the disposal of the stock and dividends, and dividing the administration of the currency to suit the interests or inclinations of the sovereign people.

The author recommends that there should be no bills issued of a less denomination than circulate in foreign countries with which we are commercially immediately connected, or at the least, not less than twenty dollar notes, that men in small business may have specie if they choose it, and commercial men may have large bills if they prefer them.

To lessen the expense of producing the bills intended for circulation as money, he recommends that the directors of the United States Bank should procure plates to be engraved and bills to be printed and executed in blank, in the best manner possible, to avoid counterfeits, so many and such bills of the various denominations, not less than twenty dollars, as shall be necessary for circulation throughout the United States for the convenient interchange of commodities; and that the directors of the United States institution shall reserve from the profits of the several banks of discount, a sum to constitute a safety fund, to be applied, according to their discretion, to the prompt and temporary relief of any casualties that may occur to any banks of discount, by which they might be unabled to meet their liabilities at the instant.

He recommends a centralized government of the currency, with the view of rendering it equally current through-

out the Union, with a divided administration; giving each
bank of discount perfect independence in the conduct of its
own affairs, to avoid the financial and political influence of
such an immense monetary power as an United States bank
and branches must possess. The capital stock, the specie received in payment, the stock, the profits made by the banks
upon the paper portion of the currency, the expenses of
conducting the currency, the reserved funds, the dividends,
and, in short, the entire government of the currency are to
be centralized, and made to constitute one perfect whole :
while the business and administration of the banks of discount are local, and perfectly independent of each other,
and of the bank of issue. Hence, the evils liable to attend
the accumulation of an immense monetary power and influence that must accompany an incorporated United States
bank are obviated.

The bank of issue, in the proposed plan, stands in the
same relation, in many respects, to the banks of discount,
that capitalists do to the banks of discount they employ for
the purpose of lending their money; with this principal
difference, that capitalists only authorize their directors to
lend the actual specie deposited with them, while the United States bank of issue deposites blank bank notes to three
times the amount of specie deposited, that the paper may
be executed and loaned, and the specie used for the redemption of their notes, as that may occasionally be required.

The bank of England lends or sells its notes to the banks
of discount of England ; they neither loan cash, nor their
own notes, generally, but the notes of the bank of England.

After the United States bank directors have procured,
engraved and executed by the officers, numbered and re-

gistered in blank, and delivered to the directors of the several state institutions, the amount intended to be put in circulation in their states respectively, the state bank directors
are to execute the bills as directors of the state banks, and
apportion them with one-third part of their amount in specie, between the banks of discount in the several cities,
towns, and districts of the states. The people of these
several localities having elected directors of their banks of
discount, and these directors having given sufficient security
for the faithful discharge of their duties, and the prompt
payment over to their successors in office of all monies
and property of the bank in their hands, may execute
the bills appointed to them to put in circulation, and loan
them upon the discount of actual business paper, having
but short periods to run, in which *no director* has an interest. Thus dividing the administration of the currency and
centralizing its government; rendering it republican, free
from credit, and from politics; equally current throughout
the Union, and always strictly convertible into specie at the
counters where it is issued.

The monthly publications of the statements of the banks
will enable the people to judge of the propriety and economy
with which each bank is conducted, and to approve or disapprove of the same through the ballot boxes.

The author has attempted to show, that currency, money,
medial commodity, and circulating medium, signifying the
precious metals and paper money of the country, whether
composed of gold and silver, bank notes, state scrip, post
notes, private individual notes, or other paper in the similitude of bank notes, intended to circulate as money, is the
instrument of measure of the *value* of all other commodities, as strictly as the established weight of the pound is the
measure of the weight of an article that is bought and sold

by weight, or the established length of the yard the measure of the materials bought and sold by cloth measure. Its
value then ought to be governed by the same laws as govern weights and measures. It should be equally as immutable and unchangeable as they are, so far as *this* property of
money is considered. But money has also another property, that of being the instrument of transfer, interchange,
and communication of capital and commodities between
man and man, by which capital is transferred; and other
commodities, through this instrument, are converted into
capital, and conveyed from man to man, and from place to
place. Hence it is seen to be a similar instrument
of the communication of capital, that books and newspapers are of knowledge. Books and newspapers are
not knowledge, nor is money capital: they are both
only the instruments by which their respective properties are communicated. Money is not used as capital
by any nation on earth, any more than the square bits of
metal, which constitute the currency of the Chinese, or the
currency composed of shells of savage nations, except in
the manufacture of gold and silver articles.

Capitalists use money only as the most convenient form
in which wealth can be kept, or transmitted from place to
place, and vested in productive capital for the purchase of
materials, provisions, payment of laborer's wages, &c. necessary to the conducting of any business they may prose-
cute.

The precious metals are used by the manufacturers of
gold and silver wares or ornaments, as capital, in the same
manner as the blacksmith uses iron and steel. And gold
and silver may, from this cause, possess their own peculiar
values, regulated by the supply and demand of them for
manufacturing purposes. But, as this demand has never

been such as to raise their price above their current value as a circulating medium, that may not have any very material influence upon their value for currency.

The importance of currency as the instrument of communication, or transfer of capital from man to man, and from place to place, may not inaptly be illustrated by its comparison with the instruments or vehicles of communication between distant places, as steam-ships, vessels, steam-cars, waggons, and carts. They are the instruments that convey capital from place to place, but they are not capital to those who hire them, unless when the owner sends them into market to be sold and left, or exchanged for money or for capital; which will not be likely to be the case, unless the channels in which they are employed are surcharged with the commodity of which they are composed : that is, the carter, who uses his cart to transfer capital from place to place, does not leave his cart with the load ; nor does the captain of a ship, sell and leave his vessel in the market with his cargo, unless the channels of commerce are surcharged, and the foreign demand for the vessel is greater than the value of the vessel to him in the trade in which he is engaged. But, when the waggoner has more waggons or carts, than the business in which he is engaged requires, he will sell not only his freight, but the instrument by which that freight was brought to market; so the captain of a vessel, when there are more ships employed in the trade in which he is engaged, than can find profitable cargoes, will sell his vessel, and invest the value of it in some other capital that he believes likely to be more productive : so, too, will specie only be exported when the channels of currency are surcharged, and the demand for the instrument, *money*, in some other business in another country offers prospects of more profitable returns than that in which it is at present employed.

Hence, it is clear, that money, like the books of a circulating library, like carts and waggons, like steam cars and
vessels, is only the instrument of the transfer of capital,
and not capital, any more than books are knowledge, or
than carts or vessels are cargoes and freight.

The proposed system of currency claims the merit of
furnishing a uniform medial commodity for circulation,
equally current throughout the union ; a centralized government of the currency, and all the beneficial effects of a
United States bank, with a divided administration of the
currency ; and, consequently, free from the evils and dangers aprehended from the accumulation and concentration
of the whole money power of the United States in one
company, or the private interest, credit power, and consecutive expansions and contractions of the paper portion of
the circulating medium issued by incorporated state banks.
It separates the bank of issue from the banks of discount;
removes credit and private interest from both, and regulates the issues by the actual demand for circulating medium
and the amount of specie in the United States.   Limits the
loans of the banks of discount, to the amount of bills apportioned to them for circulation by the banks of issue.   Re-
stricts their discounts to not exceeding three times the
amount of specie actually in the vaults of the banks at the
time of the discount, instead of discounting paper and lending money thereon to three times the amount of the paid-up
capital of the banks, as is some times done by chartered
banks, even when their deposites, independent of their circulation, may exceed twice the amount of specie in their
vaults ; and confines the lending of their notes wholly to
the discounting of *actual business paper*, having but short
periods to run.   This prevents the inflation of the currency, and consequently its ruinous contractions, with their

disastrous consequences. It separates the currency of the country from politics, by removing the necessity of legislative interference with the circulating medium, by the chartering banking companies, increasing their capital stock, or renewing their charters—thereby lessening the dangerous political excitement that not unfrequently accompanies the election of the Chief Magistrate—while it furnishes all classes of community with the kind of money they require. Issuing bills of no smaller denominations than twenty dollars, that the mechanic, farmer and laborer, who prefer specie to paper money, may receive it from that preference; and that the large trader, who prefers large notes, may find no difficulty in obtaining them for cash, at par, when he requires them for commercial purposes. It secures the perfect convertibility of the paper portion of the currency, by limiting the discounts to actual business paper, having but short periods to run, and by restricting the amount to the demand for a circulating medium, passing from hand to hand, and by being based exclusively upon the precious metals actually in the vaults of the banks at the time of the discount. It renders the currency republican, like the other elementary principles of the government, by giving the people in every part of the Union the election of the directors of the bank of issue; and the people in each state the election of the directors of state banks of secondary issue; and the people of the cities, towns, and districts, where banks of discount are to be located, the election of the directors of the banks of their respective places, as they elect the most numerous branch of their legislatures. It does not, like chartered banking companies, convert credit paper into capital, nor, by uniting itself to credit, inflate the currency beyond its proper limits; nor does it allow the directors the exclu-

sive right to have their notes firstly discounted, if they require it : for it expressly precludes the directors from any
interest, either directly or indirectly, in the loans or discounts of the banks. It applies the currency of the country
to its legitimate object, that of passing from hand to hand,
and being the necessary instrument of the transaction of the
regular business of the place, by making it exclusively the
interest of the directors to accommodate their constituents,
by discounting only actual business paper, having but short
periods to run, instead of discounting fictitious notes of
speculators, who, from their large capital or bank credit,
have frequently been able to monopolize the money of the
place, and thereby to establish the market price of its exportable commodities ; inducing the grower and producer
to believe that such speculators actually advance the price
of their products, when, in fact, they frequently fix the
price of the commodities, in which they deal, below what
the regular traders of the place would have paid, had the
money of the place been left open and free for their accommodation, and the purchase of the commodities left to
a fair competition. Yet, as these speculators have all the
money that the banks can lend, the farmers are induced to
give them credit for what they term " the advantage of the
opposition in the market." But, even if this spirit of speculation should produce temporarily an advance in the price
of some products, the farmer is not always benefitted by
such temporary rise in the commodity above its real intrinsic value, when many other commodities are reduced in
value in the same proportion.

A fair, uniform price, for the various products cf the
country, is far better for the private interest of the grower
or producer, as well as for the permanent prosperity of the

country, than occasional high prices, to be followed by corresponding low prices of the same, or other commodities of exportation. It holds out no inducement to the directors of banks to interfere with the exchanges, either domestic or foreign; freely allowing the rate of exchange to indicate the balance of trade, and the free exportation of specie to check over-trading and over-importing. Leaving the ordinary exchange transactions to individual competition; which must establish the market rate of exchange in the United States, as it does in all other countries in the world; and as it must invariably do, when it is not interfered with by banks or other artificial means. It promotes laudable enterprise, encourages industry and economy, by rendering the currency sound, always convertible into specie where it is put into circulation, and equally current throughout the Union. It facilitates commercial transactions, by inducing promptitude and punctuality in meeting liabilities, and reduces the amount of our imports to the par exchange of our exports. It provides the means of lessening the difficulties with which the several states have to contend, which have become involved abroad for funds vested in unproductive enterprizes, or have commenced greater and more extended works of internal improvements than they have funds to accomplish, by lessening the price of exchanges with the diminution of the amount of our imports, and by encouraging and promoting domestic manufactures; the directors having their interest promoted by the prosperity and satisfaction of the community in the loans of the bank, and by equalizing the currrency throughout the Union.

# AN ESSAY

ON

## BANKING, CURRENCY, FINANCE, EXCHANGES,

AND

## POLITICAL ECONOMY.

---

## CHAPTER I.

### ON THE STATE OF THE CURRENCY OF THE UNITED STATES.

Gold and Silver a small part of the currency—Convertible State chartered bank paper a large amount—Inconvertible bank paper a still larger amount.—Post Notes. State Scrip, Notes of other States, unauthorized private Notes, Checks, Deposite Notes, and Notes of Corporations and Associations, comprise the largest portion of the currency.—Small bills injurious to the issuer as well as to the bill holder—Causes explained.

The currency of the United States consists of a small amount of gold and silver coins and bullion; a larger amount of state chartered bank notes exchangeable for specie ; a far larger amount of bank notes not convertible into specie, composed of the notes of non-specie paying banks, the notes of banks of other states, unauthorized paper of individuals, of companies, and of associations, in the similitude of bank notes, issued and circulated as money ; which, with post notes, deposite notes, checks, state scrip, and bills of exchange, comprise most of the medial commodity of the United States.

And, although the constitution expressly provides, that nothing but gold and silver shall be made a tender in the payment of debts in the United States, yet, the issue of small bills by chartered banks, and the consequent abstraction of the precious metals from the circulation, has left the whole business of the country to be conducted by paper money ; which, notwithstanding the salutary and positive provision of the constitution to the contrary, has become virtually a tender in the payment of debts.

Bills compose so large a proportion of the circulating medium, that those who will not take them in payment of their debts cannot collect their dues, nor carry on business requiring the use of money.

Bank notes of small denominations, are dangerous to the banks that issue them, as well as to the currency. They expose the currency of the United States more to the dangers of over-expansion, than that to which the currencies of most of the countries of Europe are liable.

The five pound notes of the bank of England are the smallest credit paper issued to circulate as money, with which I am acquainted, excepting those that circulate in America.

The injurious effects of the issue and circulation, by the banks, of small bills, have been severely felt in every part of the Union ; and almost every state has in turn recorded the opinion of its legislature against it, by passing laws to prevent their circulation. But the power and influence of incorporated banking companies, aided by the fluctuations of currency and trade, have invariably obtained a repeal of those salutary laws, or rendered them nugatory. The good sense and intelligence of the people may, however, at last prevail. Congress may be induced to organize the people throughout the Union, simultaneously to suppress the circulation of small bills ; when the precious metals will spontaneously and instantly supply their place. The people, when once organized, will render the currency republican, separate it from credit, from private interest, and from politics.

The efforts of state legislators to correct the defects of the currency must ever be as unavailing as their attempts to suppress small bills have hitherto proved. Their actions are desultory, unconnected and temporary ; liable to the influence of private interest, or political party feeling, that may vary in the several states, and prevent their uniform action. All the states cannot be expected to pass similar laws upon this subject, simultaneously ; consequently, the currency might be changed by state legislation, but it could never be radically reformed.

Some of the states have passed laws to suppress the circulation of small bills within their own territories; but their immediate inundation with those of other states, often much more uncurrent than their own had been, aided in obtaining a repeal of the laws for their suppression, just at the moment, perhaps, when the neighboring states, from seeing the advantages of the measure, were about to pass similar laws.

The people are the only legitimate source from which to expect permanent and radical relief. Congress is the only proper body, possessing legitimate power and authority, to organize them for that purpose. When there are no small bills in circulation, all the channels and ramifications of the currency are occupied by the precious metals ; so that upon any sudden, foreign or domestic, political or financial shock, those channels are not disturbed. The farmer, mechanic and laborer, have no direct interest in it. In fact, the specie circulating among these classes may, in part, be brought into general circulation, by its commanding a premium, and thereby materially lessen the evils of the contractions of the currency, which might otherwise have been necessary to its perfect recovery. But when small bills constitute the whole circulation among the farmers and laboring clas- ses, as well as the small sums they have laid up, the panic is augmented by their general rush to obtain cash for their notes ; and if they are not paid, public sympathy is warm- ly enlisted in their favor. Their misfortunes, and the frauds of the bank, become the common topic of conversation. The evils are augmented, and the reports, that loose no- thing by being repeated, are highly colored ; the public mind becomes inflamed ; the peace and good order of so- ciety are endangered, as well as the safety of the officers and directors of the bank.

By the laws of their situation, chartered banks *must* in- flate the currency, and make it subservient to their interest by every means in their power. Contractions must always follow over-expansions : suspensions may follow them oc- casionally.

The several states of the Union, which are by the con- stitution expressly prohibited from coining money, emitting bills of credit, or making any thing but gold and silver a tender in the payment of debts, have, by legislative enact- ments, made a great variety of credit paper virtually a tender in the payment of debts. If state scrip is not a bill of credit, it ought not to circulate as such.

Currency is an instrument that should be adapted to the use of every citizen equally. The merchant, who only re- quires scissors to cut up his broadcloth, should not com- plain of the woodman, because he requires an axe in clear- ing the forest ; nor should he any more complain of the far- mer, because he prefers the precious metals to promises to pay : nor, on the other hand, should the woodman complain of the merchant, because he is unwilling to use an axe for cutting up his broadcloths, or that he prefers paper money to specie, provided it be strictly convertible and equally current throughout the Union.

## CHAPTER II.

### STATE CHARTERED BANKS.

On the trade of Banking —Banks of Deposite—Banks of Discount—Both unprofitable to the proprietors.—State chartered institutions comprise these, and banks of issue also—The former lend money—The latter lend credit—Hence, the profits of banks of circulation.

Banks of deposite, in which gold and silver are only safely kept for the proprietors, to be weighed out by their administrator, upon their orders, or the credit on the books of the bank, transferred at the will of the owners, could not be profitable to the proprietors in America; since the expense of office rent, clerk hire, other salaries, and contingent expenses, would be liable to be greater, than any increase of profits from the monopoly of the trade, by the association of capitalists in the bank; as they might lend their money as safely, cheaply, and, perhaps, as profitably, themselves, as by hired agents.

Banks of discount are institutions possessing a capital in money, which the proprietors lend by discounting promissory notes, bills and acceptances, originating in the sale of merchandize, or other commodities, having but short periods to run. As banks of discount lend only money, and not their credit, the profits of their business, above the ordinary rate of interest, would not support the expenses of

a banking house, since the loans could be made at less expense by the individuals themselves, than by officers employed for that purpose. But, supposing it would pay expenses whenever the market price of money was below its
legal rate of interest, by being a monopoly of the business
of money lending, it would not be likely to be established
in the United States, where much more profitable investments of capital can daily be made.

Banks of issue and circulation, lend only their credit;
which they do by discounting endorsed notes, made payable at the bank, due at some stated period or periods hence,
for the accommodation of borrowers of credit, who are
willing to pay the bank for the loan of its credit, due on
demand without interest, the ordinary rate of interest for
the use of ready money; believing they can purchase better in the market with the credit notes of the bank that is
well known, than they could with their own notes due
sixty days hence. They also transfer credits on the books
of the bank, and receive money in deposite, which they
use as their own. So long as their credits are current,
which may be for some time, provided they are confined
within due limits, their paper may be a convenience to the
borrower equal to their charge for the use of it. These
institutions, it is clear, must be highly profitable to the stockholders; who only keep as much specie in their vaults as
may serve to meet the demands for change, or for the convenience of their customers.

American state chartered banks are, by law, authorized
to exercise all the powers, privileges, and immunities of
these three kinds of banking. They receive deposites;
discount notes, and issue their own bills.

They do not, however, lend the money deposited with
them. They lend their own credit notes, and retain the

deposited money until the same are returned upon them for redemption in specie.

They lend their paper money, by exchanging notes with their customers. The borrower giving them an endorsed note, pa; able at the bank at some future period, and receiving in exchange the unendorsed notes of the bank, due on demand, to an equal amount, *minus* the discounted interest on the note of the borrower for the time it has to run ; the borrower, also perceiving that he can purchase merchandize and other commodities better in the market with the notes of the bank which are known, than he can with his own which are unknown, and which the law prohibits him from making in the similitude of bank notes, and issuing or circulating as money, which the bank may legally do, finds, that however well he may be known, the notes of the bank are more convenient for payments in small sums than his own could possibly be. Some discrepancy in the working of the machinery of an American bank may be reasonably expected, since the incompatible and perfectly distinct duties of these three different institutions are blended together, and all subjected to the direction of private interest. Yet, the ingenuity of Americans has assimilat·d them so nearly together, and the public mind have become so familiar with the terms used by each kind of banking, that the incongruous parts of an American compound bank appear far less unnaturally connected than they really are.

Briefly in the exercise of its functions as a bank of deposite, it receives for safe-keeping the coin and bullion of individuals, and transfers upon its books, by checks or drafts, the various amounts standing to the credit of depositors : facilitating commercial transactions, by saving the expenses of transportation from house to house, the labor of repeated countings, the wear and tear of the precious metals by friction, and the cost of assurance, or the trouble of safe-keeping. Here, however, the similarity of a bank of deposite, like that of Hamburgh, with an American bank ceases. The chartered bank receives the deposites, as was remarked, but instead of keeping them subject to the direction, checks or drafts of the owners of the credits on the books of the bank, it deposites them among its own funds, and pays them out upon the return of its own notes for specie ; unless it be in certain cases where deposites are made in parcels of the precious metals by weight, subject to the disposition of the depositor; in which case, the American bank becomes a perfect bank of deposite. For this safe-keeping, &c. the depositor may be required to pay a small sum.

So far as the last kind of deposites are made in the bank, they exercise no influence whatever over the circulation by expanding or contracting the amount.

The uniform practice of American bankers is, I believe, to put the deposites into the vaults of the banks in common stock with their own specie, and bank upon the whole amount; pay it out in the redemption of their own notes ; transfer the credits on the books of the bank at the will of the depositor, as though the identical bullion was there, and ready to be weighed or counted out by tale, to any one to whom the transfer might be made, if required. Hence, it has not unfrequently happened, that independent of their own circulation, banks have received deposites and paid them out in the redemption of their own notes, until they have not had half the amount of their deposites in specie remaining in their vaults. The depositor has the credit in the bank ; the banker discounts notes, and lends his own paper upon his right to the deposite, while the depositor, by drafts, checks, or entries on the books of the bank, transfers his deposite precisely as he would have done had he reserved it exclusively for his own use ; in which case the depositor pays for the safe-keeping of his money, while the banker may pay him a small per centage for the use of the deposite, so long as it is allowed to remain in the bank.

It appears by the report of the Secretary of the Treasury of the United States, in 1840, that there was deposited in the several banks of the United States, $75,696,857, while at the same time, the amount of specie in the vaults of the banks, was only $33,105,155. Where then is the security of the bill-holder, in case of a panic and run upon the bank ?

The specie in the vaults of the banks is actually less than one half of the amount of the deposites ; all of which may be demanded of the bank, in specie, at the shortest notice. And this is the currency of the United States !— the paper that circulates as money !—assumes the place expressly ordained by the constitution to the precious metals ! If not legally, yet virtually and practically, by displacing the precious metals, it has become a tender in the payment of debts, and the standard of the measure of all values !

Now let us see how far American banks resemble banks of discount; or, rather to what extent they yield to the influence of the salutary powers of a bank of deposite and discount. They receive deposites, as before explained. They discount notes and acceptances. But, instead of confining their discounts to actual business paper, having but short periods to run, they discount any paper that may be considered safe, for the accommodation of those who wish to borrow capital as well as money.

The banks of England, (except the bank of England,) and most of the banking establishments in the large cities

on the continent, known as private banking houses, are
banks of discount; paying their discounts in money, and
confining them strictly to business paper : while American
chartered banks discount whatever paper is offered that is
well secured, and pay their discounts in their own notes
promising to pay money on demand. A frequent rule of
discrimination (after the directors and stockholders have all
been accommodated,) between the bills offered for discount when more paper is offered than the bank is
able to do, is ; firstly, to do the largest bills, where
the payment is to be made in some eastern city, since that
affords a profit on the bill of exchange, drawn by the bank
for the re-payment of the money, of five times the amount
of the profit on its loans ; and then to proceed to select
those bills that afford the best profit, and discount to the
full extent of their means.

As European banks of discount only lend the money
furnished by the proprietors of the bank, their business of
banking does not very materially expand the currency ; as
the same money might be lent by the proprietors themselves, without the intervention of the bank : although,
where money is deposited on demand, and the deposite
loaned to another person, two men have the credit of the
same sum of money, and the currency may be temporarily
expanded by this credit. But the cupidity of chartered
banking companies does not stop here. They discount
notes, and lend money upon the credit of their specie deposites ; next lend the deposites as part of their own capital,
and yet allow the depositor a transfer of his credit on the
books of the bank, at his will and pleasure, without keeping on hand an amount of specie sufficient to meet the probable demands of their own notes for specie,
before the bills receivable held by them fall due.

European banks of discount do not expand the paper currency materially above a purely metalic currency, at their pleasure, or to the extent of public gullability.

American chartered banks, in addition to their powers of banks of discount and deposite, are also banks of issue. They lend their credit, and issue their own bills which circulate as money. Thus the circulating medium, by the introduction into it of paper money and paper credits, createable at the pleasure of the directors, to at least a certain extent, in addition to the coin and bank deposites, which before constituted the entire currency of the country, now admits of fluctuations, contractions and expansions, unknown in the business of banks of deposite and discount unconnected with credit.

As will hereafter be explained, the combining the operations of banks of issue with those of discount and deposite, has confusedly mixed together such dissimilar and incongruous things, that it has mystified the subject of the currency, as if intentionally to confuse and mislead the public mind, or divert it from the investigation of its elementary principles.

The author has attempted to direct public attention to the situation, merits and importance of the currency, in a political, as well as a financial point of view. Years of practical experience, and a minute and careful observation of the operations of the currency, composed of state chartered bank paper, its commercial inefficiency as a circulating medium, and its highly exciting political influence, have strongly impressed him with a belief, that upon the renovation or deterioration of the currency, depends the growth and prosperity of republican institutions in America, or their premature decay and ultimate destruction.

From the business of banks of discount and deposite, it is clear, that, since they lend only their money, their profits consist only of the simple interest of the same. Their loans neither inflate the currency; nor does enormous prof-its indicate extortionate charges for the use of their money, or the adoption of other means equally injurious to the per-manent prosperity of the country. Every abstraction of money from an individual, or from the public, beyond an equal and fair remuneration for the use of it, savours of ex-tortion ; for money can never be worth more in the trade of banking, than in other branches of business, only in pro-portion to capital and skill required and risk run, unless some means be resorted to not justifiable in ordinary busi-ness.

The profits of American chartered banks is chiefly made upon the loans of their credit. The sale of which, in the money market, has been authorized by legal enactments.

If this credit banking business becomes too profitable, that is, pays much more than any mercantile or other busi-ness requiring the same capital and skill, and liable to the same risk, it proves that the supply is not equal the demand; when there should, and consequently there does spring into existence, other institutions to meet the apparent de-mand. Were bank paper real wealth or real capital, the cost of producing which bore a proportion to its sale price, the value would be reduced, until the general level be-tween this credit paper and other commodities would be established. When no greater profits were made in the manufacture of paper money than in the manufacture of other commodities, the general equilibrium would be re-stored. This may be illustrated by the high price of newly invented improvements, by which former instruments, im-plements and machinery are superceded. The public

will pay for the improvement a higher profit on its production only so long as the supply shall be less than the
demand. Hence, chartered banks in America, by enjoying a monopoly of the business of banking, make unjustly
(though, perhaps, not illegally,) whatever amount of profit
they divide in their business above the fair remuneration
for the capital and skill and risk of the business, as compared with other mercantile operations.

If money is worth more than the legal rate of interest,
repeal the usury laws, and bring it into the market for sale
at its market price, like other commodities. If the dangers
of loss from the difficulty of collecting debts, and the inefficiency of the laws, be greater than necessary, pass such
bankrupt laws as shall summarily collect all the effects of
the insolvent debtor, and apportion them among his creditors equally, according to the amount of their fair and equit-
able claims, and release the debtor from further liabilities,
that he may provide for his own subsistence.

---

## CHAPTER III.

### THE OBJECT OF THE WORK.

The evils of the present currency developed.—Some able financiers invited to in-
vestigate the currency.—Preserve the spirit of the Declaration of Independence—and of the Constitution.—Render the currency republican—uniformly
current—perfectly convertible—free from credit—free from politics—and free
from private interest.—Preserve faith with creditors, foreign and domestic.—
Banks—Incorporations.—The precious metals insufficient for the currency.—
Credit rendered expedient.—Incorporated Bank credit anti-republican.—State
debts—interest.—Ten million of dollars.—Caution necessary in reforming the
currency.—The present banking system radically wrong.—Dependant upon PRI-
VATE INTEREST, and composed of credit paper.—The currency anti-republican.—
Connected with politics.—The four pillars of government—Politics—Religion—
Currency—and Literature.—The precious metals do not circulate interchange-
ably with bank paper.

The object of the following pages is to show the evils of
the present circulating medium of the United States, and
to point to a system of currency that would be less objec-

tionable, in the hope that some able financiers may turn their attention to the subject, and without connecting it with the party feelings of the day, calmly and judiciously perfect a currency adapted to the genius, habits, manners and customs of the people of these United States, consistent with the fidelity due to existing contracts at home and abroad, and an honorable protection of private and domestic, as well as foreign and national investments, with a view of producing the greatest good to the greatest number— always PRESERVING THE IMMUTABLE PRINCIPLES CONTAINED IN THE DECLARITION OF INDEPENDENCE, and THE PRESENT CONSTITUTION OF THE UNITED STATES INVIOLATE.

Let the people of this Union calmly consider in what manner the currency may be made *republican ;* rendered *current in every part of the Union ;* always *redeemable in specie at sight at the counter where issued;* be *perfectly separated from credit, from politics,* and from *private interest ;* and yet be adapted to the genius and habits of the American people, and the preservation of good faith with existing banking institutions, as well as foreign and domestic creditors.

The genius of the American people, as well as the state of existing contracts, both at home and abroad, all demand a larger circulating medium than the present disposition of the precious metals furnish. Although I am ready to admit, that, if no chartered bank paper circulated as money, and if we were free from debt at home and abroad, it would be very questionable whether a paper currency, or any other credit system, could be judiciously recommended to republican America ; but, unfortunately, this is not the case. We are in debt, both at home and abroad. Credit pervades every department of business; and bank notes are universally received as money. We have the interest of a foreign debt of ten million of dollars and upwards annually, which must be promptly met in gold and silver, or in bills of exchange or other remittances. We are, therefore, compelled to take things as we find them. And, while we preserve faith with the public and private creditor, and existing monetary institutions, we must proceed with great caution, if we would attempt to remove a long established custom ; especially if it be one that has become assimilated with our business habits and transactions. We should look with great caution, and even suspicion, upon every new system of currency ; and, in short, nothing but the total failure of all the former plans of paper money, would justify us in meddling with the circulating medium—which, like water, will find its level, and regulate itself, if left free and unrestrained by legislative enactments—but, when exclusive privileges have been once granted to individuals, or to corporations, they should be cautiously interfered with, if the public good requires that they should be removed, and not violently thrown down.

---

## CHAPTER IV.

### ON THE VARIOUS KINDS OF CURRENCY IN THE UNITED STATES.

Specie—Convertible paper—Inconvertible paper—Incorporated banks dependant upon politics—producing political excitement—endangering the republican institutions.—The elementary principles of all governments.—The farmer, mechanic, and laborer choose the kind of currency least desirable to the wealthy merchant and banker —The poor equally entitled to their choice of the kind of currency as the rich.—Specie for the producer—paper for the consumer.—Let Congress organize the people to regulate the currency.—Suppose $80,000,000 of specie—Bank upon $40,000,000 to produce sufficient currency—$20 smallest denomination of bills.—Specie $40,000,000 for small circulation—United States bank issue bills and specie.—Local banks discount bills and acceptances—give security—sell the stock to any purchaser for money—discount only business paper—issue bills upon only a metalic basis—to be current, convertible, plenty.

The slightest examination of the circulating medium of this republic, must satisfy every disinterested and well constituted mind, that there must be something radically wrong in our existing system of banking or in the business of our bankers and brokers.

Our present currency consists of a small amount of specie and bullion, a larger amount of specie-paying-paper, and a still larger amount of paper not redeemable in specie at sight.

The paper portion of our currency is so perfectly *depen-dant upon credit*, and so intimately connected with *private interest*, as to be continually under the influence of the one or the other; leaving the currency liable to those danger-ous contractions and expansions that always attend a credit currency connected with private interest : while the de_ pendence of incorporated banks upon the legislature for extensions of their charters, or for increase of their capi-tals, or for new incorporations, connects the currency of the country with its politics ; producing much of the unneces-sary excitement that pervades the whole community at general elections, and which, at some future period, may endanger the very existence of this republic. In short, the currency of these United States is *anti-republican ;* and in its operations hostile to democratic institutions.

Every government rests upon four corner pillars : their Politics—their Religion—their Finance—and their Litera-ture. And as these are well or ill devised and conducted, so are the people contented, prosperous and happy, or otherwise.

It is universally admitted, that the precious metals and promises to pay on paper, cannot circulate at the same time among the same community; the precious metals being uniformly preferred by mechanics, laborers, and men in small business, while paper money, current in every part of the Union, redeemable in specie at the will of the holder at the counter where it was issued, is generally preferred by commercial men.

To meet the preceding propositions allow me to submit the following outlines of a plan of currency :

Let congress authorize the people to elect competent financiers from every state in the Union, to meet at some convenient place, and ascertain the amount of specie in the United States, and the amount of currency that is required for the business of the country; and to bank upon so much of the specie as would be sufficient to meet the demand for a circulating medium.

Suppose, for instance, that we have in the United States eighty or one hundred million of dollars in specie, and that we require one hundred and fifty millions of money to form a currency to place this country in a flourishing condition, could we not make up the deficiency by banking upon half of this specie, which would give the whole amount of currency required, and leave the other half for a metalic circulation?

The issue of no smaller bills than circulate in England, or at the least, not less than twenty dollar bills, would bring the gold and silver reserved for the metalic portion of the currency into common circulation, while it would not in the least interfere with existing banking institutions; as their small bills would be withdrawn from circulation, as their charters expired one after another, and their place would be regularly supplied by the precious metals.

Let the United States directors execute the bills as United States directors, and apportion or divide the amount among the several states according to the demand, and take a general supervision of the state banks.

Let the people in each state elect state directors annually, who shall execute the bills as state directors ; apportion the amount set apart\ for their states respectively, between the local banks or *banks of discount* for their several states, and take a general supervision of the same.

Let the electors in every city, town, county and district, where a bank of discount is located, elect directors of the same, in the manner in which they elect the most numerous branches of their legislatures : who, before entering upon the duties of their offices, shall give good and sufficient security for the faithful discharge of their trusts, and the prompt payment over to their successors of all monies and property of the bank in their possession ; execute the bills as directors of the bank ; make their notes payable in specie at the counters where they are issued, at sight; and do all the ordinary business of directors of a bank of discount and deposite ; but at no time to circulate more paper than three times the amount of specie actually in their vaults at the time of the discount, nor discount paper in which a director of any bank has any direct or indirect interest, or on which a director's name is given as surety for the re-payment of the money.

Elect the directors of the United States institution, so that only one-sixth part of them shall go out of office annually.

To give permanency to the institution, all monev currencies should be as uniform, permanent and unchangeable as the precious metals themselves.

To obtain the necessary funds in specie, provide that capitalists may take stock to any amount of specie they will pay; that the general government may (if congress think proper,) take stock to the amount of specie they may pay, and no more ; and that the state governments may take stock to the amount of specie their respective legislatures may advise, and no more ; and that each stockholder shall receive their regular dividends on quarter days, but have no influence or control in the affairs of the bank on account of their being stockholders.

Thus the paper portion of our currency would be issued upon a purely metalic basis. No government debentures, post notes, foreign or domestic exchanges, United States or state bonds, or other public or private sureties, would be admitted as a basis for the issue of paper to circulate as money.

Such an institution as this would be wholly unconnected with credit and private interest, and free from the ruinous contractions and expansions of the currency to which our credit bank paper is constantly liable. It would not require the intervention of the legislature to renew or increase its power, and therefore would be unconnected with politics, and not liable to produce the political excitement which our aristocratical monetary system threatens. It would be equally current throughout the Union—always convertible into specie at the will of the holder at the counter where it was issued, and consequently a purely republican people's money.

# CHAPTER V.

## ON UNCURRENT MONEY.

Recapitulation of preceding chapter.—Loss to the public by uncurrent money—uncertainty—inconvenience in travelling.—Brokers rendered necessary—Their time
should be better employed in productive industry.—Cincinnati and White water
Canal Co.—Notes'uncurrent.—Private notes—Foreign notes.—Exchange ten per
cent. for the use of paper to call money—Otherwise expensive.—Small bills increase panics—Panics profitable only to gambling speculators.—The fluctuations
of the currency a loss to community.—Credit often useful.—On a new farm labor
the only exchangeable commodity.—Without credit life may be wasted in indi-
gence.—A bad state of the currency materially conducive to misfortunes and poverty.—Ten cents a day for a family, only a medium tax upon uncurrent money
in various ways.—Small bills injurious to industry and economy.—Bank paper an
incubus—a NIGHT MARE—its magic wand—The jugglery.—The history of credit
paper money, one of dishonor,waste, ambition, gambling and disappointment.—
Rag Barons in their painted Castles tax industry.—Change the scene—People
elect the directors.—Productive industry the only true source of wealth —One
man with $500 judiciously expended, equal to two men without funds in accumu-
lating wealth, in the new countries of the western states —Money makers indem-
nify themselves—mystify the science—charge for their services.

In a previous chapter, I have stated that the object of
this work is to direct public attention to the subject of the
circulating medium; to induce a spirit of enquiry into the
causes that have led to its frequent contractions and expansions, and to advise some constitutional method of rendering
the currency republican like the other elementary principles of our government; to separate it from credit, and
render it equally current in every part of the United States ;
always redeemable in specie at the counter where it was
issued; also, to separate it from politics.

I am next led to the consideration of the loss, damage,
discount, inconvenience and uncertainty attendant upon a
currency, that, although it may be made the circulating medium in one place, cannot be made to circulate freely in
other parts of the Union. This evil is loudly complained
of in the present currency, composed of the ordinary bank
notes of the state banks. These notes may circulate freely in their respective neighborhoods ; but remove them into
a distant market or state, and their circulation is attended
with loss and inconvenience to the holder. And this uncertainty in the value of the circulating medium, has given

rise to the great number of brokers, whose time and labor might otherwise be applied to some useful employment. But the inconvenience of this limited circulation does not end in occupying (at a total loss,) the time of a large number of persons in a business that does not add to the general stock or wealth of the nation, but it deprives the honest industry of the laboring man of his just reward. Suppose he labors one year in one state, and receives the ordinary currency of the place in payment for his labor. Say his residence is at Cincinnati : he receives for his labor paper purporting to be money, called *Cincinnati and Whitewater Canal Co.;* or he receives as paper money, a certificate of deposite in the *Mechanics and Traders' Bank*, with "individual responsibility," to be paid in current bank notes ; or he has received his wages in paper called *Canal Bank*, but which is only a deception, proving to be an individual promise to pay, made on silk paper, ornamented like bank notes, and merely stating that " the undersigned, who has an office *on the Canal Bank*," &c.; or he receives his pay in paper of other state banks, long after the notes have ceased to pass current in their own neighborhoods. And this is all called *currency*, and aids the idle bankers and brokers in living sumptuously upon the industry of other men, without putting a hand to the wheel themselves. The laborer's money is in the currency of the place, and he supposes he has received the value of his labor, but, on his journeying, he soon finds that his money will not pass current in the places where he travels. He must loose per-cent.-age after per-cent.-age upon every exchange he makes, until his expenses are nearly doubled by the demands for discount upon his paper money, at the various places through which he has travelled. Again, the merchant of Cincinnati must pay an average of ten per cent. to make this paper current at New York; this he adds to his profit, and the consumer must pay for all.

Ten percent. is a handsome profit in an extensive business; and this the whole community pay, in one shape or another, to incorporated companies, bankers and brokers, for the use of this bad currency.

The whole people have equal rights to any seigniorage, or other profits that are made upon coinage by the government. But in these United States, we pay annually an average of from ten to fifteen per cent. to private incorporated companies—those regulators of our finance—for mystifying the subject of currency, and furnishing a paper money that is plenty to-day and scarce to-morrow; scarcely convertible at any time but seldom *perfectly* convertible, without even a look or act from the banker that indicates the reluctance with which he parts with his specie; shewing, that even with him, his own promises to pay are considered less valuable than real money : and, therefore, although he promises to pay on demand, he prefers that the demand should never be made.

Again, the loss sustained by the paper money holder, is increased by the great uncertainty of the continuance of its circulation, or the stability and soundness of the bank ; and, therefore, goods are purchased that are not wanted, and expenses increased unnecessarily, because the holder of the money thinks, perhaps, it may not be good long, and that he may as well spend it as lay it by him. Thus few men have large or even small sums of money lying by them for any length of time. And this is another cause of the severity of the money panics, or money shocks, and contractions : there are but small sums of money to be found among the people that can be used by the people, when the banks suspend, refuse to discount, or make extraordinary demands upon their debtors for immediate payments of their long credits.

If there were no small bills in circulation, there would always be some money among the people; which, when the value of specie becomes very much increased above the ordinary rate, would be unlocked and brought out in the shape of loans or purchases at sales at auction, or some other way, and pressures would not extend through every ramification of business and of society, as it uniformly has done under a paper credit system for years past—afflicting and ruining thousands who had no influence in creating the panic, or profit in the excessive expansions and extravagance that preceded it. In short, panics are profitable only to gambling speculators. A few of whom make fortunes upon the gullibility of the producers; while thousands of honest, industrious men are ruined, that a few idle brokers, bankers, and gambling speculators, may command fortunes, often to be squandered as thoughtlessly as it has been accumulated easily; with them the maxim of "light come, light go," is generally correct.

At the first glance, one would be led to think that this money, or property, only changes hands; and that the community are none the worse for the change, and that there is just as much capital afloat, and among the people, as there would have been had it not changed hands, and these great sacrifices been made by the pressure of the times; and that individuals only suffer who are direct loosers. But look again, and you will at once see a very wide difference between this statement and the facts of the case. Productive industry is the only true source and fountain of wealth in any and every country.

Industry cannot always be productive without some capital; and here sound credit may sometimes be useful.

A. purchases a small lot of land. This exhausts his funds ; and he has only his axe to aid him in his exertions to make a living for himself, and support a small family on his new farm, Three days in the week he labors for a neighbor to purchase provisions for himself and family ; two days are spent in making little repairs about his place—building with his own hands—changing work with his neighbors— first to hire a team to draw logs for his house, then for a horse to go to the mill, then for their help to do such jobs on his place as one man cannot accomplish alone—he then has but one day left for chopping, clearing and sowing his farm. Thus the best of his life is wasted in struggling single handed with trees, bad roads, deep snows, accidents, sickness, and unavoidable misfortunes. And all this is ow- ing to a bad currency. For had he had good money, he would have saved a shilling or ten cents more a day in real money. Ten cents a day is not above the daily tax or dis- count on uncurrent paper-credit money, paid by every man of a family in the purchase of his family necessaries. He cannot get a bill changed for any thing he wants to pur- chase in small quantities ; consequently, he must buy what he does not want, or a greater quantity of what he does want, to get his bill *in part* only into small change.

What a charm, or spell, is thrown over the commercial world; that while all complain of the depreciation and in- convenience of state chartered bank paper, they tamely sub- mit to the imposition, and " spell-bound," implicitly obey its " magic wand," which, while it appears to charm paper into gold, it actually converts gold, labor and the wages of honest industry, into charmed paper money, which disap- pear the moment you attempt to grasp it.

Now let us see how much he paid for the privilege of using paper money, to those from whom he bought his

provisions and family necessaries ; for he did not go directly to the broker and give him ten cents on a dollar for specie—(which would, after all, probably been cheaper for
him to have done in the end to have converted his paper
money into change)—but he managed (as he termed it,) to
get change, sometimes by treating a friend or two who did
not need it, sometimes by buying what he did not want,
or more than he otherwise would have done of the real necessaries for his family, which were often in part wasted ;
to say nothing of his getting now and then a bad bill in
exchange, by which he looses a dollar or more at once—of
which, however, he complains bitterly.  Well, as I said
before, his average daily expenses, occasioned by bad
money, that is, money that is not good—paper money of
every description—is ten cents a day.  This sum, for four
years, the time spent in his father's neighborhood, before
going into the forest to commence business for himself,
amounts to $146—his bankers and broker's bill ! this, too,
is supposing he has kept clear of banks, and never borrowed a cent himself, or endorsed for any one else ; by which
he might have lost the whole amount at " one fell swoop ;"
while, with a sound currency, and money as plenty as any
other commodity, he would have saved ten cents a day,
which would leave him, after paying for his farm, $146 for
improvements and comforts.

How different, then, is the situation of the man of sound
currency and the man of paper money.  The one commences in the wilderness without one shilling, and continues poor through life, while the other commences with the
necessary materials for beginning in the woods ; and although their labors and hardships are very great, yet the
paper-money man has a life of wretchedness, poverty and
ignorance before him, while the sound-currency man has a

hope, and even a reasonable prospect of competence and comfort, if not of wealth. And all from this slight difference in their first beginnings.

And if this is a true picture of the baneful effects of inconvertible paper money in one instance, show me where the effect upon the consumer is not the same throughout society. I have watched paper money, and I believe its history is one of dishonor, discredit, waste, extravagance, pride, vanity, ambition and disappointment; and, in short, that if " the love of money is the root of all evil," the love of paper money is the evil itself, for it contains all the temptations to vice and immorality chargeable upon money, while it is only its shadow and not its substance ; and it is none the less emblematical of the fountain of vice for its being but a semblance of what it professes to be.

How long will men, who claim to themselves the exclusive privileges of independence, and the boasted glory of equality, bow their necks to the paper money lender, and become tax-payers to Rag Barons, in their painted paper castles ? All that is necessary is to let common sense govern, and not allow interested bank-men to control the circulating medium at their pleasure, and to suit their private interests. But make currency republican ; allow the people to elect the directors of all the financial instituitons of the country, and let the demand regulate the supply ; remove *private interest* from the regulation of currency ; make the circulating medium equally currrent in every part of the Union, and you save for the industrious laborer a competence—for the man of extensive business, a certain independence—and for all, peace, prosperity and plenty.

Here then we may again show, that productive industry, being the only true source of wealth to individuals, is so to a community. And where hundreds, nay, thousands, are compelled to labor for a bare subsistence above the tax they pay to paper money, the public looses the difference in their product, between what they now produce and what they would be able to produce with the saving of the annual paper money tax, or broker's tax. For if two men, without means, in a new country, cannot produce more profit in clearing and farming new land, than one man can with five hundred dollars, over and above the simple interest on the $500, then it follows, that every $500 collected by brokers from honest industry, to be spent in idleness, is a loss of one man to community, and of course a drain to that amount upon the labor of the industrious ; besides the loss of his own time, which might be employed in some productive enterprise or business.

The currency of the country, being left in the hands of interested individuals, is it at all surprising that those individuals should compensate themselves for its management ? And where it is left wholly to themselves to say to what amount they are to be compensated, is it at all surprising that they should arrange their plans so as to receive a regular income from the labor of the community, for their superior skill and financial powers of mystifying the science of finance, and managing said currency, so that their abilities may be in constant requisition, and they rendered independent by the gullibility of the producers ?

## CHAPTER VI.

### ON THE INFLUENCE OF BANKS UPON THEIR NEIGHBORHOODS.

The common opinion that banks enrich a place ERRONEOUS.—Flush of money—lessened productions—lessened wealth.—Foreign goods—fancy merchandize—high prices—increased expenses—money paid for every commodity —Expense of living—houses, carriages and horses must be fashionable, and the bank receives the credit.—The place prospers until pay day comes.—The scene changes.—The bankers have become rich—the producers grow poor.—The bank is to be paid—the merchant is to be paid—the mechanic is to be paid—.They all owe the bank, and where is the money to pay with ?—The evenings of years of hard industry can only satisfy for bank credits and their consequences.—Occasionally a counterfeit note, or note of broken banks, is left with the laborer.—When the price of money is high the brokers only have it for sale—new securities must be given—mortgages—judgement bonds.—The great credit farce is up.—Ask the inhabitants of the place whether the bank benefitted or injured its permanent prosperity.—Endorsers made liable—pledged securities forfeited.—The sheriff closes the drama by the unwelcome sound of his hammer.—Bank credit and bank paper, shadows, varying as the moon.—The bewitching vice of gambling thus induced.— Credit has done much towards rapidly advancing the prosperity of the Union— when properly applied and duly limited, of infinite value—its abuse fatal.— The honest and industrious support the vicious and idle.

The first effect of establishing a bank in the neighbor-hood is, that those who had no money before, soon find they have new bank bills passing through their fingers daily ; and they really believe the place is very much bene-fitted by having a bank established in it. This opinion so generally prevails throughout the United States, that I have no expectation of being believed, should I tell them that this is a fallacy—a mistake—an error; and at the very mo-ment a bank goes into operation in a place, its real wealth begins to diminish, instead of being increased. But, I should not be at all surprised if my gentle reader should be a little curious to know how this bank jugglery is con-ducted, since the transactions are made before his eyes so perfectly, that he believes it to be real wealth that is ac-cumulating around him. He sees that the village stores are better supplied with foreign goods and fancy articles than they had been before the opening of the new bank ; that many of the inhabitants who lived cheaply, plainly and even homely, now dress better—have their houses furnished and feed better than formerly ; and that even the boys, who were only employed in hard labor, are now employed by the merchants and tavern keepers, and receive their pay in money, instead of being required to take home grain or meat, or clothing, for their parents and family. Now, says the sophistical reasoner, how is it, that since the location of a bank in this place, new houses have been built, and old ones newly painted, and carriages have been bought by those who walked, or rode in plain waggons before—every body has money now, while nobody had money before. This, say they, is proof positive of the beneficial effects of a bank in the place; besides this there is an advance in the price of all the real estate in the place; every thing flourishes and looks respectful and business like. But, when pay day comes, public indignation will be kindled against the bank. The whole village inhabitants may exclaim, " woe unto ye, scribes and pharisees, hypocrites! for ye are as graves, which appear not; and the men that walk over them, are not aware of them."

Walk with me behind the curtain, and see how this wonderful secret bank money-making is conducted, and witness, in detail, the facts at which I have hinted. Here all is elegant—all is grand—all is rich!

Now let us look at the accounts, and you will see that Mr. A. the merchant, borrowed money from the bank to replenish his store of goods, and two of his neighbors, who have money plenty, and are purchasing horses and carriages and building fine houses, are his endorsers—they, too, have opened an account at the bank, and by endorsing for each other, find no difficulty in getting what money they want. And the increase of business, has justified the merchants and tavern-keepers to advance in their style of living; and to keep pace with them, the mechanics and laborers have added a slight expense to their mode of

living. And all this show of wealth is, in fact, an increased expense without a corresponding increase of income.
Time glides smoothly on, until the bank notes have to be
renewed, as they cannot then be paid, because the makers
have not realized all their visionary hopes of wealth from
credit. Bank paper, and its concomitant extravagance,
has left but little behind. Other neighbors are drawn in as
endorsers and borrowers, until the whole neighborhood
have been borrowers of credit and bank paper. They
now find, that to satisfy the demands of the bank, they
must have recourse to some stratagem to obtain a longer
credit. They have become defaulters at the bank, and
therefore the bank cannot, according to its rules, discount
paper on which their names are, either as endorsers or makers. Now steps in the convenient broker. He will lend
them money at ten per cent. for ninety days, for two or three
per cent. a month ; and mortgages, or other security, are
made to him for a sum that meets the first pressing demand
of the bank. Or, he procures for them money from some
other state or monied institution, that is glad to lend its uncurrent money on good security, at par. The bank will
not take this money, but the partner, *sub rosa*, the broker,
will give them bankable money for it, at ten per cent. discount. Now the great credit farce is completely in operation ! The village, with all its domestic habits, virtues, industry, prudence and economy, has become like a painted
castle. It may dazzle mens eye's ; but it is full of wretchedness and woe. Business is almost at a stand. The
merchant fails to meet his foreign engagements; and the
bank, finding that no more can be made out of these inhabitants, under real or pretended pressure, sues and sells out
the effects of the old inhabitants, who, one after another,
leave for the west, with the small remains of a once respecta-

ble property and competence, to tell their new neighbors of
the damages they have sustained by endorsing and being
security for others. But, trace all this misery to its proper
foundation, and it will be found in bank credit.

You will read more of the true causes of *misfortune*—
(another word for extravagance)—in money matters, in
the history of paper money, than can be found in all the
other enterprises ever undertaken by man.

Bank credit, and paper money, are but shadows of real
wealth; and those who enjoy the one, seldom ever know
the value of the other.

Gambling is a bewitching vice; it is ruinous to both
mind and body. And any extension of bank credit beyond
its legitimate bounds, is only another name for a species of
legalized gambling; and the charms it first possesses in
the food it furnishes for our vanity and ambition, soon give
place to the necessity of continuing it, to save what little
effects may still remain.

Those who live beyond their incomes, and spend money borrowed upon interest, may rely upon it, that they
never will live upon the interest of their own money.
They have mortgaged the principal for the use of the interest; and rest assured, that that mortgage never will be redeemed—that is impossible; for borrowing one sum to
pay another, and reserving interest out of the sum borrowed to pay the interest on the last loan, to preserve credit,
does not make productive capital. To borrow a new sum
to make the interest on both sums, must produce ruin
eventually.

All who have witnessed the rapid growth and prosperity
of the United States, must admit that credit has done much
in accomplishing that object, by allowing the industrious
and enterprising to anticipate their own resources. Cred-

it has done wonders in producing the rapid advancement
of this country, when compared with those countries where
credit and enterprise have been less conspicuous. Credit,
when confined within proper limits, is one of the most powerful stimulants to the production of national wealth, as is
witnessed and felt by every man who settles in a new country where capital is scarce and hard to be obtained. Yet
the abuse of credit, is as certainly ultimately fatal to the
prosperity of communities, as it is of individuals.

While speaking of credit, allow me once for all to remark, that sound, rational, consistent credit, may be and is
every day rendered useful to men in business; but that
wild speculations *upon* credit, by which men spend more
than they earn, is the kind of which I complain; and that
while speaking of the damages of bank credit, I would be
understood to mean *that* by which men of straw live by their
impositions upon the industry of others, buying what they
are unable to pay for, and involving their friends to an
amount equal, if not greater, than that of their actual wants,
to indulge in extravagance and unnecessary expenses.

# CHAPTER VII.

## ON REPUBLICAN CURRENCY.

The advantages of a republican currency over the present anti-republican currency of incorporated bank paper.—The benefits of a sound credit system uniformly admitted—Punctuality in payment important—The exclusive privileges of incorporated banking companies—Expected to make every body rich—master of every man's secret business—and establishes or ruin their credit.—Directors of banks make as much money out of the people as they can. Bank honor lends money freely, while it promotes their own interest, and sues, without remorse, while money can be made by contractions of the bank's issues. Brokers profit—or the banker only discounts notes due in N.York or some eastern market, worth 5 or 10 per cent. above their value at the bank—Or only a small part of the money may be drawn out of the bank.—The usury laws enhance the rate of interest—Money-currency—Commodity-currency—Specie not exported when bills of exchange are dearer than specie.—The business of banking is lending money, not becoming brokers.—Speculations prevent ordinary banking business—They monopolize the currency—then monopolize the trade—then regulate the prices of commodities.—Private interest injurious to currency as a commercial commodity.—Banks lend their credit to the highest bidder.—Monopoly in flour, lumber, salt, or other commodities, like a monopoly in currency, injurious.—The temptation of limited liability to fraud, in banking as in any other business.—Paper money practically made a legal tender in the payment of debts.—Incorporated banking companies have small inducements to prefer the public good to the interest of the company.—Chartered companies for all purposes anticipate the public good.—Rail roads, canals—advance prices—circulate money.—Public works unprofitable, unless they pay in tolls—immense power of internal improvement companies.

As the advantages of a limited credit have been uniformly admitted throughout the Union from the time of the Declaration of Independence to the present day, nothing need be said in favor of a reasonable credit, but to have it confined within legitimate limits, and prevent that laxity of payments that so often accompanies an over-strained credit. To continue credit sound and payments punctual, is the great desideratum of the credit system. The old maxim, that " punctuality is the life of business," has been necessarily often repeated to American debtors, and must be again and again, if it is intended that credit shall be profitable alike to the lender and the borrower, and neither suffer loss from the forgetfulness of the one or the impatience of the other.

Incorporated companies, being invested with certain exclusives priviliges, and, consequently, having distinct and separate interests from the community at large, are looked

upon as a distinct order in society ; and, by some, as possessing the power to make every body rich about them.
The directors, being chosen from among the wealthiest of
the stockholders, acquire great consequence in society,
from their having the power of giving to those whom they
choose the appearance of wealth ; allowing them such extended bank credit, and such other bank facilities as they
may require ; as well as being the repository, to a certain
extent, of the secrets of every man's finances. One word
from a director of the only bank in the place is sufficient to
give a man credit, or ruin his prospects. Yet, how few,
who vote for the election of a representative to a legislative
body, in the expectation that " he will get us a bank," think
he will place a censor upon their credit and business, who,
unless they patronize his institution and pay up punctually
too, for all the accommodations they enjoy, will be declared by him delinquents, and have their credit injured, not
only in that institution, but in such others near them as their
necessities or interests may induce them to patronize.

The bank directors of incorporated institutions, are chosen by stockholders, who vest their money or capital, in the
traffic called banking, with the view of making as much
profit as they lawfully can; under a belief that if they can
keep their money and bank upon their credit, keep other
people's money in deposite and bank upon that, they may
make an increased profit on both of these transactions.
That this is the best investment that they can make of their
money, there is no doubt, especially if they can discount
largely for each other, and use in other business as brokers
or merchants, a large share of the same capital that is professedly employed in the banking business. Directors thus
chosen, are bound to use the best of their ability to promote
the interest of the company. They have nothing to do

with the interest of the community at large any further than their interests with that community are identified. Hence, the very common error entertained among men, are frequently expressed, that the directors have done very wrong in not discounting the note of A. when they immediately after discounted a note for B. with no better names on it than were on the note of A. But before censuring a bank director for mal-practices in his office, they should reflect, that the laws of their organization bind them to make as much money as they legally can, how little you can do to him if you are not a stockholder, that can effect him, provided the stockholders are satisfied with his conduct. They elect him—they pay him—they, in short, give him his consequence in society; and he, in turn, makes as much money for the association as he can under their charter.

Bank honor means, or consists in, giving their notes with only limited responsibility without interest, for the borrower's note and interest, with unlimited responsibility of himself to the whole amount of his estate, in addition to two good endorsers, equally responsible, to the amount of the exchanged note or notes. Yet, when times are hard and money scarce, and worth more than six per cent., the borrower must flatter the bank directors, and contrive some means of evading the clauses of their charter, that renders it penal for them to charge a higher rate of interest than the law allows, as they will not lend their paper below the highest price it will bring. Among the most feasible and consistent operations for obtaining a high rate of interest lawfully, is that of making the note payable in some distant market, where the money will be worth more to the banker than it would be in his own vaults, by allowing him to charge a handsome premium on the sale of the draft for the money.

The directors may discount a note for twice or three times the amount of money to be drawn out of the bank, there being an understanding between them and the draw- er of the note, that part of the money only will be drawn— the remainder being left in deposite until the note becomes due; so that, while the bank receives double or treble in- terest for the money actually paid to the drawer, the sure- ties are held for two or three times the amount lent upon the note they endorsed. Thus private interest regulates the whole transaction. When times are easy, and money is flush in the market, it may be loaned again, as at first, upon simple interest. But, unfortunately for those who have had their notes extensively "shaved" by brokers or bankers, they are seldom ever afterwards in such cred- it as to borrow money for any length of time at simple interest.

Here again we see the influence of the ill-advised and unfortunately continued usury laws, which drive the con- scientious and cautious money lender from the market altogether, when times are critical and money is worth more than the law allows him to collect for the use of it, and thereby increases the value of what remains in the market. Circumstances may induce persons to pay a large rate of interest for a short time, rather than become de- faulters, or to purchase some very valuable cheap prop- erty, or for foreign remittances to preserve their credit abroad, and for other purposes. Money is but a more con- venient portion of the circulating medium of the country than grosser materials, when we speak of it in its most ex- tensive signification; for then it embraces every species of property that may be made convertible into remittan- ces, whether domestic or foreign. Money being the most convenient medium of circulation, will still be used as the

measure of value, though it will not be exported when bills
of exchange are cheap, that is, when the rate of exchange
is not so high as to make the exportation of specie profitable.

The proper business of bankers is, to lend money by
discounting notes; not to become brokers or dealers in bills
of exchange. But, as the sale of bills of exchange, where
bankers have friends in a remote city or country in which
the rate of exchange is against the residence of the banker, and consequently high, it is often found the most prof
itable part of the banker's business, and therefore, when
bank charters do not prohibit it, the traffic in these bills become his principal business. This, however, prevents the
bank from doing the ordinary business of banking for the
inhabitants of the place. Firstly, because the funds of the
bank are withdrawn from that neighborhood, and because
the citizens cannot pay the same per cent. consistently, that
a speculator from a foreign city or country can, who borrows
money to expend in the purchase of wheat, flour, pork, beef
or other products of the western country, to sell in an eastern market, at which place he can as well pay as at the
place where he borrows the money ; besides, he saves the
interest during the time it takes in making the remittance to
the bank where the money was borrowed; as well as having good city endorsers, his bills are worth four times the
ordinary interest for the short loan of the money. It is
true, this is often complained of by the inhabitants of the
place, who think they should have a preference to foreign
applicants for loans, without reflecting, that the business of
the company is to make as much money as they lawfully
can; and, that, until citizens of the interior can compete
with eastern speculators in the rate of interest they can
afford to pay, they cannot expect to enjoy the same facilities of borrowing money from incorporated banks.

And here, I am anxious to have it observed, that the true business of incorporated banks of issue is, to lend their cred- it as profitably as they can for the stockholders, and, conse- quently, they tax the people as much for the use of their credit as they lawfully can.

My object in this work is to show, that the money por- tion of the currency ought no more to be under the control of a private monopoly, than the cotton, flour, lumber, or any other portion of our commodity-currency ; but, that while the government reserve to themselves the exclusive privilege of coining money and regulating the value there- of, and of foreign coins, what can be more inconsistent than to authorize any set of men to issue paper upon *limited responsibility*, to make up any deficiency that may happen in the precious metals ? For, although this imaginary mon- ey is not made by law a legal tender, its effects upon the money market is nearly equal to that of its being made a tender; because it has been so generally and freely circu- lated, that the specie has been withdrawn from circulation. They cannot both circulate together among the same class of citizens, as before observed. Mechanics and laborers prefer the precious metals, and business men large paper money, always convertible at pleasure.

Self-love is the motive power of most human actions ;• and how is it possible that an incorporated company, having but one object, the dividends of the bank in view, should be expected to spend their time and money in the promo- tion of the public good, when it is entirely separate and distinct from their interests ?

# CHAPTER VIII.

## ON THE IMMENSE POWERS OF INCORPORATED COMPANIES.

The incorporation of Companies are uniformly and avowedly for the public good—but really for private advantages.—Incorporations for internal improvements possess immense power, turned to private advantage—Only profitable when they pay the interest in tolls.—The public are required to take half of the stock, or loan money for half of its completion.—This done, their success is considered certain.—The Company monopolize the hydraulics, timber, stone, land and water.—Capitalists are told of the profits of the investment—They rise in the value of the stock—Large dividends.—Municipal Corporations republican—convenient —Banking companies urge upon the legislature the necessity of capital—The danger of the withdrawal of the money of the place, to find better investments.—Credit currency is not capital—See the private motives of the stockholders—large dividends—a monopoly of the currency—limited responsibility—unlimited control of the currency.—Credit will pass as money.—Other similar Institutions will be mutual in their forbearance.—In case of hard times, the broker must wind up for us, or we must vest our funds in exchanges—become rich by our limited liability—Individuals exercise the powers of government—if they do not coin money, they make their bills pay debts.

That I may not be misunderstood, allow me to repeat, that banks are always incorporated avowedly for the public good; but the stock of these institutions is only taken by men who look to this investment of capital as the best that offers.

The arguments used to induce the legislature to incorporate companies are, that the promotion of the *public good*, in a thousand different ways require it. If it be for a rail road or canal, the legislature are told that it will increase the facilities of trade, lessen the expense of exports and imports, and shorten the distance between remote points, as well as effect the rapid rise in the value of the lands along the route ; that splendid villages will spring up, as if by magic, at its extremities, and at such points as are adapted to debarkation; in short, that it may be demonstrated to a mathematical certainty, that, although the work may not pay well in tolls on the outset, yet, that it will enhance the value of property along the route, and increase the facilities of trade to double its cost, yea, to five times the outlay, and that the public would be greatly benefitted, even although it should never pay the stockholders one pen-

ny. To do so much good, the legislature are asked to take
one-half of the stock, or to loan a large sum of money to
the company, with which to commence the work, and for
the purpose of inspiring capitalists with confidence in the
undertaking. The argument succeeds—the company is
incorporated. The law authorizes them to enter upon any
man's private property, examine it, report upon it, and if it
suits their interest to seize the same, and appropriate it to
their own use,also, to enter upon his land, cut his timber,quar-
ry his stone, and convert them to the use of the company ; and
further, to use his water privileges—out of which they
create new and valuable hydraulic powers—compensating
the owner for his property thus taken or damaged, not according to the price asked by him, but at the appraisal of
men. Here, although justice may be done between the
parties, yet men loose the rightful disposal of their private
property, through the intervention of the legislature, for the
benefit of a private company. But more of this anon.

Let us next consider what arguments are used, by the
friends of the work, to induce capitalists to invest their funds
in the enterprise. They are, the length of time for which
the charter is granted; the growth and prosperity of
the country about it, and consequent increased business;
the present expense of transportation over that section of
country, compared with the lessened cost and increased facilities about to be offered by the completion of the improvement, and the consequent increase of transportation
and business on the route, producing large dividends and a
rapid rise of the price of the stock in the market above its
original cost.

The immense hydraulic power and privileges that will
be created by the canals or slack-water navigation, of themselves are frequently represented as quite equal to the

whole outlay : then the high price at which the stock will sell in the market, by which the money may be realized on any occasion, whenever that should be desirable ; besides, that the stock may at any time be hypothecated for double the amount of money actually paid in ; and lastly, that their charter will be renewed again, should they desire it, after its expiration ; or if the legislature will not grant a new charter they will have to pay some twenty per cent. advance upon the amount of money actually expended, before they can be allowed to take possession of the improvement. Thus the stock is taken, and the interest of the company begins to show itself; but as there is such mutual dependence between the company and the public, very little inconvenience is really ever experienced from their conflicting interests.

Municipal incorporations, where all the inhabitants of a place are associated for local common purposes, are truly republican, and generally conducive to the prosperity of the place, and to the peace and happiness of the people.

Let us now examine the arguments used before the legislature to induce them to incorporate a banking company. They are reminded, that there are capitalists who wish the same privileges for investing their money advantageously that are enjoyed by the capitalists in other towns and cities where banks are established ; that the inhabitants of the city or town require the use of the capital, and all its benefits in a bank ; but that unless capitalists can enjoy the same privileges and profits for their money, that are enjoyed in other places, they will, as a matter of course, send their capital away, or move away themselves with it ; besides, the business men of the place are compelled to go to a distance to make deposites of their money, which they cannot very safely keep at home ; and when they have money to

raise upon any emergency, they must run through the place
to collect it in small sums, or post off to a distant bank for only
a small loan; and there are journeys for payments, and
postage and expenses in getting satisfactory endorsers,
and ten thousand inconveniences in living so far from a
bank; and that the bank will become a convenient safe
place of deposite for the township or county funds, and for
private funds that are now taken into a distant part of the
country at an expense and inconvenience; and that it can
do no harm, as no one is required to borrow money from it
unless they need it—and if they do, then it is quite convenient. The plenty-of-money party always prevail, and the
company is incorporated.

Let us next look into the private room of the stockholders, and hear their arguments respecting the new bank incorporating act. Their first remark is, that there is only
*limited responsibility* required, and we shall not be in danger of loosing much; we shall have large deposites to bank
upon soon, and be able to commence business upon the
payment of a small part of our capital; and those who
have not even the first instalment can borrow from a neighboring institution, and as soon as we get into successful
operation, they can borrow from our bank to pay it back
again. Thus, by keeping up a mutual good understanding
between two or three of the neighboring institutions, we
can borrow money from them to meet the instalments as
they may be required; and by loaning three dollars for
one of paid-up capital, we shall be able soon to have a fund
on hand sufficient to meet any demand that may be made
upon us by any other bank that may be jealous of our prosperity. Besides, we must have the revenues and taxes of
the country or city increased, and the money deposited with
us for safe-keeping. Our bills will circulate as well as the

specie among the people, and we shall, by receiving specie from the government, and paying out paper, be able constantly to accumulate specie in our vaults. Besides, as other banks do not return our notes upon us for the specie, but keep them as specie to bank upon, we in return will do the same, and thus, upon any examination by commissioners, we will be able to show, if not a large amount cf specie in our vaults, a large amount of the notes of other banks; and while the examinations of the banks are being gone through with, we must borrow a few thousand dollars from our neighboring banks, and in return send them our specie when their institutions are to undergo a like ordeal. This is the system adopted by bankers in many parts of the country, and by which the people, looking at their statements, given under the affidavits of their officers, are led to believe that all is quite right; and even the inquisitive legislature are satisfied.

Confidence, say they, is all that is necessary, and we may use our own funds in a broker's establishment, and lend twice as much as our own paid-up capital. And when times become hard, and the neighboring institutions begin to lessen their discounts, our broker must do most of our business at two or three per cent. a month, while we will not discount for any body except ourselves. If there appears something a little wrong in evading a law that will not allow us to take more than six per cent. interest, yet there can be no harm in the broker's doing so. If we do not enable him to make this profit in which we can share, some other bank will, and we may as well have the profit as any body else; besides, the people who wish to borrow, know whether money is worth more than simple interest to them, and what right have we to meddle with their affairs. Is it not better that it should be given to a broker than for distilled spirits, as is too often done ? When people want money they will have it at any price, and our business is to make all the money we can. And, with only a *limited res- ponsibility*, should any thing happen, and we be compelled to suspend, or even to " wind up," we shall always be the first to know of its necessity. And whoever knew of stockholders loosing money by the winding up of a bank, whether its operations had been successful or otherwise ? They can take care of themselves. In fact, we have every thing to expect and nothing to fear from the changes of the times. When times are prosperous, we will dispose of stock. When times are hard, and stocks fall, we shall be able to purchase again for half the money. By preserving our credit as individuals, whatever may be the fate of the bank, we shall have, for a few years, " the best chances" in the neighborhood for amassing property.

These, with ten thousand additional arguments, are used to induce the wealthy in the neighborhood to take stock, (paya- ble in instalments,) and pay up the whole, and receive an in- terest for the amount thus advanced before it becomes due.

Thus commences a bank that is to issue a portion of the circulating medium of the country—a currency, the metal- ic portion of which the government reserves to itself the right, the privilege, and power of coining, and the regula- ting of its value, that the public may not be imposed upon by light or spurious coin, or be left without a circulating medium while there is bullion enough for coinage—there- by allowing a seigniorage to some foreign country, or to private individuals for coining the currency of the country for them. What would be said of a government that would *incorporate a company with power to coin money*, and allow that company to make the circulating medium of whatever material or value they chose ?

# CHAPTER IX.

## THE EFFECTS OF ALLOYING THE COIN OF ANY COUNTRY.

Debasing the coin—nominally raises the value of the precious metals—virtually raises the value of commodities.—The gold bill, by lessening the quantity of gold in ten dollars, raised the nominal value of all other commodities except silver, and reduced the legal value of that in the same proportion that it nominally raised the value of gold.—Debasing the coin unjust.

When the government of a country alloys its coin, and debases its currency by lessening the value, without altering the denomination, making it a tender for the payment of the same sum after as before its being so alloyed, the creditor sustains a loss, and the public suffer an injustice that the whole commercial world must reprobate. The act is fraudulent upon citizens having particular contracts due in coin at the legal value, as rents or long leases that are due annually. How much more contemptible is it in a government to authorize a few individuals, for the promotion of their private interest, at their own will and pleasure, upon a *limited responsibility*, to issue so much bank paper to circulate as money as shall materially change its value—especially where the company have the power to fix the limits of their own responsibility, and the extent to which they will inflate the currency, and consequently the amount to which they will depreciate it; since they are capable of discounting their own and other people's notes, and of drawing the specie out of the bank, until there might not remain one shilling in the dollar of the security to the bill-holder, that the public supposed constituted the basis of the paper that they were receiving as money. Thus palming their bills upon a gullible and unsuspecting public, and filling their own pockets with good money, and failing rich, though hundreds should be made poor by the fraudulent transaction.

## CHAPTER X.

### THE EFFECTS OF BANK FAILURES UPON PUBLIC MORALITY.

Bank failures, by their frequency, cease to degrade the stockholders.

Familiarity with vice lessens its hideous form that firstly
alarmed us, till by degrees we become callous to the offensive sight, and at last indifferent. "Shame being lost, all
virtue is lost." Bank suspensions and bank failures are not
looked upon any longer as disgraceful events, how much
soever the public may be enraged against their perpetra-
tion. They have become things of every-day occurrence,
and the wealthiest and most consequential members of society often are stockholders or directors in some of these
insolvent institutions. But since these speculators have
saved some money for themselves, they have acquired respect and consequence in society. They feel themselves
above reproach, and entitled to receive that respect that
money always commands.

Now we have taken a peep behind the curtain of a newly incorporated banking company, where the initiated only
are admitted, and witnessed their machinations and fraudulent practices, which, to the uninitiated stockholders and
depositors is all fair—to them the capital stock is truly and
*bona fide* paid in. Their assets are professedly fair and
honorable. Their business moves on as regularly "as clock
work."

But *this* and *that* picture serve to show the attempts at
gullibility, by those who have the management of public
money, or private credit. The great secret is to keep all
they have, and get all they lawfully can. They make it
the interest of their directors to make as much money as
they possibly can out of every operation, by charging
interest from the date of the note left for discount, although

not discounted precisely on the day it was presented, to retain part of the funds in hand as long as possible without
interest; but to charge interest on every dollar for every
day that any individual's note lies over, or, on balances due,
if he by any means over draws his account. All this is
lawful, and has been so long and so generally practiced by
incorporated banking companies, that it has become *almost
right.*

But to our subject, the circulating medium. What common feeling or common interest have we discovered between the banker and the borrower—between the banking
incorporated company and the public ? None. There is
none. There can be none felt by institutions formed solely
for the purpose of enriching private individuals. But this
is not all. This disgraceful limited responsibility-principle holds out an inducement to fraud, to corruption, want
of faith, and utter loss of confidence, public and private.
The natural effects of limited responsibility with unlimited
public confidence, governed by private interest, is shown
in the every-day transactions of every bank in community.
They circulate as much money as they can keep afloat, and
receive their large interests, dividends, and bonuses, without one thought of the public convenience. Having literally flooded the country with their paper, and removed
their deposites from the bank to some eastern city, as New
York, or Philadelphia, they sell bills upon them at a profit:
issue post notes, or submit to some other subterfuge, to
evade the immediate payment of their notes in money on
demand. If these will not pass, they suspend specie payments, and if they fall into the hands of commissioners, or
other officers who are or may be appointed to wind up their
concerns, they loose nothing except their charter to make
money upon popular gullibility. But more of this hereafter.

## CHAPTER XI.

### ENGLISH AND AMERICAN CURRENCIES.

A comparison of the currency of the United States with other countries—especially those with whom she is connected by commercial relations.

One of the strongest arguments in favor of the circulation of bank paper as money, is drawn from the fact, that
the nations with whom most of the American commerce is
carried on, use a paper money circulating medium, thereby increasing the money currency of those countries far
above the actual amount of precious metals that circulates
among them. But while we admit the soundness of the
reasoning, so far as the comparison holds good, I am unwilling to believe, that because there are in common circulation in England five pound notes, that have been tested
by long experience to be convenient to all classes of citizens there, that one dollar bills can be useful in the United
States, while even in France, the country with which much
of our commerce is carried on, five hundred franc notes, is
their smallest denomination of paper intended to circulate
as money. Hence, I infer, that if we argue in favor of a
paper currency in the United States, upon the ground that
paper money is the currency of the countries with which
we trade, we ought to show their currency to be paper of
as small denominations as circulate among us; and that our
trade with them, the rate of exchange, and the reciprocity
of credit, are mutually effected by the currency of each
country respectively. We ought rather to conclude, that,
since England and France have found large bills only convenient and profitable to them, that we shall find a like paper money convenient and profitable to Americans. I am
unwilling to admit, that small bills are to be defended in
the United States upon the ground that large bills have suc-

ceeded in Europe ; but am quite willing to admit that the "go ahead" character of the American people may be some apology for their so anxiously desiring a paper currency ; and that, therefore, bills of as small denominations as circulate in those countries may be made to circulate advantageously in the United States; although I am inclined to believe, that, upon a careful examination of the money currency and other circulating mediums of these countries, as compared with the United States,that the latter does not require so small paper money as either of the former. England, with her national debt of £800,000,000 sterling, requires a greater quantity of the smaller paper or credit currency than France—and far smaller paper money than the United States, where there is no interest on a national debt to meet, in change, quarterly ; besides the debts of the United States are due in a foreign country, where its bank credit paper is not expected to pass, and where gold and silver or bills of exchange are the circulating medium, therefore it does not require smaller bank bills than are circulated in those countries; or, if they are required, I think they should not be of smaller denominations than twenty dollars. And in process of time even as small as these might be dispensed with.

## CHAPTER XII.

### ON THE EVILS OF SMALL BILLS.

The injury that the circulation of small bills are to the banks themselves during panics.

A fact, not generally avowed respecting currency, is, that the danger of a run upon the banks, is always in proportion to the smallness of the bills, and the amount of such bills that the bank has in circulation.

A few large creditors may be reasoned with and satisfied, without ruin to the debtor, until specie can be obtained and payment made ; but small and numerous creditors *must* be satisfied. They must have money at the instant, or they will ruin the institution with the public. Besides, as all the channels of commerce, domestic and foreign, must be filled with the precious metals or some other circulating medium, it is wisdom in a legislature not to pass any laws authorizing the issue of small bills to circulate as money, that specie may supply their place. All the minor channels will then be filled with gold and silver, and ready to support the failing resources of the banks in case of a panic, and thus prevent the necessity of importing bullion at a great private expense, and derangement of the natural commercial transactions of a country.

## ON PUBLIC GULLIBILITY.

The gullibility of the people, and blindness of legislators, have made them an easy prey to interested bankers and brokers.

The gullibility of the people of the United States have left them an easy prey to the avarice of bankers, and the blindness of legislatures, (whether wilfully blinded by self-interest or otherwise ;) and has made them the tools of interested bankers and brokers, and led to the emission of bills of a smaller denomination than circulate in other countries, or than are required to circulate in these United States·

# CHAPTER XIV.

## ON THE CURRENCIES.

### GOLD THE NATURAL CURRENCY OF THE UNITED STATES.

Gold is the natural currency of the United States—hence the necessity for small
bills on account of the bulk and weight of silver is obviated.

Gold and silver, both being a lawful tender in the United
States, lessens the necessity for small notes—since the inconvenience of carrying a large amount in silver cannot
be urged against a metalic currency, that would exist if it
was composed of that only ; besides, the gold bill, by
raising the value of gold in the United States, when coined
into eagles and parts of eagles, has rendered it the true
natural currency of this country for all amounts above $2,50.

Gold is the legal money of France, but being under-val-
ued by the mint, it commands a small premium in the market for the convenience of travellers ; and silver is as *truly*
the money of that nation as paper is of the United States.
The currency that possesses the least intrinsic value will be
pushed forward and circulated, while the more valuable is
drawn off for market or for husbanding.

### ON THE CURRENCY OF FOREIGN COINS.

Foreign coins current in the United States.—Silver the natural currency of
England.

Silver is the legal money of England for small sums ;
but gold and silver circulate indiscriminately among the
people. Gold circulates by tale, or at the market price,
and English-coined silver, of full weight, by tale exclusively ; while all foreign coin is received only as bullion.
In the United States, encouragement has been given to the
importation of foreign coins, by making them current in
the receipt of customs, at their full foreign value by

weight. Raising the value of gold at the mint a shade
above the foreign market price, has given it a slight protection against exportation, whenever the rate of exchange
is so high as to justify the exportation of specie, hence the
lessened necessity for small bills to circulate as money.

### ON THE VALUE OF THE PRECIOUS METALS.

Of the advantages that the precious metals possess over any other material for a
circulating medium.

Gold and silver possess an intrinsic value in proportion
to their abundance in a country, and the cost or labor necessary to their production, the same as iron and other metals.
They also possess an additional value from their fitness for
certain articles of ornament and use, as well as their adaptation to the use of a circulating medium, not only between
the inhabitants of one, but those of different countries. They
are produced in various parts of the globe, and as articles
of capital and industry, they possess a value, like other
commodities, dependant upon the cost of producing them,
and their peculiar value, founded upon the immutable
law of supply and demand, by which all values are determined, whether of gold and silver or of other commodities. The quantity of the precious metals found previous to the discovery of America was so small, that, by
common consent throughout Europe, they became the circulating medium from one country to another.

### ON THE COST OF PRODUCING THE PRECIOUS METALS.

The cost of producing gold and silver bears the same proportion to their market
value, as that of lead or iron.

Gold and silver have ever been considered the most inviting products of industry to which labor and capital can
be applied; but, notwithstanding, at times large quantities
of the precious metals have been found, and a few individ-

uals enriched thereby, yet, if all the time spent in searching for mines, the high prices paid for lands supposed to possess them, the rent of lands on which they are found while being wrought, the amount of money paid for laborer's wages while employed in digging and smelting the ore and refining the metal, the interest on capital invested, and the immense sums unsuccessfully expended in visiting countries and exploring unknown regions to discover gold and silver, were all duly taken into consideration, the cost of the precious metals at this moment would not be found to be less than their present value, with all the importance that is given them with the heads of kings and caps of liberty, with which coins are so splendidly embellished.

### GOLD AND SILVER REAL WEALTH.

Gold and silver are real wealth.—Bank paper only imaginary wealth.

Hence we see that gold and silver possess an intrinsic value as products of industry with other commodities. They are therefore real wealth, and not the representatives; although their adaptation to currency by their uniformity of value throughout the world, their convenient portability, malleability, toughness and durability, may have enhanced their current price; yet, their value in the arts would of itself have given to them a consequence above all other metals.

We next come to the comparison of the precious metals with incorporated bank paper, as that is now used as their representative.

### PAPER MONEY NOT WEALTH.

Paper money possesses no intrinsic value.—Its legal currency a fiction.

Firstly, paper money is of little or no intrinsic value to be converted into any other material than that of money;

and when destroyed or lost, the whole community are but
little damaged, as the entire loss falls on the bill-holders
alone. The materials of which paper money is composed
are of easy access, and possess no extraordinary properties;
consequently, the wear and tear of the circulating medium
is much less in paper money than in the precious metals.
But, since bank notes are only the representative of money,
and possessed of no intrinsic value, and merely the representative of capital, their accumulation is not an increase of
real wealth, but only its representative. Gold and silver
have their legitimate functions to perform and their natural
channels to occupy ; and when these operations are performed by paper money, its advantages cease.

# CHAPTER XV.

## ON BANKING.

### ITS LEGITIMATE BUSINESS.

The legitimate operations of banking, or the circulation of paper money.

Among the various commmercial and financial operations
known and dignified by the title of banking, three kinds
only require a particular notice ; and, as they are distinct
and wholly different from each other in their uses, operations and influence, as well as their constitutions, they require particular descriptions, that they may not be con-
founded with financial operations not intended to be treated
of in this place. These three are, banks of deposite, banks
of discount, and banks of circulation.

## OF BANKS OF DEPOSITE, DISCOUNT, AND CIRCULATION.

Their description—their uses and characteristic distinctions.

### OF BANKS OF DEPOSITE.

A bank of deposite is an institution established for the safe-keeping of coin and bullion, and the transfer of accounts on its books from one person to another; thereby facilitating mercantile transactions, saving the trouble and expense of repeated countings and transportations of the precious metals from place to place, lessening the risk and friction, or wear and tear of the coin—as was the case of the old bank at Amsterdam, and also the present one at Hamburgh. Hence, a bank of deposite neither adds to or diminishes the currency; as the checks, drafts and credits in the bank are just equal to the amount of specie which depositors have there in safe-keeping.

### OF BANKS OF DISCOUNT.

A bank of discount is an institution possessing a capital in money, which the proprietors lend by discounting acceptances and promissory notes, having but short periods to run. It also receives on deposite, at interest or not, as the parties may agree, the money of other people, re-payable on demand or at fixed periods, which it lends as its own in discounting securities. Of this class are the banks in London, (except the bank of England, and a few others,) and those of most of the private bankers on the continent. Hence the slight influence of these institutions upon the currency or credit of their respective countries. They do not increase the circulation, but only issue, or put in circulation, money that actually existed independent of any act of theirs.

### BANKS OF CIRCULATION.

A bank of circulation is an institution established for

the purpose of lending *credit* by an exchange of notes between the banker and the borrower. The borrower finding that he can do better in the market with the well-known
notes of the banker payable on demand, than he can with
his own, due a short time hence, while the banker, whose
credit is known and established, has no fear of having his
notes immediately returned upon him for specie. Therefore, for such interest as can be agreed upon between the
parties, never exceeding the rate beyond which the banker
is restricted by law, he exchanges notes with the borrower
Here then is a new currency introduced, under the influence of credit and private interest. And let us see what
the probable effects of such a bank must naturally be upon
a circulating medium. Firstly, the banker issues his notes
cautiously, and only at short credits, lest they should be returned upon him in sums beyond the amount of specie he
may have on hand. Soon, however, he finds public confidence remains firm, and his bills circulate freely among the
community, when he increases his issues, in the hope of
reaping more profits, and so continues to increase them until
all the channels of currency are completely glutted. Under all these circumstances, specie is exported; and the
only home currency left is bank notes. Prices have risen
nominally, imports have been made from abroad to supply
the increased market by the excess of currency; and this
expansion of credit extends its influence far and wide, de-
ranging the regular business of the country, raising prices
unexpectedly, and, in short, making business lively and
money plenty. By-and-bye the foreign imports are to be
paid for. Bank paper will not pay debts in a foreign market, and the note-holders call upon the banker for remittances. Specie is all the means at his disposal, every dollar of
which is drawn from his vaults, to meet these demands,

He, in turn, is compelled to call upon his debtors for the immediate payment of their notes, and finds they have expended the borrowed money in the purchase of inconvertible property, (no matter how valuable or productive, since it is inconvertible,) and they are unable to meet their liabilities.

Now comes on a money pressure, with hard times. Every man wishes to borrow, but nobody has the means to lend. The bank fails. The merchant fails. The farmer suffers. And all feel the sad effects of over-issues, and consecutive contractions, uniformly attendant upon a currency dependant upon *credit*, and regulated by *private interest*. A metalic currency never admits of such contractive and expansive fluctuations.

Of this character are the nine hundred banks and branches in the United States, with their 360 million dollars of paid-up capital. They combine all the powers, privileges and characters of these three kinds of banking, however incompatible with each other they may appear to be. Here begins the mystification of the subject of finance ; and herein lies the great evil in the currency of the United States. Dissimilar things are confusedly combined, and those who attempt to explain the secrets and mysteries of currency, have found more profit in their mystification than in their elucidation ; consequently there is a great want of correct information upon the subject.

## BANKS OF DEPOSITE AND BANKS OF DISCOUNT SAFE AND HIGHLY SERVICEABLE TO A COMMERCIAL COMMUNITY.

No evil is to be apprehended from banks of deposite, or of discount, while they are kept within the sphere of well-established principles. But change their character so as to authorize individuals concerned in them, to issue according

to their will and pleasure, such sums as they may find it to
their interest and convenience to circulate, and the usefulness of these banks are soon lost in the uncertainty, instability and dangerous fluctuations, which a few interested
individuals have the power to impart to the currency, and
consequently to inflict upon the community.

## OF CREDIT COMMERCIAL BANK PAPER.

A bank of credit circulation, to be a useful institution,
should be confined to commercial transactions. The notes
to be discounted, should be exclusively business notes; and
should be composed only of checks, drafts, bills of exchange, and of the exports and imports, which constitute,
with the addition of the precious metals, the basis of the
exchanges, being part of the transferable commodity-currency of the country and not the money-currency. And
here let me remark, that the money-currency of a country should always possess the qualities of specie, that of
convertibility and uniformity of value; which can never be given to any portion of a circulating medium,
that has to be converted into coin before it can be applied to the entire purposes of money. The money-currency, therefore, should never be connected with commercial transactions, but should always be a convertible circulating medium, unconnected with any contingency of credit
or interest, either of many or of a few individuals, or any
circumstance by which a possibility of a defeat or delay of
payment can be effected.

The individuals entrusted by the public in the management of that part of the currency of the country that constitutes the bank paper portion, should be only men of the
highest reputation for honor, integrity and punctuality, as
well as being men cautious in their business, temperate in

their habits, and unencumbered by any connection with speculations of a doubtful nature, and who should not only be holden to the whole amount of their private fortunes, but who should give good security for all money that may pass through their hands, and be strictly prohibited from discounting paper in which any director has an interest either directly or indirectly.

## CHAPTER XVI.

### ON THE LIMITED RESPONSIBILITY OF BANK DIRECTORS AND STOCKHOLDERS.

Why should bank directors and stockholders be exempt from the common responsibility and unlimited individual liability, to which parties to every contract subject the private individuals concerned therein ?

I cannot, for the life of me, divine an answer that would be at all satisfactory to Americans ; and especially to those whose business is impaired and interest endangered by the limited responsibility of those who issue their own notes to circulate as money. Certainly there is nothing found in the moral law—upon which all positive enactments are professedly founded. There can be nothing in the character of the parties composing banking incorporations, that should entitle them to this special privilege ; because they are formed of any class of citizens, who may possess a little cash, and are desirous of becoming stockholders in banks.

To justify this *limited liability* before the public, recourse must be had to the most refined subtleties, artificial expedients, and sophistical reasoning ; for bank stockholders will hardly avow the only true reason that can be assigned, that is, the *privilege of their order.*

Wealth has always been privileged, and under the guise of public good, seeks its own advancement by extraordinary requirements.

The principle of limited liability, having once been ceded to the wealthy and to banking monopolies, privilege usurps the place of right. The true ground of perfect freedom is perfect responsibility. Liberty and liability go hand in hand. Rights should only be enjoyed, upon the condition of the full performance of duties. Banking companies can show no better grounds to distinction, than merely their claim to be wealthy.

The public should be cautious in conferring upon bankers any peculiar advantages. For the moment they do it they cede to them the additional dignity of a privileged order, viz: they sell them the right to *coin* money—and then release them from the responsibility that the government claims of persons employed in the United States' mint; and even from the ordinary responsibility of common contracts! Such madness is unheard of. Such credit power never before known.

## CHAPTER XVII.

### ON THE LIMITED RESPONSIBILITY OF CHARTERED BANKS.

Limited responsibility is directly at variance with all the principles of free trade and free banking.

The breath of free trade and free banking is stifled by any legal restraint from the ordinary responsibility of all men. The first principle of free trade, or of free banking, being the most perfect and unlimited responsibility, and that of private individual and unlimited responsibility the basis of all financial operations, no man or body of men can be released from them except by positive legal enactments.

It requires the force of law to release the privileged order of bankers from the universal liability that accompanies all contracts and agreements, as well as all promises to pay money.

If it be urged, that men who entrust their funds to the management of clerks and salaried officers, are frequently less faithfully served than they would be if they took the entire management of their affairs into their own hands, the argument would be in favor of their entire responsibility rather than of their limited liability, as the only security of the bill-holder is the responsibility of the institution and that of the stockholders. If the stockholders are not liable in their individual capacities, then the security of the bill-holder vanishes like smoke.

If they intend to deal honestly, and expect people to receive their *promises-to-pay* as money, is it wonderful that the bill-holders in their turn, should expect them to be equally responsible with themselves ? The endorsers and makers of notes due to the bank, even those who have had no benefit or interest in the transaction, are each holden to the utmost farthing of their private property, for the whole amount of note or notes so given; and yet the *privileged* party require that *they, themselves*, should only be held responsible to a given amount, (which is the real or imaginary capital invested in the institution,) still they expect the public to receive their notes upon trust, and circulate them as money.

## ON THE EXCHANGE OF NOTES WITH BANKS.

Men must be truly infatuated who will exchange notes with a banker, and give good security for their payment AND PAY INTEREST UPON THE SAME IN ADVANCE, and not require the banker to give equally as good security for the redemption of his notes, in return.—This practice is truly a comment upon republican institutions.

The bandage here drawn over the eyes of the public must be too thin not to be seen through by every person who takes the trouble to look through the veil. If they claim that they are released from personal liability, by the special law of partnerships, let us look again at that law, and see when, where and how it interferes with the common principle of unlimited liability.

On the slightest reflection, it must be obvious, that limited liability is a privilege that has not the slightest foundation in natural right.

The general, if not the universal rule, of commercial transactions, is, that every individual is liable to the full extent of his means for engagements entered into by himself, or on his behalf, or jointly with others ; and it is only by the intervention of a special, that he can be shielded from the more general law. "Obligation to action and rectitude of action, are obviously coincident and identical."

Legal liability should be commensurate with moral obligation. The efficient principle of liability is highly conservative, and one from which men, singly, or in their associate capacity, should never feel themselves freed. Upon this principle rests the beneficent doctrines of commercial freedom.

Private interest, the love of gain, and the spirit of enterprise, will be sufficient to induce capitalists to make the necessary investments, to carry on whatever trade in banking the currency may require, under *unlimited responsibility*. The spirit of speculation requires no new and improper stimulus to excite it to action : it is always ready to embrace every favorable opportunity of exerting itself. Limited responsibility has a tendency to elicit a spirit of gambling.

Some one, somewhere, remarks with much appropriateness, that, " if the principles of free trade, which are but those of justice, of equality, and of common sense, do not admit of unnecessary restraints upon the liberty of human actions, much less, when properly understood, can they sanction or tolerate a limited individual liability."

### PROMISES TO PAY MONEY, NOT MONEY.

Bills promising to pay should never be received as money, unless their convertibility is secured to the bill-holder beyond the possibility of defeat.

Supposing partnerships for manufacturing, or commercial purposes, to admit of limited responsibilities and liabilities, where the parties are the only persons directly interested in the result, does it follow that a trade in promises-to-pay on paper, where the partners are the least liable to loss, and where the public are the one party making no profit in the business, and so situate as to be compelled to receive these promises-to-pay as money or cease to do business, should be placed upon the footing of co-partnerships, where all the parties concerned have the means of knowing the amount of risk they run, and when they have a prospect of gain in view in the formation of the company, and conduct of their business ?

The trader in promises-to-pay, which require little expense to manufacture, should never be placed upon the same footing with the exchanger of material products, nor his issues to the expansive powers of private ambition; especially, when it is recollected that these promises-to-pay on paper are to be the standard by which the value of all material products are to be estimated. When will the fallacy of calling promises-to-pay by the interesting title *money*, be exploded? and when will the public understand that promises-to-pay coin are not coin, and ought not of right to be ranked as money, any more than individual notes, bonds or mortgages, containing promises-to-pay coin, should? as many of these are far better secured than bank note promises-to-pay, and less liable to be defeated, yet they are seldom dignified by the appellation of money.

## ON PERFECT INDIVIDUAL LIABILITY OF BANKS.

Private Banks and Joint Stock Banking Companies, like those of Scotland, require summary Bankrupt Laws to render them safe and beneficial to the public ; even although they are based upon the broad principles of PERFECT INDIVIDUAL LIA-BILITY.

In Scotland, and other places where Joint Stock Com-panies are organized, and administered upon the sound prin-ciple of the liability of each partner to the whole extent of his fortune for the whole debts of the company, the note-holders have had better security, and the bank paper a pro-portionately better circulation—there have been fewer fail-ures or suspensions—the share-holders have more uni-formily received large dividends, while they have saluta-rily restrained the excessive expansions of the currency; at the same time proving the universal benefit of entire re-sponsibility of all the parties concerned in the institution as stockholders, directors, clerks or agents, where they have a discretionary power over the issues of the bank, and are responsible for the redemption of their notes to the whole amount of their private fortunes—the fear of loss always nicely balancing the love of gain. But even this responsi-bility of partners or stockholders, I foresee, would be lia-ble to serious objections, some inconveniences, and much liability to fraud—for promises-to-pay coin of the highest value on paper of no value, holds out strong temptations to equivocation, and to excessive issues in the hope of gain ;

often, no doubt, with the firm belief of the ability of the institution honestly and faithfully to meet her liabilities punctually.

But, when times change, and the funds of the bank are materially diminished by losses, or by the suspensions of payment of other companies, or of individuals who may hold a large portion of their funds temporarily, it is easily seen how individual liability may be evaded by the transfer of the stock of the bank to minors, to " men of straw," or to non-residents; and in thousands of ways evading the liability of their private fortunes for the demands against the bank.

If to avoid this fraudulent transfer, you make the stockholders who firstly subscribe, and those who receive transfers, severally holden, the stock would not be likely to be taken. Men of large capital would fear to become stockholders in an institution from which their private fortunes could not be released, should they desire to sell and transfer their stock, and be no longer connected with, or responsible for, the debts of the institution.

If, to avoid fraud, you should only hold the stockholders responsible for all issues made during the time they held their stock, much perplexity would naturally arise in ascertaining what amount of unredeemed bills persons having sold and transferred their stock were respectively liable for. Again, if you limit the stockholders to a given *time* after they have transferred their stock, whether that time be long or short, the liability may be avoided. The natural result would be, that the uninitiated stockholders and the bill-holders would suffer by having to pay up all deficiencies, while those who had enjoyed the profits would escape.

But the plan I propose of removing the *temptation to fraud*, and to over-trading in paper money, would protect

the bill-holder, by preventing the danger of over-issues ;
for when there is no over-expansion of the money currency, there is nothing to fear from oppressive contractions.

## CHAPTER XVIII.

## FREE BANKING.

THE PEOPLE'S SYSTEM OF BANKING REQUIRES UNLIMITED
RESPONSIBILITY, WITH GOOD SECURITY FROM THE DIRECTORS
FOR ALL MONEY THAT PASSES THROUGH THEIR HANDS.

The people should elect the directors of banks as they elect the most numerous
branches of their legislatures.

The directors should have fixed salaries for their services, (neither to be increased or diminished during their terms
of service.) Their duties should be clearly defined. They
should give sufficient security for the faithful discharge of
their duties, and the prompt payment over to their successors in office of all monies and property of the bank in their
possession.

Their responsibility to the public will increase and secure their circumspection, prudence and good management,
and consequent enlargement of public confidence.

The individual liability of the directors will sharpen
their sagacity and caution, and induce the strictest attention
to the interests of the institution, as well as to the honorable
and fair accommodation of the borrowers.

Excessive expansions of the currency and over-issues
would be prevented; as they would have two positive
limitations beyond which they could not pass. In the first
place, they could not issue more paper than was apportioned to them by the state bank of issue, for circulation. In

the second place, they could not issue that amount, unless they had one-third part of the amount in specie actually in their vaults at the time of their issues.

How widely different is the situation of a responsible director of a bank, having given good security for the faithful performance of his duties, and who has no interest in the dividends, or amount of business done, but whose direct and private interest is in the *manner* in which that business is done, from that of one whose interest consists of dividends, bonuses, and profits, and where the stockholders and directors have only a limited liability, and their interests depend upon such dividends, bonuses and profits as are dependant upon the amount of business done by the institution. It is of no great moment to the latter, whether the institution possesses any character for aught, save large dividends; or whether the public be or be not accommodated to their satisfaction, provided the directors and stockholders are largely benefitted. The gain and profits of such a bank, to the issuer, is immediate, considerable and certain, whilst the cost of the production of his paper money is relatively insignificant; and the loss of profit consequent upon a reaction, is distant, contingent and uncertain—it may be avoided—it may be thrown, as it usually is, upon the shoulders of the public. For, in but very few instances, is the return of paper upon the issuer attended with positive loss to the banker. The temptation to over-issues, therefore, succeeeds.

The losses of the bank consists in, and are principally composed of, a diminution of anticipated profits. The elected director, who has given security for the performance of his duties, cannot be guilty of any malversation without being accountable in two ways ; firstly, on his bonds, with his sureties ; secondly, to the public, through the ballot-boxes, at the ensuing election of directors,

Hence, there exists every inducement to incorporated banking companies, with limited liability, to lend their credit, and to increase the supply of their paper. Their private interest stimulates them to an expansion of the currency, by bank credit, in form of bank notes ; which, to the borrower, is just as available as capital, and to the issuer a source of profit practically unlimited, so long as the solvency of the bank is thought not to be impaired, or in other words, so long as the fund of public gullibility remains available. " Hence the constant tendency of banks is, to lend too much, and to put too many notes in circulation ;" but which may happily be obviated, by removing from the director private interest in the amount issued, and by increasing his responsibility in the faithful and popular discharge of his duties.

### THE PROPOSED PLAN OF FREE BANKING SHOULD NEITHER EXPAND NOR CONTRACT CURRENCY, NOR HAVE ITS CONVERTIBILITY QUESTIONABLE.

It is a clear proposition, that paper, perfectly, really and thoroughly convertible as this proposed must always be, can neither expand nor contract the general mass of the currency to an amount permanently greater or less than it would be with a medium exclusively metalic.

If the amount of precious metals in the United States was sufficient to fill the channels of commerce, there would be no occasion to issue paper to circulate as money, since it would only occupy such channels as would have been filled with the precious metals. Therefore, the average quantity of money, the value of commodities, and the prices of real estate, will be nearly the same, whether the currency consists of convertible paper and coin, mutually interchangeable for each other, or of coin alone. The system proposed would render the paper portion of the money-currency perfectly convertible, which can hardly be said to be the situation of *any* of our present incorporated bank paper. For, since their numerous failures, suspensions, and evasions of payment, some slight doubt must always exist, as to the continuance of the convertibility of the paper of even the most solvent banks, under a limited responsibility, while it is subject to the control of private interest and credit influence.

The issuing of post notes, due at a long period hence, is a subterfuge of the banks to augment their credit and increase their profits; and although it may not materially influence the whole mass of currency, when considered separately from the money portion, yet, when claimed to be a part of the money of the country, it is destructive of all the metalic character of the paper—its convertibility, stability, uniformity, and its punctuality—that is uniformily attached to the money composed of the precious metals.

## ON FREE REPUBLICAN BANKING.

In the United States, where perfect liberty and equality in matters of religion and literature prevail, the currency of the country ought to be free, and perfectly convertible, and as republican as the other institutions of the country.

A great desideratum among financiers and writers upon currency has ever been, to separate the incompatible functions of banks of issue from those of discount. This plan provides most effectually for their divorce. In fact, one of the leading objects of the measure under consideration, is, the restricting the supply of paper money to the actual demand for it, in exchange, and as an actual representative of specie, rendered indispensably necessary to the success of American enterprise, by the genius of their government, which, by its free and living principles inspires an almost enthusiastic ambition into every citizen.

The great and glorious Declaration, that "all men are born free and equal," is understood by the Americans, in its most extensive signification, and they sincerely feel that they are truly free and equal in the pursuit and enjoyment of wealth, happiness, honor, offices, and of religious and moral education. Hence arises their laudable ambition, and noble enterprise in every lawful pursuit and employment, likely to give honorable distinction, promote wealth, produce enjoyment, extend their circle of respectable acquaintances, the knowledge of their country, of mankind, and the world at large.

The free exercise of religion in the United States has also done much to inspire her citizens with their distinguishing characteristic go-ahead principle.

The religion of Jesus Christ ever recognized the doctrine of equality and of liberty. And the precepts and examples of the blessed Savior of mankind in this respect, far surpasses all other aphorisms and examples that have ever been handed down for the civil or moral government of the world.

This love of liberty, and respect for the opinions and feelings of others, enriches American society beyond that of all other countries, in the " home feeling" that they enjoy, even among strangers where their business, interest, or amusement, leads them. The privilege they take of asking questions, and talking of themselves and friends, upon even slight acquaintance, although it may appear officious, presuming, and obtrusive to strangers, upon their first initiation into American society, yet, after all, to persons whose political institutions, religious, literary and moral education have taught them equality and liberty, even this freedom of declaration and enquiry leads to improvement in various ways, that the formal habits of foreign courts do not admit, where every person has his own particular sphere marked out to him at his birth, and in which he must remain through life, unless he falls by crime or misfortune from his station— for he can never hope to rise above that rank except by some fortuitous event.

True, there are many honorable instances, even in England, of persons born in comparative obscurity, who have risen to wealth, and to places of power and profit under the government. But in America, such things are common and of daily occurrence, and looked upon as matters of course. Here is a case in point : it was not until the late election, that one-tenth part of the people of the United States knew that their Chief Magistrate, MARTIN VAN BUREN, was a self-made man—that he was born of plebian parentage, and that, with the blessing of heaven and his own exertions, without the aid of powerful friends at court, he had risen to fill the highest office in the gift of the people. The people in the United States are the sovereign power—and from them, either directly or indirectly, flow all the gifts of office, honor and power ; and hence the importance of its currency being purely republican, and free from politics, commercial credit, or foreign financial influence. It should be as republican as their religion, literature, or politics. If this was the case, the political machinery of the government would move smoothly on, and it would soon be emphatically, what its inhabitants now claim it to be, " the land of the free and the home of the brave."

116 DUNCOMBE'S FREE BANKING.

## CHAPTER XIX.

### A LARGER CIRCULATING MEDIUM THAN THE PRECIOUS ME-
### TALS NECESSARY.

The spirit of American enterprise—The free principles of the American government—The existing state of our commercial relations with foreign countries—
The credit character of their currencies— and the situation of existing American
contracts—all demand a larger circulating medium than the precious metals at
present furnish.

I have said that a paper currency was rendered natural,
if not necessary, to the American people, by the elementary principles of their government ; and I will here add, by
their habits of business, superior enterprise, and " go
ahead " character, and their existing contracts, both at home
and abroad ; to which may be added, the influence of the
present currencies of those foreign countries with whom
American commerce is carried on, as well as the *credit
capital* and credit confidence that pervades the Union.
Cash should never be ᵣsed as capital.

### TO PREVENT IMPROPER EXPANSIONS OF THE CURRENCY.

To prevent the improper expansions of the currency, the power to issue bank paper
must be separated from the banks of discount—the free exportation of specie
must not be interfered with—the directors of banks of discount must have no
private interests in the discounts or dividends of the bank—nor should discounts
at any time be made upon evidences of debt of any kind, but only upon the specie actually in the vaults of the bank at the time of the discount.

A subject of the most vital importance to the community,
with regard to the currency, is its constant, universal and
uniform convertibility, under every circumstance, contingency of trade, commerce or exchange. To obtain this
desirable object, remove the private interests of the directors from the discounts, by prohibiting them from discounting paper on which any director's name is given, either as
principal or surety—and remove the interests of the directors from the dividends ; separate banks of issue from those
of discount—restrict their discounts to the proportionate

actual amount of specie in their vaults at the time of the discount ; and isssue only large bills ; and you will have a key to the great secret for establishing a sound currency suitable for a free and enlightened people.

## THE ELECTION OF DIRECTORS.

The election of all the directors of all the banks by the people, without any reference to their being stockholders or not will render the currency truly republican, as well as uniformly convertible.—Always reserving to the people the power to increase the circulating medium whenever foreign convulsions or domestic afflictions shall render it necessary.

The election of the directors of the United States bank of issue, will render the first link in the chain of money-currency completely republican. Their business being unconnected with the discount of notes, or the business of brokers or exchangers of money, they will occupy themselves in learning the amount of money-currency necessary to supply the actual demand in the United States, as connected with the commercial world, and in their domestic commerce at home.

They will be able to bank upon so much of the specie as would be actually necessary to make up the deficiency of the precious metals, and no more. They should, and undoubtedly would, understand the importance of contracting their issues of money-currency in times of plenty and prosperity ; when 'convertible property and credit-currency, under private interest, were most abundant; as by that means they would have power to increase their issues, upon any reverses of trade, or convulsions abroad, by which the demand for specie for exportation, or an increase of issues for domestic circulation, should become necessary.

RIVALRY AND COMMERCIAL PROSPERITY ENCOURAGE OVER-
ISSUES OF BANK PAPER.

In times of prosperity, the love of gain, and the power of increasing their circulation, and consequently their dividends, almost at will, as well as the spirit of
rivalry between similar banking institutions, frequently induce them to over-
issue, and consecutively to contract their issues or suspend their specie payments.

Banks, exercising the powers of banks of issue, and of
discount and deposite, especially while under the influence
of private interest, are liable to over issue in times of prosperity ; and every over-issue must be invariably succeeded
by consequent concomitant contractions. So long as the
paper is convertible, the confidence that one bank inspires in
its neighboring institutions, by liberal issues in times of
prosperity, is often conducive to the over-issues of other
banks. Each bank, fancying that their credit and conduct is
quite equal, if not superior, to that of other institutions doing a similar business; and if such banks are safe in making liberal discounts, they think themselves equally safe.

But a less pardonable feeling appears too often to influence incorporated banks in their issues, that is, the feeling
of rivalry, jealousy, or ambition (aided by the love of gain,)
not to be out-done by other institutions, either in the extent of their business, or in the amount of their dividends;
nor when a reverse of fortune arrives, in their violent and
rapid contractions. Profit, however, is the ruling passion
of incorporated companies.

# CHAPTER XX.

### THE ISSUE OF SMALL BILLS INCREASES PANICS.

The issue of small bills operates against the currency powerfully in two ways; firstly, by driving out of those men's pockets who lay up small sums the specie that would otherwise have remained in them; and, secondly, when a panic arrives, by inducing such small bill-holders to demand the specie instantly of the banks, in exchange for their bills.

The issue of small bills increases the evils of over-issues in two ways. Firstly, it drives the precious metals, that would be found in circulation among a class of people who keep a little change by them, from their pockets; and from small circulation. Secondly, the persons who keep money, with a hope of laying by small sums to meet a payment on land, build a house, purchase stock, or other necessaries, demand the specie for their notes, on the least apprehension of a run upon the bank. The moment a suspicion is raised against the solvency of a bank, or against the convertibility of its notes, they exchange their bills for specie, either at the bank, or at any other market where it can be made ; and thus abstract from the circulation, at a moment of a threatened run upon the banks for specie, a part of the coin that ought to have been already laid by them in times of prosperity—thus adding increased danger from the threatened panic. And here again occurs the competition of the banks in their contractions, and their means of obtaining the "first haul" upon the public for their remittances; while the hoarding of their own specie, as well as their drawing upon such institutions as they have a legal right to expect specie from, although out of the ordinary courteous course of business formerly existing between them, increases the evils of the money pressure.

### BANK COMPETITION.   BANK NOTES ACTUALLY A TENDER.

" Competition" is said to be " the life of trade," but bank competition reverses the order of things, and by producing over-issues and over-contractions, oppresses men in business, causing the RUIN OF TRADE and the overthrow of business.

Hence the evil of having many banks, or the disadvan-

tage of what may be called bank competition—a competition once looked upon as likely to reduce the rate of interest, and increase the facility of bank loans—but which is
only found, by experience, to be one between banks, in
their readiness to issue promises-to-pay, and to inundate
the country with their notes in times of plenty, and, when
money is scarce, in their rapid contractions, and speedy
collections; as well as in devising the safest means of charging the people three, four, five, and often six times as much
for their credit, when they have them once in their power,
as the law allows. In short, bank competition seldom benefits the public. It consists in a strife to see which can make
the largest dividends, and not forfeit their charters. Such a
competition is an evil, and dangerous, both to the bankers
and the public; because it may keep in circulation a large
inflation of the currency for some time, without any sensible inconvenience to the public, until that which should be
always left as free as water, to flow wherever it is most required, having been dammed up for a time, at length breaks
down all barriers, and spreads consternation and dismay in
its course.

The channels of commerce can only contain precisely as
much money-currency, as is sufficient for all the mercantile
purposes of life. The greater the metalic proportion, the
less remains to be rapidly put in motion, producing increased alarm and confusion, by the run upon the banks in times
of panics, from thousands, who would remain quite contented, and even ignorant of any panic or danger to the currency, if they had had the precious metals for their money,
as they at all times had desired, instead of doubtful credit
paper.

Hence the great importance of furnishing each class of
society with the kind of currency they desire. Give the

mechanic and laborer his favorite metalic money—the commercial man his convertible paper of large denominations.
Thus the currency would be brought back to its original
purity and convertibility. The spirit of gambling-specula-
tion would be restrained; property of every description
be uniformly saleable at its true value ; money be equally
and regularly plenty as other commodities; the difference
of exchange, between different parts of the Union, be lessened, if not wholly removed—consequently, the advanced
price upon imported articles would be diminished to the
consumer, and importations lessened. The man who received five dollars on Saturday night in bank notes, would not
feel, that by spending a shilling needlessly he was making
money, because he got seven shillings in specie in exchange.
The man, who could save a few dollars from his wages to
lay by for some future purchase, would not fear to attempt
it, lest he should loose the whole through the inconvertibility of the paper money that he may have been required to
receive.

It is useless to say, that bank paper money, as it is called,
is never a lawful tender, and, therefore, no one is compelled to take it unless he chooses. For what business could
any man do in any city or town in the United States, who
should refuse to receive in exchange for his wares, the
common currency of the place ? Or how long would a laborer expect to find employment, should he, when Saturday
night came, tell his employer he must have the specie for
his wages ? The employer, it is true, could be compelled
to pay him in specie once, but he probably would not employ him any longer. Hence, every man in business in
community, is as effectually compelled to receive paper
currency in payment for debts due to him, as he would be
were it made a lawful tender. The poorest portion of

the currency circulates most freely, hence the apparent inundation of a country with the bills of any bank of doubtful convertibility.

## BANK SECURITIES.

The unlimited responsibility of the directors of banks and the liability of their
securities, together with the separation of banks of issue from those of discount,
will materially lessen excessive issues and contractions of the currency, with all
the evil consequences that follow in their train.

The directors of a bank of discount should give security
for all money that shall pass through their hands, as fully as
any receiver of public money would be required to for the
monies that he should receive.

The bank of discount, being entirely separated from that
of issue, would not be liable to act unduly upon the currency, by increasing its issues beyond its proper limits, or by
restricting them to the prejudice of the commercial interests of the country.

The bank of issue should be free from commercial influence, and from a credit mania. It would have one, and
only one, object in view—to *coin* bank paper into convertible currency; and to guard against excessive issues, by
which the possibility of a drain of specie from the vaults
of the bank could be produced, and ruinous contractions
rendered unavoidable.

## STOCK IN ONE UNIFORM CURRENCY PROFITABLE AND SALEBLE.

The stock in the people's free bank more profitable than that in private banking
associations, or in incorporated companies; safer from counterfeits—more saleable—and the expense of producing and conducting it materially less.

When the incorporated banks, one after another, shall
have all wound up their concerns, and taken stock in the
people's free bank, and saved nine-tenths of the expense of
conducting their institutions themselves, and become convinced that the apparent gain by excessive expansions of
the currency, is more than counter-balanced by the loss in
the succeeding contractions; that currency, being the pro-

duct of the sovereign power of the state, ought not, under any circumstances, to be subjected to the management or control of *irresponsible* interested individuals, who claim a *limited* individual liability for the very currency that they would dignify with the high sounding appellation of *money*. Then, and not till then, will be clearly observable the great benefits of having but one system of paper-money in the United States. Then this United States bank paper would be equally current throughout the Union, and less liable to be counterfeited than individual state bank notes—from the fact, that all the bills of the same denomination would be from the same engraved plate, and be executed by the officers of the United States bank ; and all bills apportioned to any one state, would be executed by the officers of that state bank ; therefore, there would be several signatures upon each of the bills, which would be familiar to all business men, and less liable, if counterfeited, to pass undetected. Another benefit would be found in the lessened expense of producing the paper for circulation, and of conducting the banks of discount.

A laudable ambition to accommodate the public, to secure popular favor and re-election, would induce directors chosen by the people, to accommodate their customers—men of business, the fair traders, and manufacturers—by discounting their *actual business paper*, having but short periods to run ; in preference to lending money to foreign speculators upon *fictitious paper*, made payable in some distant place—for, although such loans may enrich the institution, by allowing them large profits on bills drawn upon that place for the re-payment of the money when the discounted note becomes due, yet the public are uniformly injured by the transaction.

The interest of the directors, being identical with the

mass of community by whom they are elected, they will
serve them as they would desire to be accommodated themselves, honestly and faithfully.

The dependence of the banker upon the public for his
re-election, would be a sufficient inducement to obtain his
attention promptly to his business ; and further than this,
he ought never to be influenced by fear, favor or reward.
He ought to move like the clock, wholly independent of
the surrounding influences. The paper currency would
then become perfectly convertible, and equally current in
every part of the Union, and released from the dangerous
tendency to expansions, by which the history of paper money has been so uniformily marked throughout the world,
but more especially in the United States.

## CHAPTER XXI.

## ON OBJECTIONS TO FREE BANKING.

### OF THE OBJECTIONS TO A REPUBLICAN CURRENCY.

It will be urged, by persons interested in the continuance
of incorporated banking companies, and, perhaps, by those
who are alarmed at the idea of a change in the circulating
medium of the country, that there are doubts of the constitutionality of the measure, and of its utility even should it
be constitutional. To the first of these ojections, we ask to
be referred to the particular clause of the constitution containing the prohibitory article ; for as we understand that
instrument, it is clearly favorable to the exercise of the requisite power by congress to regulate the currency. And
here let me remark, that the unconstitutionality of the incorporation of banking companies, consists in representa-

tives exercising their delegated powers for a longer period than the time for which they were elected; for, as they vest certain powers and privileges in individuals, these individuals' *private rights* prevent the repeal of the law by their successors in office. This is as equally applicable to the state legislatures as to the congress of the United States.

The words of the Constitution are, that " Congress shall have power to coin money, regulate the value thereof, and of foreign coin." Hence, may it not be inferred, that whatever alters the value of the coin, is expressly placed at the disposal of congress ?

---

## CHAPTER XXII.

### CHARTERED BANKING COMPANIES ANTI-REPUBLICAN AND DISSATISFACTORY.

The people have become justly dissatisfied with the present chartered bank paper money.—They see, in this system, principles diametrically opposed to the Constitution, and to the spirit of the Declaration of Independence.

To convince the public of the importance of a republican free banking system to their permanent financial and political prosperity, and to render this question clear to the minds of persons, who, from having seen the evils of paper money, (whether it be the United States "old continental,'' or our modern incorporated bank paper, with its twin-sister, *shinplasters*,) have become firmly established in a well-grounded prejudice against all bank paper, I would remark, that we are by necessity compelled to use it, and should, therefore, render it as perfect as possible. To those who are enchanted with the idea of banks furnishing the currency, but who are in no way connected with or dependant upon them, I most cheerfully address myself; while with those who oppose the free banking system from interested motives, it is in vain to use arguments—for " convince a man against his will and he's of the same opinion still."

Allow me then to direct the attention of all Americans, with well constituted minds, to the spirit of the Declaration of Independence and of our Constitution. One spirit pervades the whole. It is the spirit of liberty; and of an equality of civil, political and religious rights and privileges. It intends the most good to the greatest number, and the utmost advancement of human happiness. This spirit should be our polar star. By its light every true American should imbue all the subordinate institutions of our government, with the same character and principles, that more than half a century's experience has proved so successful in politics. The nearer the spirit of our currency approaches that of our form of government, the less danger have we to apprehend from its imperfections.

No aristocratic, exclusive or monopolizing elements are found in the fundamental principles of our government. The sovereignty of the people, and their inalienable right to regulate their political, financial, religious and literary institutions, according to their own choice, is every where intended.

The mind is forcibly struck, on reading the Declaration of Independance, with the "WE," meaning the people of these United States, and admitting of no superior power, save the Father of all mercies. The same spirit breathes through the Constitution. And as these principles govern us, we will examine them. They are ancient land marks, never to be lightly questioned or hastily removed.

As " governments derive their just powers from the consent of the governed," so paper, intended to circulate as money, should only enjoy that privilege from the consent

of those among whom it is intended to circulate. " WE
hold these truths to be self-evident, that all men are created
equal ; that they are endowed by their Creator with certain inalienable rights ; that among these are life, liberty,
and the pursuit of happiness." Here we have, in these
" self-evident truths," a summary of the objects of human
action, and the motives by which they are governed. " The
pursuit of happiness" is here declared to be among the
great inducements to human actions; which it is the business of governments to provide for. " To secure these
rights, governments are instituted among men, deriving
their just powers from the consent of the governed." How
clearly have the framers of this Declaration been impressed with the right of the people to control their own destinies ; to regulate their own actions ; and, through their representatives, to pass such laws as shall secure to them the
full enjoyment of these great first principles of human actions.

And here let me observe, that whatever tyranny pervades
society—whether it be political, as was the tyranny that
our forefathers complained of in this Declaration—or religious tyranny, such as drove our early Puritan and religious fore-fathers to remove from a country where their
minds and consciences were enslaved, to free and independent America—or financial tyranny, such as drives the inhabitants of the old world to seek a refuge in America, from
the grasp of the tax-gatherer, the tything of the priest, the
rating for the poor, and the impoverishing effects of duties,
imposts, customs, fees, and taxes, by which they are plunder-
ed by law in open daylight. Against all these oppressions in
a foreign land, we may inveigh with as much vehemence as
we please ; but, speak against the tyranny of incorporated
banking companies, and you have about your ears a swarm
of angry wasps that would soon sting out your eyes.

But let us proceed with the opinions of our fore-fathers upon the use and end of governments; and consider the manner in which they should be treated, whenever they fail to secure to the people the objects of their institution. " That, whenever any form of government becomes destructive of these ends, it is the right of the people to alter or abolish it, and to institute a new government; laying its foundation on such principles, and organizing its powers in such form, as to them shall seem most likely to effect their safety and happiness."

Here let me ask, if an entire change in the form of government is justifiable in a nation, where lives are liable to be lost, and physical force supercedes the mild codes of civil laws, and mercy be left to weep, while military prowess and power erect their thrones and establish their authorities, how much more right have the people to change one of the elementary principles of their constitution, that has been found by experience to be incompatible with their prosperity ? But let us not charge our fore-fathers with having established our paper money currency. Let us examine the facts of the case. Let us see what the early currency of these United States was; and enquire into the causes of the defects of our present incorporated bank system.

### THE DEFECTS OF THE CURRENCY PRODUCED BY CHARTERED BANKS.

The evils of paper circulating as money, may all be traced to the connection of currency with CREDIT, with PRIVATE INTEREST, and with POLITICS.

You may trace the expansions, contractions and inconvertibility of the currency, I believe, to its connection with *credit*, with *private interest*, or with *politics*; and most of the evils of paper money generally originates from one or all of these causes.

It was not until after the failure of government notes,

(the old continental money,) that private companies began generally to issue paper intended to circulate as money.

The following is from the Connecticut Gazette, No. 1504, (New London,) September 6, 1792 : " The trade and manufactures of this state, (says a correspondent,) have long struggled under the want of a capital, proportioned to the industry and enterprise of its citizens ;—that want may now be supplied by means of the banks established at New London and Hartford. Every useful occupation, and every industrious citizen, may be assisted with money, as circumstances may require and justify ; but, in order to carry the means of the bank into the fullest effect, their bills must circulate among all ranks of people freely as money : it behooves, therefore, every well-wisher to the prosperity of the community, to give credit to the notes of the bank. Although trade may more immediately, and in a more considerable degree be benefitted by these institutions, yet, every other branch of business will come in for a proportionable share. A flourishing commerce dispenses blessings to all within the sphere of its operations, and adds to the value of the landed interests, as well as the articles in which it principally deals. The notes of the banks will be found more convenient for a circulating medium, and may be kept by the owners in greater safety, than hard money ; and none need be apprehensive of any deception in them, as the promise on the face of them will be carefully and punctually fulfilled."

The above shows the exertion that was made at that early period, to induce the people to receive this paper—the notes of the banks—at New London and Hartford as money ; and the writer declares that the facts on the face of these notes " will be carefully and punctually fulfilled." Nothing is here said of limited liability, or of privileges not enjoyed by other citizens. The reason assigned for the necessity of issuing and circulating these paper promises, is said to be " the want of capital proportioned to the industry and enterprise of its citizens." While the same cause exists, the same remedy will be likely to be applied. Credit will be attempted to be made—a substitute for capital— whose functions it cannot long perform.

## CHAPTER XXIII.

### A REMEDY FOR THE WANT OF CAPITAL. BANK NOTES ARE NOT CAPITAL.

While the discounts of banks are confined to ACTUAL BUSINESS PAPER, having but short periods to run, and no indulgence is shown by one bank to another, in not demanding their balances in specie from each other, frequently, and at stated periods, excessive expansions of the currency are less liable to occur—the channels of circulation are less liable to become surcharged—the high price of imported articles, and excessive importations, are less likely to ensue—and the necessity for the exportation of specie will in some measure be obviated.

We are now brought to an examination of chartered bank paper, when used as a remedy for the want of capital; and a wretched substitute for capital will it be found to be. That there is a want of capital in the United States, proportioned to the industry and enterprise of the inhabitants, no one will doubt; nor will any one deny that bank notes, while they were only issued in sums proportioned to the actual demand for currency, were convenient and useful; but, whenever they are sought and used as capital, they are diverted from their legitimate channels, and cease to be serviceable to a community. So much paper money then only may be circulated as can continue to circulate freely among the people without a tendency to exportation· The moment it is required to assume the character of capital, its true and legitimate powers fail, and it vanishes like smoke,—nothing remains but stained, worn and soiled rags of paper.

One continued train of abuses, impositions and frauds have succeeded each other, from the very first incorporation of chartered companies for banking purposes, to the present period. And we may here remark, that any establishment of a government currency, connected with the credit either of a state or of the United States, would be scarcely less objectionable than that of incorporated companies; as the currency of such bills would depend upon the credit of such state, or of the United States, and would be liable to be issued according to the interest of the party in power, (not less violent than private interest,) and still less secure than private paper would be under proper liabilities. The country would be liable to be inundated with it in times of prosperity. And in times of danger, scarcity, and an extensive foreign demand for specie, the government would only be able to issue more bills; which would become more and more uncurrent, as it was found to be less and less able to redeem them. And in the end, should a reversion of trade, from a foreign war, or from any other cause, continue to operate against the state, or against the Union, for any length of time, fear would be likely to be entertained that such money would become like the old continental, a mere shadow of what it had once been—and a monument of the wickedness or folly of those who attempted to give credit paper the value of real capital.

Credit is universally admitted to be useful to the promotion of enterprise, industry, and ambition. But credit must never be called capital, nor treated as capital. And in this view of the case, we again call the attention of the patient reader to the words of the Declaration of Indepence respecting the abuses of government; and leave the reflecting mind to compare the political defection of a government, in whole or in part, to the failure of any one of its elementary principles.

Every person connected with the business of the currency, knows, from sad experience, the very imperfect manner in which incorporated banks have supplied the country
with a currency in times of oppression and stagnation of
business, during a foreign demand for specie—while the
exchanges are greatly against this country—and when every man of business, however prudent he may have appeared to be, or believed himself to have been, requires aid, if
he ever requires it. What service are banks to commercial men at such times? They are far worse than useless ; for the amount of circulation, which had been long
maintained by them, is at once restricted, and they become
the first to oppress their customers, and to call in their debts
by force of law, when other means are found ineffectual
and unavailing.

CHAPTER XXIV.

THE INTEREST OF STOCKHOLDERS THE RULE OF ACTION FOR
CHARTERED BANKS.

The uniform practice of incorporated banking companies of making the interest of
the stockholders their rule of action, ought to satisfy the public, that, while the
currency of the country is entrusted to them or similar institutions, the effects
will continue to be the same as long as "like causes produce like effects."

Such institutions perform just that part in business, and
are just the organs of prosperity to a country, that they
ought to be expected to be, from their constitution, and the
laws of their situation. They are private machines for the
manufacture of princely fortunes for individuals, without
labor, and without the ordinary means of becoming useful
to mankind.

How can it be expected of a company, formed expressly for the purpose of making money, that they should forget the business of their formation, and take one thought of

the public interest, or of the general prosperity of the country. The great, and, in fact, the only object, end, aim and business of an incorporated bank, is, to make money for the stockholders. Large dividends, by safe discounts, with now and then speculative loans to each other, are the true, the only desirable business of incorporated banking companies. The good people of this republic, have had expansions of bank credit, followed by contractions and suspensions, until there can be but one opinion of the perfect convertibility of any credit-currency, for any long period, when it is based upon credit, or even connected with *credit* and *private interest*, and dependant upon *politics* for its continuance and prosperity. That incorporated banks have failed to issue paper, that is at all times, and under all circumstances, perfectly convertible, no one will for a moment pretend to deny; and, that their small notes have driven the precious metals out of the country or into their vaults, is equally true. They have ceased to perform the offices promised upon the face of their bills, by ceasing to redeem them in specie at sight.

### THE PROFITS MADE BY A BANK, ABOVE THE FAIR MARKETABLE RATE OF INTEREST, EXTORTION.

If taxation, without representation, is a just cause of complaint, why are chartered banking companies indulged in collecting, annually, such immense revenues from the people, above the ordinary rate of interest for the use of money?

But, by the quotation from the Declaration of Independence, upon the abuse of power by the government, and the right of the people to alter or change any system after it has become oppressive, or has failed to perform the duties originally assigned to it or expected of it, we are confirmed in our former opinion, that the people have an inherent right to alter the currency to suit their interests or inclinations.

The Declaration of Independence proceeds: "But, when a long train of abuses and usurpations, pursuing invariably the same object, evinces design to reduce them under absolute despotism, it is their right, it is their duty, to throw off such government, and to provide new grounds for their future security." If taxation, without representation, be a grievance, may we not complain that incorporated banking companies have long taxed the country, (without the people being represented in their corporations.) to many millions of dollars, in the shape of interest, and per centages on exchanges, for the use of their *credit ;* thereby accumulating their dividends and bonuses ? For whatever scheme may be devised, by which the currency, or money of the country, can be made to cost the borrower more than the interest and use of the same ought to be worth, is a tax of which he has a right to complain. They also collect a tax, by draining the country of specie, and continuing to issue their promises-to-pay long after they had ceased to pay them in specie ; thereby compelling the business portion of the community to pay high prices for drafts upon foreign markets, or a high premium upon the purchase of the precious metals.

What sweet, delusive language—" *a premium on gold and silver !*" The truth would sound harsh in the ears of our wealthy bankers, and their agents, the brokers, to call things by their proper and appropriate names, and, instead of saying " a premium for gold and silver paid here," say, " *depreciated bank paper exchanged here.*"

When every bank in the Union suspends payment, it is called " suspension," and the precious metals are said to be at a " premium." But if one or two banks only stop payment, they are said to have failed, and are disgraced. But crime is not crime, when the influence or power of the criminals are sufficient to prevent their punishment or disgrace.

The extent of the moral crime of incorporated banks, by circulating paper below par, can only be estimated, by computing the amount of the excess of dividends over the ordinary rate of interest made on all their circulation ; or the profits they make in times of prosperity above the regular rate of interest on money ; and the interest they charge during the depreciated state of the currency, and the suspension of specie payment by the banks—at which time they ought not to receive interest on debts due to them, unless they pay interest on their own notes. This would furnish some data for the discovery of the amount of direct financial crime that they are thus guilty of committing. This, however, embraces only a small part of the *real* mischief, wretchedness and woe they entail upon society. Their expansions induce indolence, extravagance, and excesses, that leave those who have been involved by their imprudences, in wretchedness and want.

In times of bank contractions, the honest industry and economy of many an honest laborer is swallowed up in one purchase upon credit, that he would not have made, had he known of the contraction of the currency that was about to ensue ; or, as it is familiarly termed, the hard times that were hurrying on. Thousands are thus ruined, that a few void of moral honesty may become rich.

How can a banker justify his receipt of profits, interest, and dividends made upon the promises-to-pay that he exchanges with his fellow man, after he has neglected or refused to fiulfil such promises ? Yet we often see bankers increase their dividends during the times of the greatest distress and panic. Or if they do not declare publicly as large dividends during the reverses of the currency, as at other times, yet they no doubt have less cause of complaint than the unfortunate note-holder. Their *secret partner*, the broker, makes and receives the money for them. Whether it be equally divided among all the stockholders, or only enjoyed by those who are " initiated," is left to themselves to settle. It is quite enough for me to know, that the money is lost by the public. And so long as the people loose the money on account of the inability, inexpediency or unwillingness of the directors of the bank to maintain the currency of their paper at par, the evil is the same, whether one or the whole of the stockholders receive the profits of these fraudulent and dishonorable transactions.

## CHAPTER XXV.

### ON MORAL OBLIGATIONS.

Moral obligations are above all law; and no act should be made legal that is opposed to the principles of truth and justice.

Moral honesty is above all law. And the laws of God, and of nature require, that when contracts have been entered into between men, they should be fulfilled according to their spirit, whether that spirit be exactly in accordance to their letter or not. No moral guilt attaches itself to a transaction, when the best and most honest endeavors of the parties are used to meet the spirit of their agreements, even although their letter is not strictly complied with.

### EX-PRESIDENT JACKSON'S VETO OF THE UNITED STATES BANK BILL.

The veto of the United States bank bill, by ex-president Jackson, not predicated exclusively upon the unconstitutionality of the right of Congress to pass laws to regulate the currency; but upon the unconstitutional right of Congress to incorporate a private banking monopoly.

But to return to the right that congress has to pass any law respecting the currency. That congress has exercised the power, in the fullest extent, will not be denied. That the opinions of our ablest statesmen have sanctioned that act, and that the law was discontinued by the veto of president Jackson, not exclusively upon the ground of its unconstitutionality, owing to any want of power having been vested in congress by the constitution for regulating the currency ; but because congress has no constitutional right to incorporate banking companies, by which the value of all the commodities of the country would be liable to be varied to suit the interested views of a few privileged individuals—as appears by the president's message upon that subject, and the remark that he could have given a draft of a law that would have been less objectionable, had he been applied to for that purpose.

But even had congress never incorporated a United States banking company, there is so little resemblance between the plan here recommended, and that of an incorporation of a banking company, that I maintain, that the general free spirit that pervades the Declaration of Independence and the Constitution, leaves no doubt upon the mind as to the intention of the founders of our government, as to the restrictive powers that were intended to be exercised by the general and several state governments.

## CHAPTER XXVI.

### THE POWERS OF CONGRESS.

Congress has power to create necessary offices ; and to authorise the President, with the advice and consent of the Senate, to appoint officers to execute any necessary duty or office ; or congress may, by law, themselves appoint officers, whenever such appointments are deemed necessary : how then can their constitutional right to authorise the sovereign people to appoint (elect) persons of their own choice to perform certain duties be doubted ?

The doctrine seems to be this. The general government shall pass all laws, and transact all business relating

to the peace, prosperity and good government of the United States, where a uniformity of action and operation
would better promote the general welfare than the local legislation of the several states would be likely to do ; and
*vice versa.*

It is true, that congress has never authorised the people
to elect persons, with power to examine the state of the
currency of the Union; and if the precious metals were not
found to be sufficient to serve as the medial commodity, to
bank upon such a portion of them as should be necessary
to make up the deficiency. But its not having been done,
by no means argues that they have not the right to do it.
Congress, on all occasions, when deemed expedient, creates
offices and appoints officers for any and every purpose,
without having their constitutional right to do so questioned.
How then can it be a greater stretch of power, for congress
to authorise the people to elect certain officers for certain
purposes, than it would be for them to make such appointments when they are equally necessary ? and should they
find a paper currency necessary, or desirable, to issue so
much paper as they shall deem necessary to meet the demand—provided they shall be able to obtain a sufficient specie basis for the issuing of bills enough to make up the deficiency ? For if the specie cannot be obtained, there can be
but one opinion as to the propriety of circulating paper as
money, based upon any security, promises-to-pay of individuals or of banking companies, or other evidences of debt.
Nothing but the precious metals can be, with safety, used as
a basis for the issue of paper to circulate as money. A substitute for money may, for the sake of convenience, or for
the promotion of enterprise and industy, be made to circulate as money. But when notes, or other evidences of debt,
are used as a basis for the circulation of paper to pass as

money, it becomes a *substitute* for a *substitute*. Hence the too great uncertainty and too extended contingency of promises-to-pay, to be allowed the appellation of money.

The circumstance of congress never having passed such a law, is no evidence that it has not the rightful power to do so. Congress has the expressed right to pass a general bankrupt law—which it has never yet found it expedient to do. And each state passes bankrupt laws or not to suit their respective wants.

### THE ORGANIZATION OF THE PEOPLE BY CONGRESS.

Congress has power to organize the people to regulate the currency of the country; although they may not have power to incorporate a banking company.—Giv· ing the people the means and the instrument by which they can exercise an original inherent right, is not giving them artificial rights, or artificial wants, but enabling them to supply and furnish themselves with the currency they prefer, as they are now oganized to supply themselves with education, or provide for religious worship.

The regulation of the post office department is, by the constitution, left under the control of the general government. So is the right to coin money, and regulate the value thereof. The plan proposed for a republican currency, does not require that congress shall pass any law disposing of the power of the sovereign people to one or more portions of them. It only requires congress to organize the people to exercise an inherent right upon the subject of currency, embracing the regulation and disposal of one of the elementary principles of the government, similar to that of the literature and social habits of the people. So far as education is a political measure of the government, the townships are organized, and the people empowered, to control and regulate their schools and colleges, and other means of education, according to their sovereign will and pleasure.

The constitution does not expressly declare with whom the power of regulating .the education of the people shall be placed. The local legislatures have uniformly left it with those most interested, and best competent to decide what means will produce the greatest good to the greatest number, at the least labor and expense. Hence towns regulate the administration of their common schools, agreeable to the general organization of the state for the support of common schools. Cities, and incorporated towns and villages, are, by their incorporations, uniformily empowered to provide for the education of the youth of the place ; and the people regulate their system of education in these situations as they please.

Upon the subject of religion, the original draft of the constitution was equally as silent as it is upon the subject of currency. But an amendment provides a negative clause : " Congress shall make no law respecting an establishment of religion, or prohibiting the free exercise thereof." In all matters of faith, opinion and conscience, every man should be perfectly free to follow the bent of his own inclination, provided it does not interfere with the enjoyment of the same liberty by all others. The voluntary principle of worship, and of the support of religious instruction, not only comports with the principles and practice of the Divine Author of our faith, but gloriously tends to promote equality of rights and civil and religious liberty.

The constitution, however, expressly *prohibits the states* from interfering with the currency, as fully and clearly as it provides that congress shall not interfere in matters of religion. It provides, that " no state shall coin money ; emit bills of credit ; or make any thing but gold and silver coin a tender in the payment of debts." Yet, the states issue their bonds, and provide for the sale of them in a foreign market; issue state scrip ; incorporate banking companies, with the power of accumulating all the specie of the country within their own vaults, and the means of augmenting the circulating medium at their pleasure, and to contract it whenever that will favor their own private interests; issue post notes, due at future periods; and continue their ordinary business of loaning money and discounting notes, after they have suspended specie payment, thereby perfectly draining the country of the precious metals, leaving only the credit issues of the government, or the issues of the chartered banks, to circulate as money.  The manner in which such states comply with the spirit of this provision of the constitution, reminds one of the conduct of the commander of an army, who stipulated with the besieged garrison, that upon their surrender not a drop of their blood should be spilt, but who kept his promise to the ear only— not one drop of blood was spilt, for he buried them all alive.

If paper money is not by statute made a lawful tender in the payment of debts, it is not the less so *de facto*, since it constitutes the whole currency of the country.  And neither legal enactments, nor process of law, can compel the payment of debts in a material that does not exist; or change the immutable law of trade, which compels the receipt of one article of medial commodity where no other exists.  By placing the currency under the control and regulation of the sovereign people, the latitudinous construction of the constitution will be rendered unnecessary; the states rights will be substantially preserved; the powers of the general government will not be infringed upon or extended; but the sovereign people will be *organized*, and empowered to regulate freely the circulating medium according to their own interests and desires.

## ON THE POWERS OF CONGRESS.

*The general powers of congress embrace all subjects that require to be the same throughout the Union.—The powers of the states are municipal, local and domestic.—Hence the reasonableness of the general government authorising the people to regulate the currency.*

The general government are authorised to exercise such powers as operate alike on the inhabitants of the whole United States, but which do not interfere with the internal or domestic affairs of the individual states. The powers of the state governments are to supervise and regulate the internal and domestic concerns of the citizens of their own states respectively. A state, in some measure, represents a municipality within a state or kingdom. The power of granting patents, is appointed by the constitution, to the general government; as also that of declaring war, of making peace, of passing a general bankrupt law; and, from the very nature of the subject, the power of coining money, and regulating the value thereof, and of foreign coins.

I conclude, therefore, that congress has power to authorise the people to elect the directors of all the banks; and to give the directors authority to prepare and issue so much bank paper as would be necessary, together with the specie that would circulate freely as soon as the banks shall have called in their small bills, to furnish a sufficient currency for the convenient interchange of commodities.

The separation of the banks of issue from those of discount, will lessen the facilities for the hasty improper temporary expansions of the currency, to which our present chartered bank system is so liable; since the banks of discount could not issue more paper than was placed at their disposal by the banks of issue, nor even that unless they had in their vaults one-third of the amount in specie. Thus the currency would be guarded against the rocks upon which all former systems of paper money have split. For, whether they have been United States' institutions, or state incorporated companies, they have been equally liable to the dangers from over-issues ; and have uniformly rather facilitated than retarded the reverses of trade; by which they have been driven to contractions of their issues and various subterfuges, to avoid the payment of specie for their notes. They have been compelled to make foreign loans, issue post notes, and sometimes to suspend specie payments, by their own imprudent over-issues. True, the credit of flourishing states may exceed that of a private incorporated company ; yet, when the price of state funds is below par in a foreign market, and there are no sales of stock at home, they can no more redeem their promises-to-pay in specie without loss, than could a private company. The great evil still is, credit is connected with the issue of the paper intended to circulate as money ; and the directors of the discounts are intimately connected with the borrowers, and share with them, at least in sympathy, in their political feelings, or in their private interest, their wants or their prospects of great gain.

## IN CURRENCY, CHANGES NOT ALWAYS REFORMS.

Chartered bank paper changeable—Causes— Its consequences noted.—The remedy—Its effects salutary.—Bank paper should be current—convertible—uniform—permanent.

State chartered bank paper, from its dependance upon *credit*, its connection with *private interest* and reliance upon *politics*, must, by the laws of its situation, be continually changing. Such banks issue their notes to circulate as money, upon a credit as well as a specie basis. Their credits consist of the notes of other banks, United States' and states' bonds, foreign and domestic exchanges, and various other evidences of debt. This gives the paper portion of our currency a credit character, and unfits it for the meas-

ure of all values. And how can we expect it to be otherwise, when we consider the various circumstances and contingencies attending these credits, by which their prompt
and punctual payments are liable to be defeated.

Again; its dependance upon the influence of private interest, leaves it liable to frequent expansions and contractions, to suit the convenience of those having the currency
under their control. But this is not all; its dependance upon
future legislation for a continuance of its business renders
it liable to be made the tool of party, or the slave of the
majority.

These evils in the currency cry loudly for reform. And
until this is accomplished, we shall have changes and fluctuations in it without end. Changes in bank loans ; in the
kind and quantity of the circulating medium; in the price
of labor—of bread stuffs—of merchandize—and of all other commodities. In short, the thousand contingencies that
are constantly operating upon chartered bank paper, must
produce an almost endless succession of changes ; yet, no
regular change that can be foreseen or guarded against by
the public. For neither the directors of banks, nor our
most able financiers, are able to anticipate and avoid them.

The changes by the directors in the operations cf the
banks, as well as the fluctuations of the currency, serve to
keep the business of the country in confusion and uncertainty ; while those who are dependant upon banks for accommodation, are kept in a state of constant anxiety, lest
they should be disappointed by the bank upon their next
application for a loan.

Currency should be as unchangeable when composed in
part of paper and part of gold and silver, as it would be if
composed exclusively of the precious metals.

To render the paper portion of the currency a perfect

representative of gold and silver, it must be separated from the fluctuations of trade, the speculations of individuals, and a dependance upon future legislation.

Give us a thorough and permanent bank reform. Assimilate the paper portion of the currency as nearly as possible to specie ; secure the bill-holder against the depreciation of the notes, and the public against over-expansions and consecutive ruinous contractions, and you will thus lay the foundation for universal prosperity in the United States.

## CHAPTER XXVII.

### MORAL PRINCIPLE ABOVE ALL LAW.

Moral honor above all law.—The passage of depreciated paper at par, a departure from moral rectitude—The fluctuations of the currency fosters a gambling propensity—A radical reform in the currency necessary.—The founders of our government had their attention directed more forcibly to politics and religion, than to currency.—Render currency republican, and it will become the key-stone of the arch of the republican edifice, of which it is at present but a defective and dangerous anti-republican corner.

This gambling propensity may be said to be the first step towards moral depravity. Men seldom commence the most abandoned course of conduct at their full speed. They are generally led on from step to step. And ultimately loosing all regard for moral obligations, acknowledge no bounds to their ambition, except the words of the statute. With them, if it is lawful and defensible in a court of justice, it is right ; and consequently justifiable. A liability to pay whatever we contract to pay, whether the law compels us to do it or not, is the result of natural obligation. It arises from the operation of the moral law ; it results from the very nature of man as a moral agent. Being legally released from an obligation, morally binding, does not lessen the moral obligation. But doing away with the legal obli-

gation, ought rather to strengthen the moral obligation ;
since the creditor, whose claim is morally the same as before the legal discharge of the debtor, has only the moral
obligation to rely upon. Faith, honor and honesty, among
men, do not depend upon legal obligation; but upon moral
honesty, binding mankind to rectitude of conduct. Therefore, whatever tends to lessen respect for moral obligation,
should be avoided as dangerous to society.

The man who circulates counterfeit money, is punished
by law as a felon, and an enemy to society ; and the man who
passes bills of a broken bank, is treated with not much less
severity. But he who issues bills that are five or twenty
per cent. below par, is a gentleman banker—complained of
a little by those who suffer at the moment of their loosing, to
be sure,—but he is a wealthy banker or broker, and he is taken by the hand, and, wherever he goes, he is quite the gentleman. He has made money out of the public, and no enquiry is made respecting his moral honesty.

Oh! the depravity of the times ! when men may defraud
each other openly, and smile and be smiled upon in turn.
When will the American people see the dangerous rock, of
want of moral honesty, that is certain destruction to every
individual who is wrecked upon it!—and it is not less so to
states than individuals.

The want of moral principle leads to wretchedness of
character and conduct; from which, without reform, the
chances are, that little good will ever arise either to individuals or to states. Strict integrity and punctuality in deal-
ings; truth and honor in words and actions ; industry and
economy in habits; generosity and philanthropy in manners;
always respecting the property, the feelings, and the opinions of others, comprise some of the important duties of society that we respect and commend. And how is it sur-

prising that we should be dissatisfied with having our pockets picked in the dark, by the man who exchanges our commodities—by him who professes to give us money, but only
gives us depreciated paper—and in finding that every man
in the neighborhood has been so often defrauded in the currency that they have been required to receive for debts in
change for large bills, or other ways, that they feel themselves justified in passing uncurrent money upon every body
that will receive it.

This is evident, from the uniform habit that pervades
community of passing the most depreciated money first;
for, whatever is to be bought, or for every payment
that is to be made in money, the poorest kind must
first be passed. This evinces a laxity of morals, and a want
of strict punctuality and moral rectitude at which every lover of liberty should shudder—for liberty can only live while
supported by virtue and morality—and every relaxation in
the morals of the community, is one step from the straight
path of republican simplicity, honor and liberty.

Strict moral obligation requires, that the spirit of every
engagement should be punctually and faithfuly fulfiled and
complied with. . The passage of uncurrent money, for a
full and valid consideration, is as substantial a departure
from strict moral honesty, as the passage of base coin,
forged notes, or notes of broken banks. Yet, such is the
laxity of American morals upon the subject of currency,
that few men now think it a crime, to pass money, that is
but a slight shade below par, for its nominal value; and
hundreds are daily found in the market, offering their uncurrent money in payment of small articles, in the hope of
getting specie change; believing that ninety cents in change,
is as good to them as a paper dollar. True, this is but the
exchange of one commodity for another; and were the un-

current money only passed to those who know its exact value, and who did not intend to pass it again to any body who would receive it through ignorance of its real uncurrency, or who would take it with the hope of passing it again upon some unwarily traveller or country dealer, the crime would be far less; yet the principle and its effects upon the morals of society are the same.

A country in debt is never free and independent. There was never a truer remark than, that "the borrower is a slave to the lender." And as true as this is with regard to individuals, so true is it with regard to states and nations. When morality is lost to either, all is lost. Thus, when nations, or the commercial individuals of a nation, are in debt, the whole community are in debt.

A new order of things has silently crept over society. Men are attempting to live by their wits, by contracting debts that they cannot pay—the fashionable term of suspending payment, is following the payment in uncurrent money. These, and an entire disregard to moral honesty, are links of the same chain; like the stealing firstly one pin, and ultimately coming to the halter. So the passage of uncurrent money lays the foundation to a depravity of morals, that would allow a man to contract a debt that he could not pay, and live luxuriously upon credit, without earning the salt to his porridge.

I know my homely style and my plain metaphors will leave me subject to the severest criticisms. And I know, too, that few critics are severer than those who find their craft in danger. I know that if any benefit is to be derived by the public from my remarks, it will be just so much out of the pockets of the money sharks ; and that just in that proportion I have to expect to receive their unlimited castigation. But how little will that be felt by me, if the currency should assume its proper place among the elementary principles of the government, and become one of the strong-est props to the republican edifice. What moral educa-tion is to the politics of a republican people, strict converti-bility and punctuality is to finance and currency. Without the first, a republic could not long continue : without the last, a commercial country could not long flourish and prosper.

If, after all that has been said of the advantages of reform, and disadvantages of any change not producing a radical reform, there should be those so sceptical as to refuse their assent to the proposed plan upon the ground of its being an experiment, or of its being an innovation of long established usages and customs in business ; to them let me remark, that, on this continent the great experiment was made by civilized man of the attempt to construct society upon a new basis; that it was here for the first time that theories, hitherto unknown, or deemed impracticable, have produced a grand spectacle for the admiration of the world—unknown in the history of the past, and unequalled in its beneficial re-sults to mankind—surpassing the expectations, or even the hopes, of its warmest and most enthusiastic admirers and supporters.

If then, after more than half a century, some parts of this great fabric, or some circumstances connected with it, should be found not perfectly similar to the whole edifice—if, in an entirely new system of government, in which the action, practice and experience of all former governments have been invested, there should be found some relicts of former institutions incompatible with the harmony, beauty and strength of this splendid living temple—would not this be the place to examine into the causes of any and every dis-crepancy that are found by experience to exist, and that time, habit and usage have not been able to adapt to the place originally designed for it to occupy. In short, if, while the whole attention of our fore-fathers have been directed to the establishment of a government freed from the evils of a monarchy, they have lost sight of the currency of the country in the general and highly important character of the first principles of a republican government, is that at all surprising. They secured themselves against the evils that had most vexed and perplexed them. The church they precluded from any connection with the state. Literature they left free and unrestricted by any religious creeds and sectarian requirements. And they happily secured to all, equality in civil and religious matters, as well as in political honors and offices.

But currency being a vexed question, and one respecting which very little had been said and done, and one from which little danger was at that time apprehended, attracted but slight notice. The Constitution briefly says all, that, under the then existing state of commerce and of society, could have appeared necessary : " That congress shall have power to coin money, and regulate the value thereof, and of foreign coin,"—evidently not anticipating any monopoly in the currrency—but that the precious metals alone should constitute the legal money of the country ; and that congress should, at any future period, make such further provisions respecting the completion of the currency as time and experience should dictate.

The defects of the present paper money currency are now universally admitted, and the necessity of some reform loudly proclaimed. Then, is not a time of peace, a time of plenty, a time of quiet respecting any great political movement, and a time when the importance of the currency is becoming known, and when intemperance and licentiousness are giving place to temperance, order, decency, and respect for sacred and divine things—is not this time the proper time for the public consideration of the subject of currency, with a view to its permanent improvement ?

In making any great alteration or improvement in the system of paper money, reference ought to be had constantly to the great leading principles contained in the Declaration of Independence and in the Constitution, that the fundamental principles of the government should all be made to coincide, and that the ancient land-marks of the government should not be thoughtlessly thrown down or removed, but that every addition should perfect the glorious plan of human liberty and of human happiness.

America, by giving money its proper value, and rendering the currency sound, stable, and always perfectly convertible into specie, would hold out inducements to the wealthy foreigner to visit our shores, as well as to him who has but his labor to depend upon for his sustenance.

---

# CHAPTER XXVIII.

## PERIODICAL BANK STATEMENTS.

The defects of bank reports—Their mystification.—The necessity of full statements—To this end a centralized government necessary.—The proposed plan.

Every person, who has carefully examined the bank statements annually made to the Secretary of the Treasury of the United States, or the statements of banks of almost any states in the Union as made to their legislatures, must be forcibly struck with the very imperfect manner in which many of these statements are made out—the absolute ignorance, shire neglect, or wilful misrepresentations and misstatements they contain.

In some of these statements there appears to be a studied mystification of the required facts, as if they were made exclusively to comply with a clause in their charters, but with the evident determination of defeating the intention the legislature had in view in inserting the clause. There could be no need of such subterfuges and concealments, if the banks intended to deal honestly, frankly, fairly and openly with the public.

Every facility should be afforded the public for obtaining all the necessary information, to enable them to comprehend the subject of currency and banking. Every explanation should be given that could be reasonably required to make the statements of the banks clear to the most common understanding. But, as if concealment was the object of some of these bank statements, they contain imperfect, heterogenous and fraudulent statements; by which, those banks that make such mystified statements, must succeed in evading the searching inquisitiveness of a vigilant committee, to whom they are referred, if the committee have not time to ask the officers of the banks for explanations, or to unravel their mysteries in committee.

This, however, is not very surprising, when we consider that there are now in the United States nine hundred banks and branches, created by some thirty independent states and territories, including the District of Columbia, without any uniformity in the government of the currency except the natural law of private interest, by which all chartered companies are governed.

These nine hundred credit aristocracies may have some important principles that are common to them all ; yet, having no common head, no centralization of government, by which their accounts and statements could be directed to be made similar, and no blanks prepared expressly for their use, whatever ignorance they may be guilty of, they may reasonably plead that want in justification of their errors.

In the proposed plan, the monthly published statements of every bank of discount throughout the Union, as well as the quarterly published statements of the banks of issue, including the statements of the banks of discount, are considered important; as thereby the public may be appraised of the expansions of the currency, and in some measure enabled to guard against the commonly ruinous effects of over-expansions and consecutive contractions.

These periodical statements should be made so clear and plain, as to be as easily comprehended by every man who can read them, as any common statement of a merchant's account.

The quarterly bank statements, in addition to their ordinary matter, should contain all their liabilities and assets—particularizing not only the debts and resources of the banks; but the immediate liabilities of the banks should be distinguished from their deferred liabities; and their immediate resources from their deferred resources. The amount of specie received in deposite should be distinguished from the amount of bills of other banks, and from deposites made of their own notes. Without such statements it must be impossible for the public to arrive at any thing like a correct knowledge of the true condition of the currency; or that the people, for whose benefit these statements are made, should be able to judge of the amount of paper money at any one time in circulation; or the amount necessary, to-together with the specie that the absence of small bills will always keep in circulation, to promote and obtain the greatest possible permanent prosperity of the country.

And, in addition, the quarterly statements of the banks of issue should contain accounts of the prices of money in foreign countries ; and the rates of exchanges between the U. States and the countries with which the American commerce is carried on ; and, when any cause, out of the course of the ordinary supply and demand, varies the rate of exchange temporarily above or below what it ought to be quoted, that cause should be stated and explained, as well as its probable effects upon the demand and supply in the United States.

By no means the least important of the measures, proposed for rendering the currency perfectly convertible, and uniformly current throughout the United States, in the accompanying plan, is the contemplated regularly published, clear and correct statements of all the banks, both of issue and discount.

When we consider the importance which the banking system of the United States must exercise over the property and industry, and consequently the prosperity of the country, we cannot refrain from urging upon the public the importance of free banking. By this plan the people will be required to express an opinion, through the ballot-boxes, upon the measures and policy of the banks of discount in their immediate vicinity, and of the states and United States institutions at stated periods. Hence, the importance of publishing clear, particular and correct statements of all the business of all the banks. A uniformity in these statements, could be provided for in the same manner as are the returns of the post office, by furnishing the banks with similar blanks, requiring only to be correctly filled up to make complete returns from the banks of discount to their state banks of issue, and by them to the United States bank of issue, for publication, for the information of the public.

The removal of private interest in the concealments of the returns of the banks, will lessen the temptation to fraud and false statements; and the supervision of the state directors will be likely to detect any inaccuracies that may inadvertantly creep into their statements.

A bank should not interfere with exchanges, either foreign or domestic. In fact, there would be no domestic exchanges; or, at most, none above the actual expense of the transportation of specie from one part of the country to another. This system would soon reduce our imports to the par exchange of our exports; domestic exchanges would soon find their level, by the reduction of the imports of the place to its exports, until trade would be equalized throughout the Union.

The tariff might then be confined to the encouragement and protection of domestic manufactures. In all other respects the trade would be free with all the world, as is the trade between the different states of the Union.

## CHAPTER XXIX.

### ON EXCHANGES AND BANK MONOPOLY.

History of the incorporation of banking companies.—Expansions and contractions of the currency, the natural effects of the laws of their situation.—The high price of domestic exchanges—of foreign exchanges—the result of bank monopoly.—Speculators monopolize the currency, the trade, and regulate the price of commodities —High prices increase importations.—Specie not returned for the sale of bills in a foreign market.—Eastern speculators increase western importations.—Exchanges between two places the barometer of trade.—Bank contractions reduce prices as much below par, as their previous expansions had advanced them.—Effects of bank monopoly on exchanges.

Capitalists apply to congress, or to state legislatures, for the passage of an act of incorporation for banking purposes. The law is passed—the stock is taken—the money is paid, and business commenced. Bank notes are prepared for circulation. The newspapers of the place give them a puff or two; the community read the puffs, and exaggerate in their neighborly news the benefits of the new bank.

Their note exchange is opened : the villagers or citizens present their notes, well endorsed by each other, for exchange ; the board examine into the stability of each endorser, and register, for future use, their abilities and responsibilities. Notes are exchanged: the bankers give their unendorsed notes, with *limited liability* without interest, due on demand, for the borrower's note, due sixty days hence, (the interest for sixty-three days having been deducted and retained by the bankers,) with two good endorsers— all three of them being liable for the whole amount of the endorsed note to the extent of their entire fortunes. And this is the *equality* of incorporated banking companies !

Bankers may reasonably ask, what right have the public to expect us to hire a banking house, employ clerks, incur the expense of obtaining bills, and the trouble, risk and responsibility of conducting a bank, merely for their convenience and accommodation ? The answer must be, certainly, none : nor do the directors of the bank feel they have been elected by the stockholders for any such purpose. The bankers have sought and obtained the privilege of exchanging notes with their neighbors, or whoever may be disposed to exchange notes with them, for the purpose of pursuing the trade of banking as being the most profitable business, and the best mode of investing their capital that offers. The directors and stockholders do not fancy that the public have any more right to claim their services, unless it be to the interest of the bank to accommodate them, than they have to claim the services of the merchant who sells them broadcloths.

The object of the merchant in investing his money in broadcloths, is not the accommodation of particular persons, in a particular place, but the investing his money in stock that would be the most productive. He offers his broadcloth for sale, at just as great an advance upon the cost and charges, as he believes the people can be made to pay. Hence it is clear, that the accommodation of the inhabitants of the place, by the merchant, any farther than promotes his interest, is no part of his object. His business is to make money by selling his goods in the best market. He receives nothing but current money in payment for his goods, provided he can sell them for that. He is not actuated by sympathy for the poor half clad inhabitants of the place, only so far as they have the means of paying him for his goods. This is precisely the situation of banking capitalists. They firstly obtain the *exclusive* privilege of banking; then invest their capital in bank stock; issue their bills; discount the best notes that are offered, and charge the highest interest the law allows; for the laws of their situation compel them to make as much money as they legally can. In locating their banks, they do not seek the poorest places, for the benefit of the poorest people, within their knowledge, nor do they select the notes of the most needy inhabitants of the place for discount : but they locate their banks where the people are able to pay them a handsome profit for the use of their *credit*, and they loan their money to persons, who, with their sureties, they deem quite competent to repay them the principal in due time—the interest they secure in advance. All this, too, is in strict accordance with the laws of their situation.

The directors of banks are selected by the stockholders from their supposed superior skill in banking, and their ability for making the most profit upon their capital stock invested, that can be made. They, therefore, sell their notes to those who are able and willing to pay the most for them, upon precisely the same principles that the merchant sells nis broadcloth. They both accommodate their customers, for their respective interests only, not for the interests of their customers.

If the merchant, who asks five dollars a yard for his broadcloth, finds a customer who will pay him that amount for all his stock, he sells it all to him at once; and if he will pay him that sum in a draft upon some well known house at par, where the bill will be worth to him five per cent. above par, who complains of the merchant for selling his stock to this purchaser, in preference to selling it out to his credit customers, who, perhaps, already owe him as much as they are able promptly to pay ? But when bankers loan to speculators all the money of the place, because the specu- lators will repay the bank in a distant market, where a draft will be worth five or ten per cent. above par, the former customers of the bank complain, as though they had a right to *command* the loans of the bank ; yet all this is strictly in obedience with the laws of their situation, which compel the bankers, as well as the merchants, to make their capital stock produce as much profit as they legally can.

The merchant imports and sells as much broadcloth as he profitably can; firstly, for money, then for credit, as long as he believes his sales will be profitable to himself.

So the banker issues and loans as much of his credit pa- per as he can keep afloat, and get pay for, to the uttermost limits of his credit. Substituting for the specie that should be in his vaults, every evidence of debt in his possession, including the notes of banks and public and private bonds and securities, and upon these credits he issues bills, intended to circulate as money, without the specie necessary to meet the prompt redemp- tion of his notes, if that should be demanded.

The channels of currency become surcharged. The ex- portation of the commodity that exceeds the actual demand follows. The only exportable portion of the currency is the precious metals; consequently *that* will be exported. Brokers become the convenient agents of the banks. Specie is sold at a premium. The banks lessen their discounts, call in their debts, and thus contract the circulating medium at their will. And all this, too, is in exact accordance with the laws of their situation; and the immutable laws of supply and demand.

In this state of the currency, the bank makes its principal business dealing in exchanges, as this affords larger profits than loaning money at six per cent., since the scarcity of money that the bank has itself produced, has raised its value to two, three, four, or perhaps five times the lawful rate of interest. Here again the evil effects of the monopoly of the present chartered bank system of currency is felt and deprecated; for, by this monopoly, the prices of domestic and foreign exchanges are advanced or varied, to suit the interest of these monopolizing chartered companies.

The people suffer much inconvenience, also, from the want of small change in specie, owing to the banks hoarding it up in their vaults, or collecting it for exportation, to enable them profitably to draw bills upon foreign markets to which they export it. This also raises the price of exchanges, and of all imported articles of merchandise.

In the western states, at this moment, the expense of obtaining a bill on New York of one hundred dollars, is often equal to the expense of importing from New York the very articles purchased for the money there.

Reader, if you are an elector, and have voted for a supporter of chartered banks, remember, that through him, you vote for this very state of things, which you so much deprecate. If you will read this little volume, your own common sense will enable you to judge, whether or no the author has shown you a safe, certain, feasible remedy for the various defects of our present chartered bank paper. If you approve of his plan of republican free banking, as one of the sovereign people, it is not only your privilege, but your bounden duty, to encourage its immediate adoption. If you have a choice in the kind of money you are to use, have you not a constitutional right to enjoy the gratification of that choice, as well as the banker or speculator, who may be interested in, and therefore contented with, the present uncurrent bank paper ?

While a few privileged individuals, enjoy by law the exclusive monopoly of the business of banking, of the exchanges, and of the currency, specie must become more and more scarce ; exchanges more and more uncertain, and the price of the same higher and higher, with every evolution of trade.

Bankers will sell their notes, their drafts, (and through their agents, the brokers,) their specie, to the highest bidder. That is, they will make the best market of their credit, their capital, and their legal privilege of banking, that is in their power, For this is in exact accordance with the laws of their situation.

The speculator, who purchases commodities in the western country, for sale in the eastern cities, can pay for the loan of his money in the eastern market at much less expense to himself, than the regular trader in the western city, whose business is purely domestic. He monopolizes the money, by paying the banker (indirectly, probably,) more than legal interest ; and this enables him to monopolize the business or trade in which he is engaged, and to regulate the prices of the articles in which he deals, by which the producer receives less for his products, or manufactures, while the consumer pays more for them—making a dead loss to both, without any other benefit than that of supporting, in comparative idleness and luxury, a large number of bankers, brokers and speculators.

Self-interest, being the motive power of most human actions, and the only avenue to the favors of chartered banking companies, the speculator finds abundant means of monopolizing their favors ; which he does, by making his notes due in a distant market, where the sale of the draft for their re-payment is worth more than it would be in the vaults of the banks ; and in numerous other ways, the speculator increases the dividends of the banks above the ordinary rate of interest or profits they make on their regular loans.

He next establishes the prices of the commodities in which he deals, to suit his own interest, relying upon the bank for such credit as he may require—not from their preference for him, for he well knows they have no such preference. He relies upon their own interest—he is secure and must succeed.

The business of banks of issue is to lend their credit. This done, they have the power to regulate the exchanges, that is, the price of bills between distant parts of the United States, and even between the United States and London.

Self-interest being, as was just remarked, the law by which monied corporations are governed, the double profits made upon the discount of notes, where the re-payment is to be made in a distant place, induces the bankers to extend their discounts to the utmost verge of their abilities, and often far beyond their means of redeeming their notes in specie when demanded.

To save their charters, banks frequently firstly resort to

contractions, then to suspensions of specie payment; or
they convert their banking house into a broker's office, and
commence buying and selling exchanges; or they turn their
business over to their agent the broker, to make as much
money out of their bank monopoly as they legally can. To
this, also, they are impelled by the law of their situation.

Banks, however, frequently resort to various other subterfuges to avoid suspensions, and yet to retain their charters, after they have expanded the currency far beyond
their power to redeem their notes in specie, and beyond
the abilities of the channels of currency to contain—when
the exportation of specie, by the immutable law of supply and demand, must ensue. Among the schemes
practiced, are those of issuing post notes—notes due at as
distant a date as may be made to circulate, sometimes bearing interest and sometimes without interest, drawn in the
similitude of bank notes and circulated as money, to the
full extent of public gullibility.

This flush of money serves to increase the amount of
sales of foreign merchandise for domestic consumption. It
delays, but does not remedy the evil. Yet, with this excess
of paper money, prices do not rise, perhaps, as high as
might have been expected from the unlimited discounts of
the banks ; as the speculator, by monopolizing the money
of the place, has been able to fix the price of the article he
wishes to purchase lower than the competition between the
regular traders of the place would have made it, had the
money of the place been left free from the interference of
monopolizing speculators, who, by the aid of a monopoly
of bank credit, would not only regulate the purchasing price
of his commodities, but also influence their sale price, which
men with small capitals would be unable to do.

The speculator may be enriched—the bank may be profited—but the farmer, the mechanic, and laborer, frequently receive of even this inflated inconvertible bank paper, less than they might have received in cash for their commodities, but for this chartered bank monopoly.

But the worst of all remains to be told. After the money has been given by the bank to one or more foreign speculators, *no specie is returned to the bank from the distant city* for the bill that was received for the loan to the speculator. It was merely an exchange of liabilities; by which are formed facilities for extending and increasing importations beyond the natural limits of supply and demand, or the sound principles of trade and commerce. The banker receives either his own notes for the bill, or what is still worse, he discounts a new fictitious paper, the private note of some debtor in the place where the money is due for the bill, and after deducting the exchange, the bank has established by this monopoly, and the interest, the balance becomes a new credit. Inland importations are thus increased—foreign importations are also thereby enhanced—the balance of trade is turned against the western consumer—and, ultimately, against the United States with foreign countries. The American debtor in a foreign market, must pay an advanced price on bills of exchange, or a premium on gold and silver to meet his remittances; the country becomes drained of its specie; bank loans are limited; the price of commodities fall below their cost of production; enterprise and industry are checked; public and private confidence become shaken; the bonds of society become relaxed; respect for the laws are diminished; the passion of self-love predominates; and private interest, the love of *gain*, and the desire of *power*, sway the destinies of this great nation; and as the word of a Despot directs the fate, the peace and prosperity of his government, so does the *private interest of incorporated companies* rule the destinies of this otherwise powerful and happy people.

The legally privileged order of bankers, with brokers and speculators, may become rich, but the people must become poor. And will the people, who make and unmake those privileged orders, still madly support them? I say, no. Show them how to avoid the iron rod of these bank task-masters, and they will not submit to them. The mechanic, the farmer, and the laborer, know that the banks are a heavy annual tax upon their labor—destroying their habits of industry and economy, and inducing luxurious extravagance and indolence, and not unfrequently intemperance; while the commercial community admit, that improper over-expansions, by the immutable law of supply and demand, must produce consecutive contractions of the currency—the natural effects of banking monopolies, and of the laws of the situation of incorporated companies.

# CHAPTER XXX.

## ON COMPARISONS OF THE CURRENCY WITH THE GOVERNMENT.

The government and administration of the proposed bank compared to the political machinery of governments.—On the difference between the centralization
of government with a centralized administration, and a centralized government
with a divided administration.—The administration, in monarchies, more centralized than the government; as well as in mixed monarchies.—The concurrence of the people's representatives necessary to the government.—The centralization of municipalities in monarchies.—Republican townships have numerous administrators—each independent of the others—each under a centralized
government.—The courts.—The people, through the ballot-boxes.—Proposed
plan CENTRALIZES the GOVERNMENT of the currency, like the general government of the Union.—Divides the administration of the currency—This resembles
the administration of townships.—One bank of issue—Numerous banks of discount—Directors of both responsible to the laws and to the sovereign people.—The
stock, specie, issues, reserved fund, dividends and government centralized—The
election of officers, the discounts, loans, collections, securities, and entire business
of the banks of discount, divided.—The old United States Banks, with centralized administrative powers, directed the operations of their branches, discounts,
expansions and contractions of the currency, and dealt in exchanges—The
whole currency subservient to their interests.—A centralized administration of
the currency dangerous to republican institutions—injurious to trade and commerce—by its own laws a monopoly.—In republics, government should be centralized—administration divided—the law powerful—The administrator insignificant.

In monarchical governments, the *administration* of the
government is even more centralized than the government.

In mixed monarchies, as those of England and France,
the government is in part divided, and the administration
contralized : the people, or portions of them, elect one
branch of the legislature.

In mixed monarchies, where the concurrence of the
three branches of the legislature is requisite to the passage
of all laws, the house of representatives possesses at least
a negative power over their enactments, but without possessing any influence over their administration. The administration is centralized in the Chief Magistrate, executed by the persons of his appointment, in his name, and according to his will and pleasure, subject to his removal from
office, and to fine or imprisonment at his pleasure.

In municipalities, under a monarchy, the administration
is centralized. The mayor is the head of the corporation,

## 166      DUNCOMBE'S FREE BANKING.

and the aldermen and common councilmen are more or
less dependant upon his concurrence in all important measures.

In townships in America, the administration is divided
between a great number of independent magistrates, elected by the people for distinct magisterial and administrative duties. In one township, may be found from twelve
to twenty magisterial officers, administering the several
functions of the township ; each independent of the others,
amenable to the superior courts in their individual capacities, and accountable to the people at their annual election.
Wherever they are not altogether independent of each
other, it is the *government* of the township that connects
their duties, and not its administration.

In the United States, the laws provide for the organization of townships, and prescribe general rules of government ; still the administration of the township is independent of either the general or provincial government, each
township officer is as independent of every other body or
officer as is the president of the United States—they, like
him, are bound by particular laws, and accountable to the
sovereign people, through the ballot-boxes, when they become candidates for re-election.

For the purpose of rendering the currency of the country republican, the plan here recommended proposes, that
the government of the currency shall be centralized, upon
principles somewhat analagous to those of the general government of the United States ; and the administration of the
currency divided, as is the political administration of the
townships.

Upon the plan of the proposed free banking system, the
bank of the United States is made the bank of issue ; and
the directors are entrusted with the power of issuing and

promulgating general rules for the uniform government of the state banks of re-issue, and of the local banks of discount, but without power to interfere with either, beyond certain clearly defined limits—nor in any way with the *administration* of the banks of discount, any more than the general government of the Union interferes with the administration of the townships.

The government of all the issues of currency, whether of the precious metals, or of the paper intended to circulate as money to supply the deficiency of the precious metals, occasioned by their exportation, should be centralized. It should be under the immediate control and regulation of the whole people, through directors freely elected from every part of the Union. That the stock subscribed, and the specie received thereon, may be equalized throughout the Union; that the reserved fund—for the safety of the bill-holders, to be applied to the relief of any local bank, whenever any casualty shall render it temporarily unable to redeem its notes at sight, and for that purpose should be subject to the disposition of the directors of the bank of issue. This reserved fund is intended to redeem at the instant, such notes of the banks of any state as shall not have been redeemed on demand, until such bank shall be again able to meet their notes in specie and re-pay the amount thus borrowed.

And also that the dividends may be apportioned equally between all the stockholders, in proportion to their respective amounts of stock.

To illustrate this point more clearly, we will suppose, that the business done by the bank at New Orleans, would enable the directors of that bank to have divided ten per cent. upon their business, with the bills apportioned to them, upon the specie in their vaults, while the bank at Boston may not have been able to divide over six per cent. per annum;

and supposing this difference in the amounts of their dividends throughout the Union, when the profits of all the
banks are summed up, the rate would be found to be eight
per cent., which would be paid to all the stockholders equally. This, too, would aid in giving the currency a uniform
circulation throughout the country, since the government
would be uniform, central and identical—with the administration divided, and adapted to the wants, interests and inclinations of the people in every part of the Union.

The old United States banks possessed centralized administrative powers, from which financial and political evils
were seriously complained of. The mother bank regulated the amount of business that each branch was to do ;
and directed the kinds of business that each branch was to
be engaged in. If dealing in foreign or domestic exchanges was likely to be more profitable than lending money,
this was, by order of the parent bank, made the business
of the branches, as well as of the parent institution. The
currency was expanded where the bank or a branch wish-
ed to sell bills of exchange, that the temporary flush of
money might raise the price of exchanges ; and contracted
at such points as she wished to buy bills, that the temporary scarcity of money might lessen the price.

The bank and branches, having the whole monopoly of
the exchanges, and from her being the only dealer in exchange, the power and influence of her immense capital,
and almost unlimited power of augmenting and diminishing the amount of paper at any one point, whenever it
suited her interest, as well as from her greater facility of
making remittances from place to place, and her better and
more perfect, as well as more extended organization for immense financial operations, enabled her to fix the rates
of exchange to suit her private interest. By contracting

the currency, for which purpose it was only necessary to refuse or delay her ordinary discounts for a few days, she
could enhance the value of money for immediate use, and
thus lessen the price of bills of exchange in the market to
suit her private purposes.

The unjust and improper exercise of the influence and
powers created by the *centralized administration* of the
United States bank, has very justly alarmed the lovers of a
sound currency and republican institutions.

In the proposed plan, the immense dangerous power and
influence of a mammoth bank, with a centralized administration, is entirely removed, while the benefits of a centralized government of the currency are increased and retained.

Thus we see it is the *centralized administration* of the
currency, which is so much to be feared, should congress
charter another United States bank, with branches throughout the Union, and not the *centralization* of the *government*
of the currency.

In a republic where the people are the sovereign power,
the administration of the government cannot be too much
divided, nor the government too much centralized; that the
power may exist, but the representative not be perceived;
that the law may govern and be powerful, and the administrator be insignificant and concealed. In this particular,
the elective system possesses superior excellence, and is
admirably adapted to the conduct of the finances and banking of the United States.

In a centralized government and divided administration,
consists the excellencies of the United States constitution :
numerous independent magistrates, with duties well defined, govern the country.

In the centralized government, with a divided adminis-

tration, consists the superiority of the present constitution
of these United States, over the first confederacy of the
several states, as well as over all other former confederacies
of republican states, ancient or modern. The government
is general, and its principles of action and of operation uniform, with local administrations, adapted to promote the
interests and immediate relief of the wants and inclinations
of the various parts of the Union. The administration is
divided, and the administrators directly responsible to the
people for the faithful discharge of the duties of their respective offices—each in his private person and individual
capacity through the courts of law.

The government of the United States is an unit, while
the administrative authority is almost entirely restricted to
the townships.

Deroqueville says, "in no country does the law hold such
absolute sway as in America :

"The administrative power in the United States presents
nothing, either central or hierarchical in its constitution,
which accounts for its passing unperceived.

"The power exists, but its representative is no where
to be perceived,

" The magistrates are numerous, and the law carefully
prescribes a circle of action for each, while they have a
right to perform their functions independently of any authority."

## CHAPTER XXXI.

### ON THE CENTRALIZED GOVERNMENT OF THE CURRENCY, AND ITS DIVIDED ADMINISTRATION.

A centralized ADMINISTRATION of the currency, from the laws of its situation, anti-republican.

When the administration, as well as the government of the currency, is centralized, by the laws of its situation it is anti-republican, and dangerous to the perpetuity of republican institutions, as well as to the equality and liberty of the people, by connecting in the hands of a few irresponsible individuals, the immense power and influence of all the money of the country.

In the system of currency hereby proposed, all this monetary power and influence is entirely removed, and all its dangerous financial and political effects obviated, by the division of its administration; while the perfect uniform convertibility of the paper intended to circulate as money, and the equalized circulation of the currency of each state, throughout all the states of the Union, will be happily provided for by the centralization of the government of the currency.

# CHAPTER XXXII.

## OF BANK INFLUENCE.

Of bank influence.—The bank of Upper Canada—the only bank in Upper Canada in 1830—capital $400,000—Government stock $100,000—eight directors—Governor appoints two directors.— Grievance Report, at the Colonial Office, (Eng.)—Political influence complained of—Officers of the bank generally tories—Bank agents are tories—The committee of the Assembly, in 1830. upon the bank, ask for information—that refused—Parliament is dissolved, and the capital of the bank increased, without giving the information sought —The House of Representatives report upon the United States Bank—Mr. Clayton chairman—Members of Congress charged with being interested—Editors of news-papers subsidized—Directors parties to this improper influence—Responsibility to public opinion—Monied interests control the press, and influence representation, and a bandage over the people's eyes.—The dangerous effects of an United States Bank and branches—a tremendous engine in the hands of a corrupt administration, by the laws of its situation—A chartered bank must support a friendly administration—must make as much money as it lawfully can—The bank would be made the fiscal agent of the government—The bank and government would perpetuate each other.—A credit aristocracy dangerous to republican institutions.—Bank operations—how rendered serviceable.—The Bank of England—notes lawful tender—based upon credit—Connection dangerous to American currency.—Political and financial shocks—effects in England felt in America.—Specie exported in 1839, at a loss—benefit to the Bank of England.—United States Bank and branches could control elections—Republicanism would cease.—Rothschild, Baring, Wilson, govern the United States—war—peace—manufactures—capitalists—The remedy—separate currency from credit—from private interest—from politics—render it republican—The people elect the directors.—Private interest of the people in the government—Elect directors of banks of discount—Bank of issue separate.—Gold and silver the true elements of a sound currency.—Directors give good security—bill-holders secure—Issue no small bills—paper money made current and interchangeable—More specie in the vaults of the bank than bank notes in circulation.—The object of this book is to produce a sound currency—centralize the government of the currency—divide its administration—modify the usury laws and the bankrupt laws, and have money sound and plenty.

By the following, it will be seen to what extent a bank, connected with the government, may oppress a people.

In 1830, when this account was sent to England, the capital of the Bank of Upper Canada, the only bank then in the Province, was £100,000 Province currency—$400,000—one-fourth of which was owned by the Colonial Government, who appointed two of its eight directors.

GRIEVANCE REPORT C.—(From the appendix to a Memorial received at the Colonial Office, England.)—" The government and its officers have the bank under their control, and direct its vast powers at their pleasure. It is not necessary for me to assume it as a fact, that they use their powers, (one of which is to loan millions, yearly, of paper, for which they are not individually responsible to the bill-holder,) for the purpose of rewarding political partizans. The history of all political parties in such a government as that of Upper Canada, will enable the reader to draw a proper inference. The bank has agents in the several Districts, who are believed to be in the receipt of large incomes drawn from the agencies.

" They are usually found among the most active partizans of those in authority.

"In the year 1830, the Assembly appointed a commitee on the currency, with power to enquire into the management of the bank, which had solicited an extension of its stock. I was chairman of that committee, and reported certain resolutions for information desired from the bank. The house, by an unanimous vote, sustained the resolutions, and the bank refused their information, contrary to the terms of its charter. The dissolution of that Parliament enabled the bank to obtain its charter, without disclosing the general condition of its affairs to the body, which granted it a large additional share of the power of the government. The report of the majority of the committee, appointed by the House of Representatives of the United States, to examine into the proceedings of the directors of the United States Bank, before renewing its charter, and made this year to Congress, by Mr. Clayton, shows, that members of Congress, and editors of public journals, had been tampered with, and the press subsidized, to a very great extent, and that the whole board of directors had been parties to this undue influence exercised. If these things are in a government like the United States, where there is a general responsibility to the public opinion acknowledged by public men, what may not be presumed in a secret institution like the Upper Canada Bank, in the hands of the politicians?

" If a capitalist's monied interest can succeed in influencing representation and the press, that representation will become more and more its instrument, and a bandage over the eyes of the public, ' the powerful, and in the hands of a bad administration, the irresistible and corrupting influence, (observes Mr. McDuffie,the chairman on the ways and means, in his report to the House of Representatives of the United States, 1830,) which a government bank would exercise over the elections of the country, constitutes an objection more imposing than all others united. No matter by what means an administration might get into power, with such a tremendous engine in their hands, it would be almost impossible to displace them, without some miraculous dispensation of Providence.' "

If we should ever be so unfortunate as to have a corrupt Executive at the head of the general government, of the United States, with the whole currency of the country subject to the disposal of a few interested individuals, as directors of an United States Bank and branches, at the time of a general election, would not such an Executive perpetuate themselves during pleasure? A chartered bank must support the administration which will patronize it: by the laws of its situation it cannot do otherwise. It has been created for the purpose of making the most money out of the public, with the least labor and cost, that can be legally made. It has nothing in common with the community. Its object and entire business is that of making money. A corrupt Executive would find no difficulty in securing its support, by affording it an opportunity of increasing its profits; perhaps appointing some of its officers to the Treasury Department of state—making the institution the recipient of the public revenue ; and, if necessary to secure its utmost support, allow it a large deposite of public money to bank upon, free from cost, and even to allow it a profit, a per centage upon the receipts and disbursements of the public revenue. Such an institution would perpetuate itself by perpetuating an administration that would use it for political purposes ; every debtor in the United States (and who would not be in debt with such a credit currency,) would be directly or indirectly pledged to the support of the bank and the party that would support it. A monied aristocracy, or rather a *credit aristocracy*, at home, would regulate the affairs of the nation—if we were fortunate enough to escape the grasp of foreign mercenaries, which probably would not long continue—but liberty and equality, with republicanism, would exist only in name. The American Republic would soon follow in the tracks of most former republics, and its glory and excellence fade and be forgotten, or be blotted from the page of history as a dangerous dream of imaginary happiness.

While upon the subject of bank influence, it may not be amiss to suppose an incorporated banking company doing the business of the money currency of these United States. The directors to be men with whom private interest, and the importunities of numerous hungry money borrowers could have no effect. That during times of foreign and domestic prosperity, they had restricted their discounts to the *actual* demand for currency, and that, consequently, during the reverses of the money market, they had been able to increase their discounts and relieve the pressure in the United States, however severely it may have been felt abroad. Would not the financial and political power of such a company be dangerous to the liberties and commercial prosperity of the nation ? For it should be recollected, that so far as credit is connected with the currency, the American money market is in much danger from the effects of shocks in the English money market, owing to the circumstance that the basis of the circulating medium in Great Britain is credit, and that the capital of the Bank of England is in part composed of their irredeemable national debt; and that, consequently, if ever the credit of the British government should be shaken, that shock must be felt almost simultaneously by the Bank of England—and *vice versa.*

The Joint Stock Banks generally pay their debts in Bank of England paper, which, by the bye, is lawful tender in the payment of all debts except its own; in fact, the loans of the different banking houses in London, are mostly composed of the notes of the Bank of England. Should a panic occur in the money market of England, the holders of bank of England notes would immediately demand specie for them, and when the specie should all be drawn from the bank, as a matter of course, it must suspend specie payment, or avow its insolvency—(what a false, yet fashionable, term for bankruptcy is *suspension ?*)

In such an event, the currency of the United States would be involved in the shock. A run would be made upon American banks, upon the first moment of the arrival of the news of the run upon the bank of England for specie to save the bank of England from ruin, and, perhaps, the nation from revolution. American stocks, previously owned in England, would be re-sold in the American market at such prices as would command purchasers, and specie would be hurried to England to meet the high prices that it would be likely to command there. We have seen gold and silver exported to England, during the late threatened panic there, by the friends of the bank of England

in the United States, to meet the emergencies of the bank
of England, as well probably, as to profit by the first high
prices of specie after the banks should have suspended. What
effect this timely transportation of specie may have had in
preventing the threatened suspension, I am unable to say,
and the circumstance of the exportation of specie in 1839,
at a loss (since remittances could have been made in bills
at less expense,) is only referred to to show the intimate
connection that exists between the monetary affairs of England with America.

But to proceed with the investigation of the political
power and influence of an incorporated banking company,
we will ask, what would be likely to be the course adopted
by a *corrupt government*, about to be removed by the votes
of American freemen? Would it not be likely to purchase the support and influence of a few individuals, who
could control the whole currency of the Union? and if so,
could not such an institution exercise an immense power
over the liberties and fortunes of the people? Could not
the directors of the paper portion of the currency, although
consisting of but a few (perhaps otherwise obscure,) individuals, fearlessly say to the Executive of these United
States, support the bank, and the bank shall support you—
oppose the bank, and the power of the bank and branches
shall oust you from office. The necessities of the one, and
the laws of the situation of the other, must produce an al-
liance, offensive and defensive, between a credit aristocracy and such a political party. The bank, using the legislature, as Mr. Jefferson said, as a bandage to blind the
people's eyes : the subsidy of the press, which would be the
natural consequence of such a combination, would leave
the public bound hand and foot, and delivered into the
hands of their oppressors.

Republicanism would only exist in name. The stock of the bank would gradually glide into the hands of foreign capitalists; and we should have the nominee of some foreign Rothschild, Baring, or Wilson, as bank agent in each of our principal cities, regulating the kind and amount of currency that the free born sons of America shall receive and use, while foreigners retained entire control of " the sinews of war," and the instrument of wealth in peace.

How could the American government conduct a war against England, extend commerce, or even increase domestic manufactures, with the purse strings of the treasury in the hands of capitalists, whether foreigners or Americans, who were opposed to the measure ?

The uncontrolled and uncontrollable passion for gain, common to Americans, renders it far more necessary that the currency of the United States should be sound, than that of any other country.

The remedy we propose for the defective state of the currency is, to organize the people, with power to regulate the currency of the country, as they at this time regulate its political machinery, through persons independently and freely elected by the people—persons who have no more direct interest in the business of the bank, than an officer of the government has in its finances. One common bond of interest should support the currency, as it supports the political machinery of the government; but no private interest should be allowed to intervene, to separate the people from the government, or to strengthen the natural hostility of political parties.

All the elementary principles of the government should conduce to the equal support of the whole people, and to the strengthening of the institutions of the country. Hence the importance of changing the elementary principles of the currency of the United States, from aristocratic to republican.

The strength of a republican government consists in the private interest that each citizen has in its support, and in its healthful administration. The union of public with private interest should be promoted by the general organization of the people, for the exercise of all the powers and privileges consonant with this object. They should exercise the same influence over its monetary affairs, that they do over its literary, religious and political institutions.

Currency, to become sound, must have the paper portion of it as perfectly separated from the influence of private interest, from credit, and from politics, as are the precious metals.

The bank of issue must be separated from the banks of discount. The issues of paper to circulate as money, should only be based upon specie. No notes of other banks, public bonds, or debts of the United States, or of the several states, foreign or domestic exchanges, or other evidences of debt, either public or private, should be had recourse to or used as a basis for the issue of paper to circulate as money. Gold and silver coins, and bullion, are the only true elements of a sound currency ; and so long as these only are used as a basis for the issue of paper to circulate as money, and the business of the banks of discount is limited to discounting only actual business paper, having but short periods to run, the currency may easily be preserved sound.

The directors should be precluded from any interest in the discounts, and held responsible to the people for the faithful discharge of their duties, which should be all clearly defined, and well adapted to the promotion of the greatest good of the greatest numbers, at the least expense, or danger of loss to the public.

The securities given by the directors, should be such, that, with their salaries, and their hopes of re-election, the public might rest safe and contented in the enjoyment of the currency, to which common benefits they are entitled and ought to enjoy.

The issuing no small bills, would bring specie immediately into circulation, for all sums below the amount of paper issued : while the perfectly interchangeable character of the paper, would put it on a par with gold and silver throughout the Union ; and while it would be preferred by commercial men for large business and remittances, gold and silver would be gladly received by men in small business.

All the small channels of currency would be filled with the precious metals. Every class of community would have the use of the material for money, which they choose from the preference of the other classes of society, for that material least desirable to themselves.

Removing the necessity for legislative interference with the banks, either to increase their capitals or extend their privileges, by organizing the people to regulate the currency, as before recommended, will check the dangerous and improper political influence and interference of chartered banks with elections.

And as to there not being specie enough in the United States to form a basis for the circulation of large bills, sufficient to do the actual business paper of the country, such apprehensions are groundless, and those who have believed that we were indebted to chartered banks for all the money we have in circulation, may be a little surprised to learn, that, for the last six years—during the greatest fluctuations of the currency—in times of unbounded prosperity, as well as of the greatest oppressive financial contractions of the currency—during suspensions of specie payments, and consecutive suspensions of business, from Maine to Georgia—there never has been, at any one time, not even for one day, as much bank paper in circulation among the people, as the amount of specie, proved by the oaths of bank officers, to have been in the vaults of the banks at the periods stated. This fact at first appears a little startling; but it is no more strange than true, that there has not been, for six years past, as much bank paper in circulation in the United States, independent of the deposites in the banks, as there has been specie actually in the banks at the time. The question then arises, how can this be true, and money continue so scarce, unless there is something radically wrong in the elementary principles of the banking system?

The leading object of this work is, to illustrate principles upon which paper may be issued, to meet the deficiency of the precious metals, occasioned by the exportation of specie, that will be invariably interchangeable for gold and silver, current throughout the Union, as · easily to be obtained as other commodities.

By centralizing the government of the currency, and dividing its administration; separating the bank of issue from the banks of discount; limiting the discounts to not more than three times the amount of specie in the vaults of the bank at the time of the discount, and to only actual business paper, having but short periods to run, in which no director has any interest; separating currency from the influence of private interest, credit, or politics; issuing no small bills, that men of small business may have gold and silver, and the commercial community large bills, from the choice that each would have for the kind of currency least desirable to the other; rendering it republican, by giving the people the election of the directors of the currency, as they elect the most numerous branches of their legislatures, **must**, from the nature of the immutable laws of supply and demand, and of cause and effect, give us a currency always convertible, uniformly current throughout the Union, and, with proper modifications of the bankrupt and usury laws, as easily to be obtained as any other commodity. Currency would then become the firmest, as it is the most natural, bond of union between the people and the government of their choice.

## CHAPTER XXXIII.

### A CHARTERED UNITED STATES BANK AND BRANCHES.

Its benefits—how obtained. Its evils—how avoided.

A chartered United States Bank, with branches, possess decided advantages over the present state chartered banks, in a financial point of view, in various ways; but whether these benefits are not more than counterbalanced, by the numerous evils that accompany them, remains to be investigated.

A chartered United States Bank, with branches located conveniently throughout the Union, for the accommodation of the business of the country, if confined to the legitimate business of banking, (that of lending money, by discounting only actual business paper, having but short periods to run,) would undoubtedly possess great and important advantages, in the monetary affairs of the country, over the present local, state chartered banks, by rendering bank notes equally current in every part of the United States; and thereby lessening the enormous expense of making remittances from one part of the Union to another, and removing the inconvenience of defraying travelling expenses.

It would also do much toward equalizing the quantity, as well as quality, of the circulating medium throughout the Union—and of giving a more uniform value to merchandise, and other commodities of importation and exportation; while its notes, from their extended credit, would require less specie deposited in the bank as a basis for their issue— both on account of their having nothing to fear from the hostility of neighboring rival banking institutions, which would not exist; or from any demand for specie for exportation, as the bankers (if they chose,) could guard against over-issues, and thereby prevent the surcharging of the channels of circulation, without which there would be but little to be apprehended from demands of specie for exportation. This would also release a large amount of specie from banking, to be profitably employed in commerce.

The centralization of the government of the currency in the proposed plan, gives the directors of the United States bank, the bank of issue, the sale of the whole of the bank stock, the apportionment between the several states of the specie received therefor, and the bills intended to circulate as money; the preparing such bills for circulation; the right of reserving a safety fund from the profits of the bank, to meet, temporarily, any contingencies of a local bank, by which it might be unable, promptly, to redeem its notes in specie at the instant of the demand. Also the equalizing, and declaring the dividends of the banks, and thus removing the spirit of interested rivalry between the banks of discount; the power to cause the publishing of regular, full and lucid bank statements, at stated periods; and forms for the banks of discount to fill up, of their monthly published statements and reports, that they may be made uniform; with also as perfect a control of the government of the currency, (without interfering with the administration of the

local banks, the banks of discount,) as an United States
bank and branches could have. This would render the paper portion of the currency always strictly interchangeable
for gold and silver, equally current throughout the Union,
and free from the influence of private interest, credit or politics ; securing the bill-holder from a depreciation in the
value of their bills, and the public from the dangers of excessive over-expansions of the currency, and the ruinous
effects of its consecutive contractions, or of suspensions by
the banks, of specie payments, with their destructive influences upon manufactures, agriculture and commerce. Thus
giving the public all the advantages of an United States
bank and branches without any of its dangerous financial or
political effects or influences.

The evils to be apprehended from an United States bank
and branches, are principally of two kinds, financial and
political. Its financial evils spring principally from the
concentration and monopoly of such an immense monetary
power in the hands of a few men, for their own exclusive
benefit ; men who have a distinct and separate interest in
the business and conduct of the bank, from that of the great
body of the people, and who are not dependant upon the
people for their election or continuance in office, or for their
salaries ; but whose business, by the laws of their situation,
is to make as much money out of the people as they legally
can. To accomplish this, they loan their money in large
sums to foreign speculators, to the almost entire exclusion
from their favors of the regular traders, manufacturers,
and business men of the place. They discount the fictitious
notes of speculators in preference to the regular business
notes of their customers, because the speculators will pay a
higher price for bank credit, than the business men of the
place, are willing to give—which they can well afford to do,

by paying their loans in places to which they export their
purchased products, or by other means—since they thus monopolize the money of the place, which enables them to control the business, and regulate the prices of the commodities in which they deal, as well as the exchanges between
the different places in the United States, and between the
U. States and foreign countries. By this operation, the producers—the farmers, the mechanics and manufacturers—
receive less value for their labor, their grown or manufactured articles of sale and exportation, than they would have
received from the regular dealers of the place, had the money and business been left free to their regular competition ;
but which they were precluded from, by the speculators
monopolizing the whole of the money.

From a similar cause, consumers have to pay more for
the necessaries of life than they otherwise would have to
do, while bankers and brokers are thus enabled to live
sumptuously by their legal chartered privileges, upon public gullibility.

The political evils of a chartered United States bank and
branches, grow, in a great measure, out of the same causes
that produce its financial evils. Among the most prominent of which, is, that of the centralization of the administration and concentration of action of such an immense monetary power as the whole of the money of the country must
possess in the hands of a few individuals, who are in no
way responsible to the people for their conduct ; but whose
interest is directly opposed to that of the other inhabitants,
while they are dependant upon succeeding legislatures, for
a renewal of their charters, a continuance of their powers,
or an extension of their privileges, which connects their interests more or less with the political parties of the day,
and which, at general elections, materially increases politi-

cal excitement, and violent party feelings. The bank having all the money of the country at its disposal, as well as
most of the credit and business capital under its control, it
must regulate the elections, to suit its own interests.

One old maxim is, that " necessity knows no bounds ;"
another, that " the borrower is the slave to the lender." If
these maxims be true, how can we expect to see political
independence in men who are in debt and in distress ?
Their private interest in the continuance of their existence,
which seems dependant upon credit bank paper, must induce them to support the plenty-of-money party, without
inquiring or even caring for the political ability of the can-
didate honorably to discharge the duties of the office to
which they are about to elect him.

Nor can we expect it to be otherwise, while credit, currency and politics, are thus blended together, by the necessity for frequent legislation upon the subjects of banks and
currency.

By what means, short of the immediate interposition
of Divine Providence, could such a bank party ever be defeated at an election of our Chief Magistrate, while they
can command the votes of their debtors and dependants.

In a credit country like ours, next to the question, " what
is to be made by this operation ?" is, " how long a credit
can be had ?" followed by " what must be the security ?"
If these questions are answered favorably for the purchaser, the bargain is concluded. The price, quality, and mar-
ketableness of the article, are often considerations of apparently minor importance. And much of this practice has
grown out of the abuse of bank credits. Hence the importance of a sound, uniform currency—unconnected with
politics or credit, and uninfluenced by private interest, to
the freedom of elections, or to the election of just and en-

lightened representatives, or to an independent legislation.

A suborned press, and a bribed and dependant legislature, are only fit guides for a weak or corrupt people.
They are the stepping stones by which an aristocracy of
wealth, or of credit, and a government for the benefit of
the few at the cost of the many, ascend the throne. Orders
and distinctions of classes, among the people, are thus
easily formed. And, although they may not at once present us with kings, lords, and commons—church and state
dignitaries—naval and military subjugations—these must
assuredly follow in the train, or the people must rise in their
might and disenthral themselves from the financial and po-
itical trammels of chartered bank paper, with its paper aristocracy.

For all these evils, the people have a certain, safe, and
effectual remedy, in the management of the currency themselves. They are competent to elect the directors of their
political machinery, to select the church in which they are
to worship, and to employ their religious instructors and
teachers ; to choose officers of their schools and colleges,
as well as to elect the administrators of their townships and
municipalities. Then how is it possible they dare not trust
themselves with the regulation and conduct of their banks?
Certainly the regulation of the paper portion of the currency cannot be beneath their notice, while the regulation of its
metalic portion is, by the Constitution, restricted to the
operation of congress alone.

The remedy consists, in dividing the administration of
the currency, by giving the people the election of the directors, and by separating the banks of issue from the banks
of deposite.

The election of the directors of the banks of discount,
by the people interested in its loans, will give them the

same control of the currency that they have of the other elementary principles of the government; the directors being prohibited from discounting paper, in which a director is interested.

The history of the late United States bank, and the manner in which it bought and sold bills of exchange, to promote its own interests; and the history of the Philadelphia United States bank, with its speculations in cotton, its attempt at the regulation of the currency and exchanges, domestic and foreign, are all too fresh in the memories of the business public to require to be detailed here. But, as I am writing principally for the youth of these United States, who may not recollect this part of the history of our finances, it may not be amiss briefly to refer to their records ; especially as they hear from fame, with her thousand tongues, that the United States bank and branches furnished a convenient currency—that her bills would pass currently throughout the Union—without being told what sums she abstracted from the pockets of commercial men, by her bold measures and powerful influence upon domestic and foreign commerce, through her interference in commercial speculations, and by her intermmeddling with the exchanges.

We all feel the necessity of a circulating medium, uniformly current throughout the Union ; and many among us feel this necessity so great, that they would be willing to risk the consequences of a chartered United States bank, with all its dangerous financial and political effects, present and future, for the sake of this one good. The aged and experienced upon matters of currency and banking, who have not been blinded by their own interests, will not readily be again ensnared in charters to companies of individuals for banking purposes, but young men, you may be again ensnared as we have been. Have patience with me, my young friends, and in my plain homely way, I will show you, how you may have a currency still *more* perfectly current throughout the Union without a chartered bank, and that too, without the possibility of its interfering with the exchanges, commerce or politics ; which, from the laws of its situation, a chartered United States bank and branches inevitably must do. Self-interest being their motive power, they must make all the money they legally can. Well, we admit, that the U. States bank and branches did make the currency of the country much more equal and convenient, and lessen the cost of bills of exchange between the different parts of the country below what they are under the management of the present state chartered banks. But was that the best paper medial commodity that could be obtained ? Were not its financial and political evils greater than its benefits ?

In that institution, as in all state chartered banks, private interest was a leading feature that stamped all its transactions : domestic and foreign commerce, and inland and foreign exchanges, were made tributary to its interests. The United States bank, with its branches, was nearly the first bank that dealt much in exchanges, particularly in inland bills. It at first commenced dealing in exchanges sparingly, as if conscious of the impropriety ; but, finding the public complaints less than the increased profits, it ultimately monopolized the business of exchanges—buying and selling bills upon points where its branches were located, and fixing the rates of domestic exchanges to suit its own interests, and dealing in foreign exchanges and commercial transactions.

Previously to the incorporation of the last United States bank, the business of buying and selling bills of exchange

between different cities and states, had been left, as it ever
ought to be left, to individual competition. This established the market price of bills of exchange throughout the
Union, as it is established throughout the commercial world,
and as it must invariably be conducted whenever it is not
interfered with by legally constituted monopolies. Up to
that period, banks had generally confined their operations to
lending money, or lending credit: generally to the latter
business in the United States. It should ever be remembered, that banks of circulation lend credit; while the proper business of a bank of discount is to lend money. Neither of these have, of *right*, any exclusive privilege over
exchanges, nor should they have the power to interfere
with inland bills ; yet such was the course adopted by the
United States bank, and since followed by state chartered
banks to the great prejudice of the currency and detriment
of commerce. The United States bank, however, possessed this decided advantage over state chartered banks—
that, having branches in every part of the Union, it avoided
the expense of maintaining agents to transact its business at
the points where its drafts were made payable, and it had
no necessity for increased funds to meet demands at such
points, as it chose to make its drafts payable at, as its own
branches furnished all that was required. The evils of this
operation upon currency consisted in part in a bank tax
upon all bills of exchange, and a flush of money, followed
by a corresponding scarcity, whenever the interests of the
bank required it. Currency should always be perfectly
free, and convenient for every one to use at will, and transmitted with as little cost from one part of the country to
another as possible ; for every shilling that is unfairly collected on exchanges, is not only just so much loss to the individual, but also to the public. The consumer has it to

pay. If it goes into the wrong pockets, into the hands of those who have no right to it, the public are the loosers.

The practice of banks of dealing in exchanges, *appears* to facilitate commercial transactions : and, to a superficial observer, would not be thought capable of any injurious effects upon commerce or currency, either public or private ; as the public have no interest in common with the person from whom they purchase their bills. Their only enquiries respect the certainty of the payment of the bills upon their maturity, and the rate of exchange they have to pay for them.

The public appear to forget, that the bank, by withholding its discounts for a few days, when and wherever they wish to purchase bills, may produce a temporary scarcity of money, and thereby lessen their price, perhaps one or two per cent., to promote the private interest of the bank. This private or individual *exchange dealers* could not do, as they have only a given amount at any place where they may wish to draw bills upon ; hence they cannot expand the currency, by liberal discounts, when they wish to sell, and contract them again when they wish to buy. This practice of the United States bank and branches, may be very profitable to the stockholders ; but just as much as it puts into their pockets, it takes from the pockets of the fair trader and regular business men. Suppose then, the currency of the country conducted by one general chartered United States bank, located at New Orleans, with branches in Cincinnati, New York, and other large cities. At one season of the year remittances are uniformly made from New York to New Orleans ; at another season of the year remittances are mostly made from New Orleans to New York. How easy would it be for the mother bank, at New Orleans, to expand its currency at the time that remittan-

ces were to be made from that city to New York, and advance the price of exchanges and to contract them again at
the times when they expect to buy exchanges. The same
thing may be done at New York by the branch at that place,
and in fact by any of the branches throughout the Union.

They have only to expand the currency at the time and
place where they wish to sell, and to contract their discounts when they wish to buy exchanges. All this may
be done without materially increasing the amount of the
business of the bank, or augmenting the amount of the circulating medium : the bank contracting at one place while
she expands at the other, and *vice versa.* Thus remitters
have uniformly higher prices to pay for exchanges, than they
would be charged, if the business of exchanges was left to
individual competition. The dealers in exchanges have
been literally driven from the market, by the superior facilities for the business, of the old United States bank, with
her large capital, large credit, and power of increasing or
lessening the price of exchanges, by diminishing or augmenting the currency at will.

Whenever a privileged chartered banking company monopolizes any business, and by superior capital, superior
credit, or superior local advantages, drives the regular dealers in the business out of the market, she regulates the
price of buying and selling the articles in which she deals,
and thus monopolizes them at her own will. Having all
the money, she can have all the merchandize at her own
price. The public are uniformly the loosers.

The loaning large sums to private speculators, produces
the same injurious effects upon the growers and consumers.
The grower gets less for his produce, and the consumer
pays more for his necessaries. This is loudly and justly
complained of by the commercial public. But how much

more would this be felt under the financial influence of one chartered United States bank and branches than it is at present ; when, from the laws of its situation, the injurious effect of bank monopoly, and bank preferences by a few individuals, must be felt, just in proportion to the extent of the credit paper that this mammoth paper money-making engine had put in circulation, and as it had acquired public confidence and extended its commercial influence. With the incorporation of such a monster, we may hopelessly bid farewell to a sound currency—farewell to flourishing com merce—farewell to growing manufactures—farewell to republican principles, and the blessings of equal, civil and religious liberty. Nothing but the kind interposition of Heaven could save us from utter ruin.

## HOW TO OBTAIN THE BENEFITS OF AN UNITED STATES BANK AND BRANCHES, WITHOUT ITS EVILS.

Its benefits recapitulated—The importance of a uniform measure of values—not produced for the future by a U. S. bank and branches.—On the U. S. bank's monopolizing powers—superiority in the fund market—desirable stock—accumulation of credit only delays payment—or changes the creditor.—Republicans should avoid long credits, and the payment of interest.—Elect the directors of the banks by the people—Centralize the government of the currency—divide its administration—render it republican.—Leave the exchanges to private competition.—Upon the issue of small bills.—The material of least value circulates.—Banks do not increase the amount of money—their circulation is less than the specie in their vaults, independent of their deposites.—Something radically wrong in the elementary principles of banking.—Chartered banking—their constitutionality.—The competency of the people to regulate the currency, considered.—On preserving the metalic character of the currency.—Instability of chartered institutions considered—payment must be made.—A sound republican currency produces plenty of money.—The United States the first perfect example of self-government.—Their currency a defective principle—a relic of aristocracy.—Discrepancy of the workings of the government machinery, remove this—extend liberty and equality.

The public benefits of an United States bank and branches we have seen to be, the producing a current circulating medium (or nearly so) throughout the Union ; and consequently a present uniform measure of values, wherever this United States bank paper formed the whole currency. While we have also seen, that, although the *present* measure of all values is thus made uniform throughout the United States, yet that the past and future measure of values, can by no means be relied on as established by any one or more chartered banks, owing to the constant fluctuations of their paper currency, and to their being controlled by private interest, by credit and by politics—as every over-issue lessens its value, and every over-contraction increases it. The price of a days labor yesterday, may be the price of two day's labor to-day, and the price of three day's labor to-morrow, owing to the uncertainty of bank paper.

The liberal discounts of the banks, or the contractions of their circulation, which must, by the laws of their situation, be varied to meet their interests, credit, or political party requirements, all influence the value of money and of other commodities, and leave it fluctuating and uncertain.

The proposed plan of a currency is intended to possess decided advantages, in every respect, to any chartered company, without the ruinous commercial effects of the monopolizing of the currency and exchanges of an United States bank and branches. It must declare larger dividends and reserve larger bonuses, than any other safe investment of money in America. The stock will be more uniformly current and saleable in the stock exchange market, and consequently posses this great and important advantage over most other stocks; that it will be money in hand, when that is desired, drawing the highest interest while it is retained, and convertible into other stock, money, or commodities, at an advance in times of plenty of money, and at but a slight discount in the worst of times; thus it will become desirable stock for the investment of money. We have also seen, that the accumulation of credit only defers the pay day; it does not create actual means of meeting payments—it only changes the creditor and the credit—and the longer the payment of any debt is deferred, and the more interest that has been allowed to accumulate, by adding interest to interest, the greater must be the sacrifices and exertions to meet the ultimate payment of the debt. From which we infer, the safest way for a republican debt-paying people to do is, to get out of debt as soon as possible,and cautiously avoid becoming involved a second time. To accomplish this, credit must be separated from currency ; politics must be separated from currency ; private interest must be separated from currency ; the bank of issue must be separated from the banks of discount; and currency must be rendered as republican as our other elementary principles of government, by leaving it to the disposal of the people, through the election of directors from among themselves, of persons having the same common interest with themselves.

The centralization of the government of the currency, will give the public all the benefits of a chartered United States bank and branches, while its divided administration will prevent its monopoly by a few private individuals for their own benefit, and that of speculators. It will prevent the bank from interfering with exchanges, or with commerce ; and confine its operations to its legitimate business, that of lending money, by discounting only actual business paper, having but short periods to run.

The election of the directors by the people, will render the paper portion of the currency as republican as the precious metals ; as current throughout the Union as gold and silver, for which it must be uniformly interchangeable ; while the issue of no small bills will furnish every class of society with the material they prefer for money, from the choice of other classes, for that material least valuable to themselves.

It is a fact, not frequently remarked, that there has not

been, for ten years past, upon an average, more paper money passing from hand to hand, independent of the de- posites in the banks, than the actual amount of specie in the vaults of the banks, upon which this amount of paper has been issued. It is true that the reported amount of paper in circulation has generally exceeded three times the amount of specie in the vaults of the banks; yet, as the deposites of the banks consist principally of the notes of other banks, the actual circulation of paper money, after deducting the deposites, is less than the specie hoarded up in their vaults. The bad management of the currency by chartered compa- nies, lessens the actual amount of circulating medium be- low the necessities of the public, and below the ablities of the specie in the country ; compels commercial men to pay a large interest for bank credit, and keep on hand in deposite a large amount of bills ; while these privileged bankers enhance or diminish, at their pleasure, the amount of money in circulation, and the prices of all commodities, and increase the facilities or difficulties with which money is to be obtained. The few individuals who now have the man- agement of the monetary affairs of the country, as directors of chartered banks, would not be less capable to regulate the currency as directors of the banks, if they were elected by the people, than they are at present from that cause. They are at this time considered competent to control the issues and discounts of the paper that is to circulate as money in the place, when their interest is directly opposed to the in- terest of the community; how much more likely would they beto render general satisfaction to the public, if they were only interested in the prosperity of the place, and the metalic character of the currency ? Besides, if these individuals, who are now selected from so small a por- tion of the community, as are stockholders in chartered banks, are found competent to the regulation of the paper portion of the currency, would it not be reasonable to suppose that from the whole community, directors of the currency could be found far more capable, and far more desirous of regulating the currency for the general prosperity of the country ; and of preserving its metalic character, and the equilibrium of the circulation ; as well as the uniformity of quantity and consequent absence of fluctuations, contractions or over-expansions, by which the measure of all values is rendered indefinite and uncertain, as it must ever continue to be under the chartered bank system. Whether the paper be issued by one large chartered bank, or by many small companies, the effects must be the same ; instability, and uncertainty must attend it. The radical defects of the currency must be removed, for accumulating credit upon credit, will not obviate the defects of the currency ; it extends credit, and thereby delays the time of payment ; but that is all—payment must be made sooner or later, or interest must be added to interest, accumulating the debt, and endangering its ultimate payment. With a sound republican currency—with money plenty, that is, as easily to be obtained as other commodities—with domestic commerce and manufactures encouraged, by the loans from the bank being made to the fair traders of the place, by discounting only their actual business paper, having but short periods to run—the true growth and prosperity of the community will be best promoted.

Under such a state of finances, currency and exchanges, America would flourish ; her citizens, from the Atlantic to the Pacific, would prosper ; and this continent would become one vast republic, where civil and religious liberty would reign triumphant. She might then well be styled, "The land of the free, and the home of the brave."

A sound currency in the United States would do more toward extending and establishing FREEDOM THROUGHOUT THE WORLD, than the combined forces of armies and navies.

The United States first showed the world the example of a great people governing themselves; and becoming prosperous and happy under their own institutions.

If the currency of the country is found to be defective, from its containing the relics of feudal or monarchical principles, let that aristocratic tendency be excised; let the grand experiment, commenced with the establishment of our constitution, be here perfected ; let all the elementary principles of our government be made perfectly republican. The present discrepancy of the workings of the machinery of the government will instantly disappear—all the various parts will harmonize, become strong and pleasing— while they perfect the peace, prosperity and good government of these United States, and extend the blessings of human liberty over the habitable globe, " until all the nations of the earth shall know the Lord, from the rising to the setting of the sun."

CHAPTER XXXIV.

ON THE EFFECTS THAT THE CURRENCY OF A COUNTRY HAS UPON ITS INDEPENDENCE.

Currency one of the pillars of the government.—Frequent legislation upon the political machinery of the government injurious.—Provided against by the founders of our government.—Religion and literature made independent of each other,
and of politics—in this also is seen the wisdom of our forefathers.—The liberty
of speech, freedom of the press, social habits, all free—but currency less perfectly f-ee by practice than by the constitution.—Causes explained—Love of
gain—Spirit of enterprise—Sectarianism serviceable—susceptible of abuse—
kept within proper limits, salutary to the public welfare.—Currency should be
left at the disposal of the whole people—they require no new powers—they only
require organization by congress.

As has been before stated, the currency of the country is one of the pillars upon which the fabric of government rests; and, therefore, ought to be as immutable as its religion or its literature. We have shown in another place, that great evil would result from a constant, or even frequent legislation, upon the political machinery of the government; and that to prevent the danger of such a course of policy, the framers of our constitution have wisely provided, that the form of government cannot be altered, or, in other words, the constitution cannot be amended, without careful, lengthy, and public consideration, as well by the people themselves as by their legislature.

The religion of the country, too, is quite independent of its politics. Every man is allowed to worship God according to the dictates of his own conscience. He may pay one or more clergymen, or he may not pay any; he may pray or worship as long, as loud, and as often, or as little as he pleases; he may purchase as many or as few church pews as he chooses; and whatever he does, or does not do, in matters of religion—provided he does not outrage decency, or disturb the public peace of society—cannot be made a test for office, or a disqualification to any situation under the government, or within the elective powers of the people: all this is happily provided for by our inimitable and glorious constitution.

Our literature, too, has been left free and unrestrained by legal enactments. Our schools, seminaries, and colleges, are opened to all—whether he be Jew or Gentile, Protestant or Catholic, it matters not—the honors of our institutions are free to all who seek them; although he be a citizen of another nation, and a subject to a King, yet republican America offers him free access to our schools, and equal competition for the honors and degrees that they confer. And all this, too, is wisely provided for by our constitution, that no religious creed should close the doors of our colleges upon such citizens as were unwilling to subscribe to the thirty-nine articles of faith, or other religious tests.

And here again we see the wisdom of the framers of our government, that no legislative enactments are annually required to entitle the people to become educated. Their social habits, too, are as free as their public presses. And this credit too, is to be ascribed to the wisdom of our venerable forefathers. One thing, however, they could not provide against, without violence to the spirit of the constitution, and that was, the exportation of specie from the country. How ridiculous then to complain of it. It is a part of the active business of the country, and should be left free, like water, to flow where it tends. The love of gain is of itself an honorable ambition, (when not inordinate) to be above the wants of the necessaries of life. This love has led to noble and great privations and sacrifices, to acquire a competence—and few people in the world have shown more laudable enterprise than the Americans—yet, this love of gain leads to the use of small bills, which drives the specie out of circulation; but, like sectarianism in religion, by which much more religious instruction is obtained than would be secured without it, it is susceptible of much abuse; yet, when confined within true bounds and proper limits, it becomes salutary to the public welfare.

The currency of the country should be left to be regulated by the people. They require no new powers to make them quite independent in finance. All they require is, such an organization as would enable them to exercise the powers that are inherent in them, and constitutionally secured, to regulate their currency without the intervention of the legislature, or without the aid of private companies, or foreign or domestic credit. The currency of the country should be as free from either private interference, or polit-

ical party influence or credit, as are the religion, the politics, or the literature and social habits of the people.

The hands of the people would become strong, through
the election of their financial directors, after the same manner as they elect their political directors. They would
thus separate currency from politics.

The currency of the country may also be divided into
*money-currency* and *commodity-currency.* The money-
currency should be composed of the precious metals, and
paper based upon the precious metals, and always convertible into specie : not subject to any contingency or circumstance that would alter, change or defeat the value of it, or
endanger its instant convertibility. The credit-currency
should be composed of every species of convertible
credit—bank notes of incorporated companies, (although
bankers should never be allowed a *limited responsibility,* as
this would render their credit imperfect,) deposites, foreign
and domestic exchanges, checks, bills, drafts, convertible
merchandise, and commodities of exportation and of importation.

I have chosen to add to every species of credit, the commodity-currency of the country, composed of such goods
as are certain of making remittances, at some price, in any
market to which they may be shipped, as well as to illustrate what I mean by a money-currency and a commodity-
currency, the better to enable me to direct public attention
to a system of mixed specie, and *paper money currency* that
shall be equally and invariably as convertible as the precious metals, by producing so much paper only as would
occupy the channels of commerce, not supplied with the
precious metals, that mechanics and laborers may have a
metalic currency, and the merchant and commercial men
may have large bills for commercial purposes.

If any doubt remains as to the preference given by different classes of business men to each species of money for a currency, let them be enquired of, and their answers should decide the question of the currency. If they severally require different kinds of money, why should not each class of citizens be gratified with their choice of their kind of currency? The whole of the paper, however, should always be convertible at will at the counter where it was issued.

In making the distinction here laid down, between the different kinds of currency necessary to the transaction of extensive business, I wish not to be understood as expressing opinions that have been matured by thorough investigation, and perfected by experience, but as simply advancing ideas that are entirely original with myself; and drawn from an examination of the currencies of Europe and of the United States, as well as of the North American British Colonies.

The currencies of every country have more influence over the people than standing armies and navies. Their direct personal interest in the support of the currencies and finances of a country become its firmest bulwarks. This has been clearly illustrated in England, by the effect of their irredeemable national debt, in the firm support given to the government by the fund-holders.

The English people pay annually, in interest on the irredeemable national debt of Great Britain of £800,000,-000 sterling, and in support of the civil administration of the government, the army and the navy, independent of the immensely expensive municipalities in the kingdom, a much larger sum than is collected from any other people, with the same means, in christendom. And, although the name of the immortal Pitt, as associated with the national debt of Great Britain, may be  damned to everlasting fame, yet the public economist cannot avoid admitting what all, who trace effects to their causes, must see, in the association of private interest with the monied interest of the kingdom, the operations of his master spirit; and that, if he exclaimed, when the thought first entered his mind, "my country never dies," that he clearly saw such a connection of private interest between the government and the people must be perpetual, and must (as every day's experience shows,) support the Throne, Lords and Commons, in all their extravagance, when armies and navies, without the aid of the private interest of the citizen, would be unavailing. In this light, his plan of a national debt, owned by the citizens of the country, having the interest paid punctually, the funds themselves being always saleable in the market, like any other commodity or public stock, and therefore, always convertible through the government agent, the Bank of England, (which has for part of its capital a government debt,) into money at the pleasure of the fundholder.

There is also another example of the wonderful power and influence of money over the governing and the governed. The government support the bank, renew its charter, whether popular among the great mass of people or not, so that it is desired by the monied portion of the nation; and the bank, in turn, loans the government an additional sum for the privilege of its charter. The bank of the United States, and some banks of states, have *given* a bonus for their charters. Oh, what a mockery of independence in legislation !

To bribe the whole government—Kings, Lords and Commons—is no crime ; while to bribe, or even offer a bribe to one or more members of the government, is a capital offence.

Well, to proceed. The funds being always convertible

at nearly the same price, renders them desirable property
to the capitalist, as it is money at interest, and always convertible at his pleasure ; and few, if any, among the fund-
holders, ever enquire, with Yankee inquisitiveness and cu-
riosity, whether this debt, of which the English funds are
composed, ever will or will not be paid off or redeemed.
To fund-holders it is quite enough, that their respective
portions are convertible ; and so far as they are individually concerned, their portion may be paid off any day that
they desire that it should be—for they can realize the money for their funds, with a slight increase or diminution, as
the money market is flush and the country prosperous, or
otherwise. Hence, the wonderful power of the English
nation. Private interest is brought to support the government by means of heavy duties, imposts, and various direct
taxes, to furnish the means of paying a large and extremely
expensive army and navy ; and, by tithes and taxes, to support an extensive church and state establishment; and by
poor rates, to provide for the poor—which, while it serves
to keep the people in awe of present pains and penalties
or future punishment, it provides places and situations for
thousands of persons, the younger sons of a half-starved
aristocracy, who would be unable to support themselves
without the aid of church and state.

The governing power of every country are always content
with their own administration of the laws; and where the
governed can be kept poor and ignorant, any government
will satisfy them, or if it does not satisfy them, they learn,
by sad experience, that to complain injures them instead of
benefitting them—and they thus remain silent, and toil on.

And, but for the cheap publications, and the reduction of
the duties on bread-stuffs, ale, and the coarse and common
materials used by the masses and the poorer classes, they

would be as easily governed as so many sheep or bullocks. Hence the question becomes one of serious moment, in England, whether education, without morality, promotes or lessens the happiness of the people. The reduction of taxes upon knowledge, has opened ten thousand new and politically dangerous channels of knowledge to the common people. " Knowledge is power" every where ; but in England that power is more rapidly acquired in the dense population of large cities and towns, and from the immense large manufactories, where reading is becoming popular, and where every man may drink his mug of half-taxed ale, and read his half-taxed newspaper, at half the expense of former years, and where their constant intercourse with each other, enables them to communicate any information that interests them throughout the whole establishment, and from one large establishment to another, with telegraphic celerity.

## CHAPTER XXXV.

### THREAD-NEEDLE LANE THE CENTRE OF MONIED ATTRACTION.

Thread-Needle Lane, the Bank of England, and the Stock Exchange, regulate the currency of the world —The great credit mart.—The magic power of exchanges.—Self-love the motive power.—Fluctuations in the currency injurious to trade.

Thread-Needle Lane is the point of monied attraction ; around which the wealthy merchants and bankers of Europe and of America assemble. It is the great credit mart of the world. With the Bank of England are deposited the revenues of the British nation, and the products of the commerce of the western and much of the eastern hemisphere ; and from thence issue *credits* that pass currently throughout the continents of Europe and America, in bills of exchange and drafts, as the precious metals do in other countries.

On looking at this immense operation of credit, we are led to enquire, by what strange magic is this wonderful machinery moved—exercising its influence among political friends and foes alike ? The enchanting power of money, and of private interest, operates like a charm upon every man, woman and child, throughout the universe ;—and in this is found all the wonderful secret that so much astonishes mankind.

Self-love has found a pander in the credit system ; and in that joy, all patriotism, distinction of country, religion, sect or party, are swallowed up and forgotten.

The stocks of the old and new world are priced, and the exchanges with each regulated according to the amount of exports and imports, that the one requires of, or can supply, of the other. At this point, then, the great credit currency of the world is brought to be weighed, valued and balanced. Here each trader receives his wages, whether it be much, or whether it be little, and returns to his native land to replenish his stores, and again to visit this centre of monied attraction, and enrich himself by these exchanges. If he resides on the western continent, or in the United States, he returns to a western exchange, say New York, and here he finds proper food for his avarice and ambition— the various American stocks and exports of the north and south are all before him. One thing only gives him vexation: the currency of the country changes with the credit of the country ; and what he left, on his leaving America, as a sound currency, he now finds either doubtful, or perhaps, swept away by the influence of some counter-current in trade or credit, that he had not foreseen or anticipated, and he readily concludes, that the money-currency—that currency by which every other material is valued—should be uniform, and invariably the same. This is found to be the case with the precious metals, and he wonders why convertible paper-money should not be equally uniform in its value, and equally as easily obtained at one time as at another.

## CHAPTER XXXVI.

### TO RENDER THE PAPER PORTION OF THE CURRENCY AS STABLE AS GOLD AND SILVER.

Separate currency from credit, and from private interest—Limit its issues to the amount of its bills—to the amount of its specie basis—to the actual demand for the discount of business paper.—Separate issues from discounts.—Allow the free exportation of specie, to check over-trading.—Without over-issues no fear of contractions.—Careful supervision—frequently published reports—check excesses.—Elect directors—preclude them from temptation to over issues.—If the bills apportioned to a bank are not equal to the specie—loan specie, if necessary, to meet the actual demand for currency.—Issue no small bills—their injurious effects.—In England, with the issue of one pound notes, the specie disappeared, as if by magic.—The precious metals preferred by a majority of the producers.—Disadvantages of uncurrent money—from six to ten per cent. tax paid in prosperous times for a paper currency.—Producers and consumers support all the bankers, brokers and idlers—who live upon the depreciation of the currency, or by the circulation of uncurrent notes.

To render the paper portion of the currency as stable, and immutable as gold and silver, *money-currency* must be separated from the *credit-currency*, which is controlled by private interest. Restrict the issues of paper, to circulate as money, to the actual demand. This may be done in two ways; firstly, limit the quantity to be issued in each state by directors, whose business it shall be to understand the money trade of the world, and who can have no private interest to blind their eyes, or mislead their judgments, whereby, they being placed above suspicion, may calmly consider the demand, and order a supply to meet it. But again, should this demand be more than a metalic basis could be found to justify, that demand should be lessened, by lessening our imports. This would again produce a salutary check upon

over-issues; for, be it remembered, that without over-issues, there is nothing to be feared from over-contractions.

The United States bank directors should never discount
paper, put bills in circulation, receive deposites, or in any
way exercise any power over the credit of the currency in
its local circulation, farther than by apportioning to each
state the amount, beyond which they cannot exceed their
issues; and to take a general supervision, and publish the
reports of the several state institutions quarterly, or oftener
if necessary.

The several state institutions, in turn, would apportion,
according to the demand, the amount intended to be circulated in their state, between the local banks, or banks of issue, of their state; take a general supervision of the branches, and publish their monthly reports : as well as furnish
the general bank with regular quarterly statements of the
business of the several banks of issue, in their state; while
the banks of issue would be restricted to three times the
amount of specie actually in their vaults at the time of the
issue. If specie accumulated in their vaults, beyond the
amount of bills given them to circulate, they would not necessarily suffer from the loss of the use of the specie, as
they could loan it as any private individuals might do.

By issuing no bills of smaller denominations than circulate in England, the general or universal credit-currency
would not be impaired, and the precious metals would occupy similar channels of commerce on both sides of the
ocean. Small bills are that portion of the paper money,
that supplants the precious metals in any country. And
we have the experience of France and England, and repeated experiments with small bills in the United States,
against their circulation—and only one argument in their
favor, that of convenience, growing out of the parsimony

and private interest of incorporated companies in this country.

In England, during the circulation of their " one pound notes," the precious metals disappeared. And upon the calling in of all the one pound notes in England, a slight inconvenience was experienced ; but this was but tempo- rary, and soon yielded to the far more healthy state of the currency, in which five pound notes are the smallest paper money-currency that circulate in that country.

In France, their ablest financiers have never yet been able to discover, under any emergency, any advantage to be derived from giving the people a credit paper-currency, that they might not be satisfied with, under any little politi- cal discontent or financial derangement. And how discern- ing Americans can find profit in using the credit of private companies, in lieu of their own legal metalic currency, is more than I can comprehend, if such is the fact ; but I have yet to be convinced, that the mechanics and laborers are desirous of having paper money supply the place of the precious metals for small sums.

If they could realize the daily loss they sustain in the do- mestic market, by having small bills to change instead of sil- ver dollars, the loss from fire, from accidents, and from coun- terfeits, as well as from *uncurrent* money, I am convinced, not one out of one hundred would be willing to pay six per cent. to the banker for paper money, that costs him six per cent. more to circulate it after he has it.  His only source of consolation for this loss is ; firstly, that he does not pay the six per cent. for the use of the paper to the bank, that being paid by the borrower ; and that, if we had no small bills, money would be so much scarcer, and we should be troubled for change, and that wages and prices would be materially reduced.

This reasoning, at the first blush, appears consistent; but remove the private interest of the banker from the scales, and with it will disappear his sophistical reasoning. Wages will not be lessened, but they will be paid in money, by the removal of small bills; and change, instead of being more scarce will be more plenty and convenient, and the people will see, that whatever number of brokers and unnecesary bankers are supported out of the profits of the currency, is just so much of the wealth of the country, and consequently, the currency taken from the common stock and consumed : for it is useless to say, that this gives employment to so many men, because in America men can always find profitable employment in some productive business, and men are as much wanted as capital. Besides this loss of men and money, the extravagance and luxurious living of bankers and brokers, when their profits are enormous, produces a corresponding desire to extravagance among other classes of society, by which the whole community are impoverished; for whoever lives upon credit beyond his income, is an injury to community to the extent in which he lives beyond his earnings.

## ON CREDIT CONNECTED WITH PUBLIC IMPROVEMENTS.

We have seen that the *private interest* of stockholders, in incorporated companies, and the *credit* upon which paper intended to circulate as money is issued, have expanded the currency, and nominally enhanced the value of property in the United States—increased importations, facilitated extravagance in living, in dress, in houses, in horses and carriages, in furniture, in personal ornaments, and in ten thousand almost nameless ways—while it has lessened exertions to earn and honestly procure property by the sweat of the brow.

The soft bed induces longer indulgence on it. The easy spring sofa prolongs reclining after meals: while fashionable idlers make, and expect to have returned, their frequent morning and evening calls ; all of which draw largely upon the time of the tradesman and mechanic, and increase his expenses, while it lessens his means of supporting them. Bank credit has laid the foundation for this deranged state of things, and bank credit must be continued and increased if they are supported.

Foreign merchandise should never be bought upon credit by the consumer, as it requires the exportation of money, or some other commodity, to meet the payment in a foreign market ; such articles, therefore, should not be consumed until they are paid for. The general adoption of this practice would lessen foreign importations and encourage domestic manufactures.

Formerly, fine houses were not attempted to be built until the builder was quite prepared—both with materials and money to finish and furnish them when completed. But times are strangely changed ; the fashion now is, to buy every thing you want, or fancy you want, upon credit, if you can get trusted. Credit is now universally used for capital ; and if a man has a credit at the bank, and wants to build a house, or ornament his place, he commences with as little apparent thought of how or where he is to obtain the means of ultimately paying the bank, as he would if pay day could never come, or the money he received from the bank was an old deposite of his own. Is it, therefore, any wonder that the newspapers are filled with notices of sheriff's sales, offering in the public market, not only the house or other improvements made upon credit, but the lot on which it is built, and all the comforts secured by years of industry and economy ?

States have followed in the same mad career. The opinion of a party has been mistaken for public opinion ; the
statements of interested individuals have been received as
the unbiassed opinions of creditable witnesses. The success of one enterprise, or work of public improvement, after being emblazoned from Maine to Georgia, is made the
grounds of an argument for commencing public improvements upon credit in other parts of the Union. For instance, the Erie canal and Schenectady and Albany rail
roads have proved profitable investments of capital, and
have afforded great public convenience and accommodations. Hence it has been inferred, that canals and rail roads
could be made in every state and section of the Union upon
*credit ;* and that they would all be equally profitable and
advantageous. For this purpose, as the states had no surplus revenue, or special fund that could be pledged for the
payment of the interest of the money, bank credit has been
used as capital, and hundreds of thousands of dollars have
been invested in the stocks of public improvements upon
bank credit as capital. This error has proved fatal to the
enterprises and to the speculators themselves. Many of
these new and expensive public works could not pay if
completed : and they cannot be completed upon bank credit when that has ceased to exist. The works that have
been commenced, and those in actual operation, although
they cannot pay for some time to come ; yet, as they are rapidly falling to decay, they require legislative relief promptly and immediately. The system of currency hereby recommended, will afford them ultimately, permanent relief,
by encouraging domestic manufactures and agriculture—
thereby increasing the interchange of domestic products
with foreign countries, while the money will be retained
by the reduction of our imports to the par exchange of our

exports : our currency will become equalized throughout the Union, convertible, current, convenient, and free from inflations and consecutive contractions.

The bank paper credit party expend their money before they have earned it. States, relying upon bank credit for capital, have expended their resources before they have been collected. Bank credit and foreign credit are used by both as capital. No one thinks of giving or receiving cash for commodities : bank notes are the only medial commodity ; whether they are at par or otherwise they are made to answer for a circulating medium.

England has a mortgage on nearly one half of the states of the Union ; and unless the management of the currency be taken out of the hands of incorporated companies, and given to the people, it must, by the laws of its situation, of credit and of incorporated bank paper, have a mortgage upon the whole Union.

Nothing now but strict economy can save the states from bankruptcy—both the people and the state governments.

The government of the Union may retain its credit and remain solvent, unless it should madly endorse for the states, or in other words, assume the payment of the state debts. Then would the *government* and *people* of these flourishing states be reduced to the situation of tenants of the bankers and brokers of England ; paying them annually in coin, a rent for our public works, for credit bank paper to circulate as money among us, and for our very houses and farms. But no, this cannot be !—" The sons of America were never born to be slaves." England, nor her Rag Barons, shall ever hold under their jurisdiction one foot of ground in this " land of the free and home of the brave." *Credit*, with what a siren's voice, dost thou charm the ear ! What witchery is there not in thy inviting smile !

How fascinating thy offers ot *wealth !* How easy a trade
to learn, is spending money ! While credit lasts, how few
feel that pay-day must soon come ! And habits of extravagance once established are hard to be broken off. But the
charm of unlimited credit must be shaken off—this spell of
bewitching enchantment must be broken. Men must return to habits of honest industry and economy, and learn to
earn before they spend their money, or this country can never emerge from the abyss of debt, credit, extravagance,
misery and dependance into which bank notes and bank
credit have imperceptibly plunged them.

The following extract shows how independent the United States may become whenever they shall will it to be so.
Our resources are ample for domestic prosperity and happiness : our imports should be limited to the par exchange
of our exports.

"AGRICULTURAL STATISTICS OF THE UNITED STATES.—The Philadelphia North American contains a very valuable table with the
above title, and containing a statement of the agricultural products
of all the states but three, viz: North Carolina, Michigan, and
Kentucky. From which we learn that the largest wheat growing
state in the Union is Ohio—the amount 16,000,000 bushels ; the
next largest, Pennsylvania with 13,000,000 ; the next New York,
11,000,000; and the fourth, Virginia, with 10,000,000. The largest
amount of Indian corn raised in one state, is in Tennessee—42,-
000,000 bushels; Virginia, 34,000,000 ; Ohio, 33,000,000 , Indiana,
28,000,000; Illinois, 22,000,000; Alabama, 18,000,000; Georgia,
17,000,000 ; Missouri, 15,000,000.

"New York is the greatest potatoe growing state ; amount 30,-
000,000 bushels. Maine comes next with 10,000,000; and next
Pennsylvania, with 8,000,000.

"The greatest cotton growing states are Mississippi, 289,000,-
000 lbs.—Alabama, 240,000,000—Georgia, 148,000,000—South Carolina, 134,000,000—Tennessee, 128,000,000—Louisiana, 87,000,-
000—Arkansas, 23,000,000—Virginia, 10,000,000.

"Louisiana is of course the largest producer of sugar, amount

249,000,000 lbs.; New York comes next, with 10,000,000 lbs., the produce of our forests.

" Tennessee, as she is first in corn, is also first in swine, number 2,795,000. Ohio stands next, with 2,000,000.

" New York stands first for wool; next Ohio, Vermont, Pennsylvania and Virginia.

"Tennessee again stands first, for tobacco, amount 26,000,000 lbs.! Maryland, 18,000,000—Virginia, 14,000,000. We regret we have not the returns from Kentucky. In corn and tobacco, we think she shall rank with the best of her sisters.

" New York stands first for lumber; value $3,788,000. Next Maine, $1,808,000. For products of the orchard New York stands also first; value $1,732,000. For products of dairy New York is again at the head; value $10,000,000. Vermont next, $4,892,000.

" The ' Agricultural Statistics,' from which the above extracts are made, abundantly prove, if indeed any proof were wanting, that this country possesses within herself all the elements of greatness. We can raise and manufacture within our extended territory every article necessary for our sustenance and clothing. Why then continue to pay out millions every year for French silks, French wines, English iron and English broadcloths ? There must be a reform in this particular, or we shall never be free from embarrassments."—TROY WHIG.

Congress must organize the people to exercise their financial powers, as they now exercise their political privileges. The people must elect directors from every part of the Union, to regulate the paper portion of the currency ; to ascertain the amount of specie in the United States, and the amount of currency necessary to the permanent prosperity of the whole people ; issue paper upon so much of the specie as shall be necessary to meet the demand for the currency ; procure, engraved in the best manner possible to prevent counterfeits, so many bills of the various denominations necessary for circulation, of not less than twenty dollars, and execute them in blank as United States directors ; apportion these bills between the several states, according to the de-

mand for a circulating medium in each state, together with
a specie basis sufficient to authorise their circulation under
well-established principles.

The people in each state should elect state directors, to
apportion the bills and specie furnished to each state by the
United States bank directors, between the banks of discount, to be located in the several cities, towns and districts in each state, where banks of discount are designed
to be located, and to take a general supervision of the same.

The electors in each city, town or district, where a bank
of discount is to be located, should elect directors of those
banks annually as they elect the most numerous branch of
their legislatures; who, before entering upon the duties of
their offices, should give good security for the faithful discharge of their duties, and the prompt payment over to
their successors in office of all monies and property of the
bank in their possession ; and who should be precluded
from discounting any notes or acceptances in which a bank
director has any interest.

This will effectually remove *private interest, credit* and
*politics* from the currency.

These directors, being freely elected by the people, and
having no private interest but that of their re-election, will
direct their whole energies to the promotion of the public
good, the accommodation of the fair trader of the place, and
the preservation of their own popularity by the correctness
of their whole published financial conduct.

This will render the paper portion of the currency useful to the large commercial dealer, while the precious metals will benefit small dealers particularly.

The banks will then discount only the actual business
paper of the traders of the place, having but short periods
to run, instead of preferring the fictitious notes of specula-

tors ; since the regular dealers of the place will have the election of the directors. And thus the credits of the bank will be applied to the promotion of domestic manufactures, and works of permanent utility.

The officers of the United States bank will thus be rendered responsible to the whole people of the United States for the manner in which they discharge their duties, and dependant upon them for their re-election. The officers of the state banks will stand in the same relation to the inhabitants of each state ; while the directors of the banks of discount will be responsible to the electors in their respective cities, towns and districts, through the ballot-boxes.

The separating the bank of issue from the banks of discount, will lessen the danger of expansions of the currency, and its ruinous consecutive contractions.

The issuing no small bills will fill the small channels of currency with gold and silver, and lessen the excitement from any political or financial derangement, whether in Europe or America.

Specie being the only true basis upon which to issue bills to circulate as money, instead of notes of other banks, public bonds, private securities, or foreign or domestic exchanges, that has been too often used by chartered banks, will render the currency perfectly convertible on demand at the counter where it was put in circulation, and equally current throughout the United States.

Currency must be allowed freely to flow wherever it is demanded, even although it leave the country, which will enable the exchanges always clearly to indicate the state of trade between trading countries.

The exportation of specie should be unrestrained by banks, or other artificial means, as the only sure check to over-trading and over-importing. The tendency of coin to go into other markets, when not interfered with, checks, most effectually, the tendency to excesses in business, in expenses of living, in imports, and in consumptions.

## THE OBJECTIONS TO A PAPER CURRENCY CONSIDERED.

To those political economists, who maintain that the system of currency here proposed, by authorising the circulation of more paper than there is specie actually in the vaults of the bank at the time of the discount, gives the notes of the banks a credit character that endangers its convertibility, and thus overthrows many of the arguments used in its favor, and weakens the force of all. To these perfectly philosophic objections, allow me to reply : that, upon the first view, that impression is strictly natural; while, upon a more thorough investigation of the elementary principles of currency and banking, I trust we shall find, that paper may be made strictly convertible, equally current throughout the Union, and as little liable to expansions and contractions of the currency as if it consisted exclusively of gold and silver. But first let me premise, that, if paper had not been used as a substitute for gold and silver, and made to circulate as money, both in Europe and America, we should be the last person to recommend the introduction of bank paper credit, or in fact any unlimited credit, either foreign or domestic.

But we are compelled to " take things as we find them;" and, since chartered bank paper has raised the nominal value of landed property, the expressed value of contracts, of merchandise and other commodities, far above what they would have been estimated in a currency composed exclusively of the precious metals, justice to all parties requires that we should not hastily change their measure of value, but allow the people to manage that matter them-

selves, lest the shock occasioned by the change should overturn our other valuable political, religious, civil and literary institutions. For rest assured, that bankers, brokers and
speculators, with their long train of attendants and dependants, will make a desperate battle in defence of privileges
which they have exclusively enjoyed, until they almost fancy themselves entitled to command them as a matter of
right.

In the United States we have nominally a mixed currency, composed of paper and gold and silver, which were
originally intended to have been perfectly interchangeable
for each other and equally current throughout the Union.
But, by degrees, through the intervention of small bills,
the metalic portion of the currency has been withdrawn
from circulation, until their perfect interchangeability has
been lost, and their uniform current circulation throughout
the Union destroyed. Our enquiry then necessarily is,
how has this transmutation of the currency been produced,
and what were the agents, or causes, by which it has been
so imperceptibly accomplished? for, since "like causes
produce like effects," if we admit into this system of mixed currency, under the plan of free banking herewith proposed, the same principles that brought about the present
inflation, deterioration, and consequent inconvertibility of
the paper portion of the currency, we shall assuredly have
ultimately the same expansions of the currency, the same
depreciation in its value, and the same interchangeability
of the paper portion of the currency, that exists at present.
But if we have discovered, and provided for the removal
of the cause of these evils, we shall have nothing to apprehend from any bad effects upon the currency from the
introduction of paper for a certain portion of it.

We have seen, in another place, that the medial commod-

ity in one country and nation, differs frequently very materially from that of another nation ; and that, although no
kind of money except specie is useful as a measure of values, or a medium of the transfer of other commodities, in
the country where this particular currency is not received
and used, yet bank paper, square pieces of Chinese metal,
and shells, all possess some value with neighboring nations
who are trading with the people using any particular kind
of money, as the bits of metal used by the Chinese for money. Now, so long as the medial commodity is uniformly
perfectly convertible into whatever may be desired for
commerce or consumption, it is quite immaterial of what
that instrument of common circulation is composed—the
cheaper and least expensive material being, from principles
of economy, naturally preferred, since whatever expense
can be saved in the value of the currency, is so much added to the general fund of productive industry or commercial profit.

So much paper then as can be made uniformly perfectly
interchangeable for gold and silver, is preferable to gold
and silver from these causes, as well as from its greater
convenience for commercial transactions. Our next enquiry then is, how this perfect convertibility of the paper portion of the currency is to be preserved ? In answering
that question, we are almost instinctively led to ask another
question, viz : by what natural law, or from what defect
in the organization of the system of the paper portion of
the present currency, was its interchangeability destroyed ?
The discovery, exposure, and remedy of this evil, constitutes the business of this publication.

In this work we have endeavored to show, that all the
defects in the constitution and organization of the paper
portion of the currency, may be traced either directly or

indirectly to the influence of *private interest, credit* or *politics ;* and that much of the bad administration of the currency is attributable to the banks discounting fictitious paper, dealing in exchanges, and checking at times the free circulation of specie by the issue of small bills, and by artificial means obstructing the free exportation of specie, by which the exchanges are prevented from indicating the exact state of trade with foreign countries, and thus inducing over-trading and over-importing. The remedies have been described and treated of previously, and will be more fully explained hereafter. They consist, briefly, in giving back to the people privileges at present conferred upon state chartered banking companies.

It must not be forgotten by us, in our over anxiety to render currency republican, that our other elementary principles of the government are republican, and that we must expect, in attempting to change the character of currency from *aristocratic* to republican principles, that is, in attempting to expose to public view the anti-republican principles and other defects and incongruities of the currency, that we shall have to meet in array against us all those who are interested in the continuance of the present credit currency by chartered companies for banking purposes, and associations under general banking laws. They will be followed by all the aristocrats, who think the government already too republican, and that the people are incompetent to govern themselves even in the matters already entrusted to them. Not far from this array may be expected to be found the timid, who always fear to meddle with the elementary principles of government, as being too sacred and too important to be spoken of familiarly ; and at the same time too difficult of comprehension to be likely to be improved by alterations. Then next comes a class of

dependants upon credit, and who cannot hear the most unlimited credit spoken against, without instinctively starting
to their feet, and arming themselves for the defence of the
credit system ; they shout for credit, the whole credit, and
nothing but credit; (how little they understand the subject of which they speak.)

With all this formidable array against us, we shall have
but little prospect of arousing the sober, honest, producing
farmer, mechanic, and laborer, to enlist in our cause. The
merchants are either in debt themselves to the banks, or to
the wholesale dealers, and they want money to be continued quite as plenty, whether it be good or bad, as it is now ;
or if they are not dependant themselves upon credit or the
banks, many of their debtors are, and they fear to lessen their means of paying them—as if the proposed plan
was likely to lessen, instead of increasing the quantity of
the circulating medium, and the facilities of obtaining it.
The wholesale dealers are indebted abroad, and they have
large stocks of goods on hand ; and plenty of money makes
high prices, and by the laws of their situation, they are violently opposed to even the investigation of the subject.
They will be well satisfied, I trust, when they have seen its
successful operations.

The learned profession of the law may be expected to
take the lead in debating the question, and in writing for
the press against us ; by the laws of their situation, it can
hardly be expected to be otherwise, as it must lessen much
of their most profitable business, and besides they they are
professionally aristocrats. Rendering the currency sound
and republican lessens the distinction and difference between the ranks and classes of society, that all who occupy
the highest rank, wish to have as broad and distinct as possible. Besides this, they have a direct interest in combat-

ting our principles; for, as we check legislation upon any subject, we lessen the complexity of the laws, and consequently lessen the necessity for the greatest number of expounders of the laws. Again, by lessening excessive credits, we deprive the profession of the law of one half of their livings. I will venture to predict, that upon a careful examination of any extensively practicing lawyer's docket, you shall find that half of his business has grown out of excessive credits or bank loans; hence, how is it possible that they should not be uniform in their opposition. I know many pure patriots among this learned profession, who are as honorable as any class of citizens in America; yet, by the laws of their situation, they are opposed to us; and those who magnanimously prefer the public good to their own interests, as bank solicitors, bank lawyers, and associates of bank directors, and associates with the aristocrats, of the court and of the state, have greater sacrifices to make than can be expected of many; but rest assured, there will be some honorable exceptions in favor of a purely republican government, which ours cannot be until the currency of the country shall become as purely republican as our politics, religion, literature and social habits.

I have thought it necessary to examine the array that will be likely to be brought against us, and their reasons for their opposition, that, while we attempt to defend ourselves against one attack, we do not lay ourselves open to many others still more powerful. I am aware, that my ideas upon this subject are somewhat crude and indigested, but they are purely original; however much I am indebted to other authors for my language, I believe I shall never be charged with having borrowed my ideas, as I have not seen or heard them advanced before I have advanced them on several occasions, both in public speeches and private conversation and correspondence.

But to return to the charge, that, as our system admits of the circulation of more paper than we have coin in our vaults, it becomes a credit paper, and liable to the objections common to a credit currency. We have frequently remarked, and will here again remark, that the exchanges always indicate the state of trade between two countries; and that the tendency of coin to flow abroad, is the only effectual preventive of over-trading and over-importing. Now I prefer, and would show many reasons why the currency of the country should only consist of the precious metals, were it not for two reasons; the first is, that at the present prices of every transferable material, there is not metalic currency enough to conveniently exchange the various commodities, and transact the business of the country. The varying the nominal value of property would interfere with existing contracts between debtor and creditor, which should always be preserved and maintained inviolate. The inflation of the currency of foreign countries, with whom we have commerce, and especially the inflated state of the currency of England in particular, by their using credit paper as a circulating medium, is a powerful argument in favor of the continued use of paper to circulate as money here. England is a country of credit and punctuality of payment: their very existence, as an independent nation, rests solely on the punctuality with which they meet their engagements. And their punctuality in meeting the payments of interests as they become due, has produced a perfect convertibility in the funded or bonded debt of England; consequently that debt has become a capital to the nation. In a republic, a debt could never be made a permanent support; because of the equality of conditions, the obnoxiousness of taxes, and the frequent changes in the administration, must render a national debt unpopular and unsafe.

The party in power never will tax themselves, unless under circumstances of a very great emergency, and then only for a very short time, and to a small amount. While in a monarchy, where the few govern the many, the case is reversed. The law makers and its administrators are not in any way accountable to the people for the manner in which they discharge their official duties; or at most, not more frequently than once in seven years; unless at shorter intervals the Throne may dissolve the Parliament, when the government may choose its own time for the dissolution. Thus the accountability of the governing power to the governed is remote and uncertain, and frequently may be altogether avoided. The few tax payers after all, who can exercise even the elective franchise in their limited *viva voce* manner, renders the *few* "perfect lords" over the *many;* to which may be added the long list of sinecurists, pensioners and officers, and others, upon full pay and upon half pay—with an immense constabulary, policemen, army and navy, at the beck of the government, to aid the tax-gatherer and the collector—with the immense wealth, power and *religious* influence of an established church : all dependant upon the continuance of the payment of the taxes, and the collection of the revenue, for, not only their comforts, but many of them are dependant upon this source for their very support from day to day. But most of all, and far stronger than all these, is the *individual private interest* of every fund-holder in England; he has a direct and positive interest in the support of the government equal to the amount of the public debt he holds.

We have before remarked, that if we had precious metals sufficient to supply the demand for currency, we should not have occasion to issue paper to circulate as money ; but, since the gold and silver in the country is insufficient to

serve all the purposes of American commerce and enterprise, we are compelled to make the best substitute in our
power. We have before seen, that in countries without
banks, and even without coin, or with but a very limited
quantity of currency, the people have uniformly invented
and instituted substitutes for coin. We have seen shells in
one country, skins in another country, square bits of metal
in another country, and beef, pork, live stock, horses, hogs,
grain, lumber and iron in other countries, all substituted
for currency, or for coin to circulate as money ; and even
the smallest private promissory bills or notes, to be paid in
flour, in grain, or store pay, when specie and bills have been
entirely withdrawn from circulation, have been allowed to
circulate—sometimes only as change, at other times, and in
other places, they have constituted the principal circulating
medium of the country.

Hence we conclude, that if all the bank paper that now
circulates as money in the United States, was to be withdrawn from the circulation, the specie remaining not being
a sufficient instrument for the whole community to use,
some other medium would be used instead of the present
bank notes. I am not desirous of lessening the circulating
medium below the full supply of the actual demand ; nor
do I propose to withdraw the present bank paper from the
circulation, until its place is fully supplied by a better currency, as the charters of the banks expire one after another.

# CHAPTER XXXVII.

## ON EXCHANGES, AND THE MYSTERY INVOLVED IN THEIR COMPUTATION.

Exchanges left free to private competition, favorable to commerce.—The business of banks is lending money, not dealing in exchanges.—The free exportation of specie regulates the price of exchange, and checks over-trading.—The exportations of merchandise better than being in debt.—Accumulations of credit, whether of banks, states, or of the United States, only delay payment.—Exchanges effected by the sale of public stocks in a foreign market.—British banks' endorsed bills.—The United States Bank the first dealer in exchanges.—Philadelphia United States Bank—its business—its losses—its censures—influence upon prices, on exchange, on cotton—Mr. Biddle and Mr. Jordan blamed—Their conduct natural—Like many others—only more known—wider extended operations.—The dangers of chartered companies.—Legitimate banking.—Legal alteration of the value of the precious metals unjust—lessens stability.—Legal enactments may delay the exportation of specie, but it must ultimately come.—The old computation of the pound sterling incorrect—explained—recent computations.—The par exchange 9¼ per cent. above the computed par—It should be quoted in dollars and cents, on the par exchange.—British gold and silver received as coin—when of full weight and fineness, by tale—light coins by weight.—American coins in England pass only as bullion.—United States bank and branches injurious to commerce.—Suppose a company chartered to regulate weights and measures.—An United States Bank and branches more dangerous now than formerly—more business—more influence.

The exchanges should always be left perfectly free and open to private competition in the cash and bill market.— When that is the case, there can never be any danger of bills rising above their true value, or falling below their real worth ; neither buyers or sellers of bills can suffer much from any attempts of private individuals to monopolize the bill market, either domestic or foreign, as the buyer, if he suspects the price is too high, can export specie (where the cash market is open and free,) at about one per cent.

Private individuals cannot control the cash, or expand or contract the floating currency, at their will and pleasure, as banks can, to meet their own interest of buying and selling bills. The true business of banks of discount is lending money, by discounting *real business paper*, having but a short time to run.

Removing the interference of the banks with the exchanges, except they guarantee bills for a regular per centage,

as being often better known than individuals, and less liable
to inconvenience, from being unexpectedly required to alter or change the remittance or money at a moment's warning, and as being more generally informed of the customs
and forms used and required in foreign markets ; and allowing the free exportation of specie, whenever the actual
rate of exchange shall demand it, will most effectually prevent over-trading, by warning the importer of the danger
of importing goods that cannot be sold, especially when it
must cost him much to obtain remittances to pay for them ;
and whenever he finds the specie leaving the country, he
knows that more goods, bills or money have been imported
than there is means in the market to pay for, and he will
not madly " carry coals to New Castle."

He knows that goods cannot be safely sold upon credit,
when there is nothing coming into the market to meet the
demand for remittances ; and, if he cannot sell for money,
a prudent merchant would make his remittances with the
same material that he imported at a loss, sooner than remain involved. This has frequently been done during the
recent fluctuations of the market, at a loss of importation,
exportation, interest, shipment, re-shipment, insurances, and
damage of ordinary wear in transportation not assured
against. But even this may still be a better business for
the importer than any sale he could make in America for
cash, and his situation may be such that he cannot sell them
upon credit, the only way they could have been disposed of
at a nominal profit. If the best market for his goods, is
the place from whence they were imported, they should be
re-shipped and exported to that market. That is, if the sale
of English goods in the English market constitutes the best
remittances that can be made to pay an English debt, or
if their sale in it is better than they are in America, then the

merchant is justified in re-shipping his goods to make his remittance, even although it be at a loss.

In times of great money pressures, temporary relief may be afforded to the merchant by the introduction of some new credit, after the ordinary credits have been exhausted by over-straining in over-trading ; as by the addition of the credit of a bank to ordinary private bills, and remittances made by individuals, or by the introduction into the market of a new commodity, as of state stocks, or of United States bonds. These, for a time, while the amount of the sales are being drawn for, will relieve the money market, and lessen the rate of exchange against the selling country, or perhaps even produce a balance temporarily in favor of that country, where the rate of exchange had been too high for bills to be in the market, as the exportation of specie would be less expensive than the purchase of bills for remittances.

The banks in British America pursued an honorable course toward bill dealers, until they become dealers in exchanges themselves : they endorsed or guaranteed the bills for individuals at a small per centage. But since they have become dealers in bills of exchange themselves, the practice of guaranteeing bills, I believe, has been generally discontinued, as I supppose they find it more profitable to regulate the rate of exchange to meet their interest in the bill market, than guaranteeing bills for others. They thus have exchanged one positive public good for two as positive evils. The first is, the purchaser must pay higher for a bill than he would have done, had the price been left to private competition, as it is in every other part of the world, and was in the United States, until the United States bank interfered with exchanges. The other is, it disturbs the balance of trade, as indicated by the reported price of exchanges,

which should exactly indicate the state of trade between
two countries, that importing and exporting merchants may
not be misled in their commercial transactions.

The guaranteeing of bills, by banks, for a per centage, is
no doubt exceeding their legitimate business; yet the evils
that grow out of it, since it left the remitter free to get his
bill guarantied or not, as he chose, is far less than the monopoly of the whole business by the banks.

The United States bank, that established this monopoly
within the last twenty five years, possessed decided advantages over private individuals for dealing profitably in exchanges, both domestic and foreign, owing to her numerous
branches and complete organization, as well as her immense
power of increasing or lessening the value of money and
of exchanges, wherever and whenever it suited her purpose. She could thus make a profit upon every variation
of the exchanges. Since the cessation of the operation of
the United States bank, the Philadelphia United States
bank, and other banks, that have been engaged in exchanges or merchandise and other operations, have been an additional tax upon the importer and remitter; they have been
apparently convenient, but really very expensive.

The Philadelphia United States bank, with other banks,
that have since dealt in exchanges and merchandise, have
frequently very sensibly influenced the price of exchanges
and of other commodities. It will be admitted by all, who
have witnessed the operations of the United States bank of
Philadelphia, that she alone kept the price of cotton above
what it would otherwise have been, perhaps ten or fifteen
per cent., for more than two years, by her influence upon
trade, commerce and exchanges; but she as well as the
public, have suffered seriously from the consequences, and
her officers and directors are receiving severe castigations

from almost every part of the Union. But why vent all
the spleen of a disappointed loosing public upon Mr. Biddle, Mr. Jaudon, and the other directors and officers of *that*
institution? What they did was perfectly natural. In fact
it may be said to have been almost unavoidable ; it was in
strict accordance with the laws of their situation, and
what hundreds of other chartered banks have done, and
are daily doing. The only difference is, the capital, credit
and skill in the business of this institution was far greater
than that of the ordinary banks ; and consequently, when it
failed of success in its speculations, a much greater number of persons were involved in the failure, and the amount
of loss was actually much greater than that of any other
one bank, both to the bank itself, and to those connected
with its speculations. And, as a light placed on high is
seen at a greater distance than small lights that are placed
low, so this institution, by its high credit and immmense influence, better illustrates the principles and conduct of ALL
chartered banking companies than smaller examples; in
fact the frauds of smaller banks can now no more be seen,
in presence of this immense culprit, than stars can be seen
in presence of the sun ; still no one doubts the existence of
the one more than that of the other. For although small
banks have been less sinners, yet their sins have been the
same, or others not less profitable to themselves or less a
tax to the public, only in proportion to their lessened ability to accomplish extended operations, or the superior vigilance of the public and rival institutions over them. As an
example, witness the greater uniformity in the currency of New England over that of the more western
states. Their sounder currency is probably, among many
minor causes, to be principally attributed to the vigilant
supervision of the public over the banks, and to the uni-

form practice of the banks in demanding balances due from
each other at short and regularly stated periods, by which
their circulation has been confined within na, rower limits,
and their business much more generally restricted to the
discounting of actual business paper, having 1 ut short periods to run.

Whenever a bank departs from its legitimate duties, that
of lending money upon the discount of actual business paper, having but short periods to run, the currency becomes
inflated, and its convertibility endangered. It is all the
same to the currency, whether it be fictitious notes that are
discounted or bills of exchange, or cotton that is bought
with bank notes, they each inflate the money currency.
These operations may enable a few individuals to amass
splendid fortunes at the public expense ; but the public and
the uninitiated stockholders being the loosers, cannot fail to
reprobate their conduct. When will the public learn wisdom by experience ? when find instruction in the past ?
Never—never, until they take the business of regulating
the paper portion of the currency into their own hands ;
and instruct their peers to conduct banking to suit their
own real wants, and for the accommodation of their actual
business: then every day's experience will be a lessen for
future improvement.

The interference of the banks with exchanges, commerce
or credit, has precisely the same effects upon the measure
of all values—the money-currency—that altering the legal
value of the coin of the country, by the government, has
upon its exactness as a measure of value ; excepting that
the latter is a political as well as a financial frau l.

The law may give either gold or silver, or both of them,
higher legal value within the government of the country
where the law exists than they previously possessed, but it

is the market price that establishes its real value, which must always be found by an examination of the exchanges, and the price the coin bears in foreign markets.

If the legal value of any coin (as of the American Eagles, and parts thereof,) be raised or lowered above or below its former value, this operation expands or contracts the currency precisely as do the over-issues and contractions of the circulation of the banks.

Money, like water, will finds its level, and whether that level be high or low, with regard to the surrounding objects, is not very material, so that there be a sufficiency of the one or the other for all the operations which they were respectively designed to perform.

The increasing the circulation by legally raising the value of gold and silver, or either of them, or by the expansions of the currency by the increased issues of the banks, raises it above its former level, the channels become surcharged and must flow out; but as neither paper money nor depreciated gold and silver will circulate in a foreign market, the precious metals will be exported, and the coin that is alloyed will only pass as bullion, valued according to the weight of the fine metal it contains, and its exportation is attended with this additional loss. It is true that this loss may dam up the channels of circulation for a time, and retard its exportation, by advancing the price of bills of exchange, and of all other exportable commodities; but all this, instead of having a salutary and beneficial effect upon our commerce, trade or exchanges, has directly the opposite effect, since it raises the nominal value of commodities, and increases their accumulation, not in proportion to the actual demand, which should always regulate the supply, but according to the apparent demand which is thus placed above the necessary supply. And, although it may delay

the exportation of the precious metals, yet this is of slight
importance, since it does not increase the productive wealth
of the country, that being the only true source of profitable
remittances—all other operations being merely changes in
credits, oi alterations in the quoted exchanges, without any
real change in the exchanges.

The par exchange between the United States and England, under the original law establishing the mint, and authorising the coinage for the United States, passed in 1792,
authorised the coinage of silver dollars, of the value of
Spanish milled dollars, to contain 17 dwt. 8 grains of standard silver, an 1 that the proportions that gold and silver
should bear to each other should be as one to fifteen, that is,
one ounce of pure gold should be worth fifteen ounces of
pure silver.

However, by un act of congress, in 1789, the pound
sterling was declared to be worth four Spanish silver
dollars and forty four hundredth parts of a dollar, in the
estimating advalorem duties upon British merchandise
at our custom houses. By later computations, it appears
that the computed value of a pound sterling at $4,4444,
was below the par at the time—the true par having been
found by later calculations to be $4,5657, which was $2\frac{7}{10}$ per
cent. above the computed par. By the acts of 1832, 1834
and 1837, the British sovereign (the pound sterling,) has
been made equivalent to $4,8665, equal, within a fraction,
to $9\frac{1}{2}$ per cent. premium on the old computed par, which is
the true par on London under the present laws.

Previous to the passage of what is called the gold bill
in the year 1834, the eagle contained $247\frac{1}{2}$ grains of pure
gold. By that act, and by the act of 1837, the eagle is
made to contain $232\frac{1}{5}$ grains of pure gold; and one ounce
of pure gold is made equal to sixteen ounces of pure silver.

The prices of bills of exchange show the state of the trade between two countries; yet, strictly speaking, exchange in its operation has relation only to the precious metals. A bill of exchange is merely an order for the delivery of a given quantity of one of the precious metals, at a given time and place, dignified by the name of " a bill of exchange," and magnified and mystified by special legislation and by financial usages and customs, until a few persons only attempt to comprehend it. I have just shown, that the par exchange between England and the United States is about $9\frac{1}{2}$ per cent. premium above the old computed par. This is well understood by commercial men ; but yet they will not reduce their table and ordinary computation of the exchanges to that par, and publish the difference, which would show the real rate of exchange—but all questions of finance, banking, currency, and exchanges, must still be involved in some mystery, otherwise the influence of money would be lessened if not reduced to its actual worth, and value ; and there would be another principle of equality developed by the American government. To do this, all that appears indispensably necessary, would be to quote the exchange on London in dollars and cents for the pound sterling, instead of designating the per centage above or below par, according to the old computation. This might be done by subtracting the par premium on the sterling pound, according to the old computation, from the rate exhibited, when the rate of exchange exceeds that amount; and subtract it minus that amount when it is below that amount. This would make the quotation quite clear and intelligible to every reader.

If the par value of the pound sterling be $4,8665, and the rate of exchange should be so much in favor of the United States as to reduce it to $9\frac{1}{2}$ per cent., that is, to the old computed par, it should be quoted at $4,4444, or at 9½ per cent. discount, instead of being quoted at par, as it would be according to the present practice ; by which the subject is mystified, and the attentive and superficial observer misled into a belief, that the imports and exports of the country were equal, that is, that the total amount of American exports were equal to the total amount of their imports, and that a merchant in New York can purchase, with an ounce of pure gold, or an ounce of pure silver; a bill on England, which will entitle him to receive in England, an ounce of pure gold or an ounce of pure silver.

By the laws of the United States, British gold and silver coin, of full weight and standard fineness, are receivable in the payment of duties, at about the value of their amount of pure gold, or pure silver, when coined at the American mint.

When exchange is at par, the English merchant at Liverpool or London, with a given sum of British standard gold, or standard silver coins, can purchase a bill upon New York that will entitle him to receive from the drawee of the bill in New York, a like sum of British standard gold, or silver, or its equivalent in American gold or silver. The coins of full weight and fineness of the two countries, which are the respective equivalents of an ounce of pure silver, or an ounce of pure gold, or of the standard fineness of British silver or gold will express that par.

The injury that would be done to domestic and foreign exchanges, by an incorporated United States bank and branches, doing the whole banking business of the country, can only be comprehended, by supposing a mercantile company, chartered to promote commerce, (nominally,) with the exclusive privilege of regulating the length of the yard-stick and shortening it again at their pleasure, and of increasing or lessening the weight or measure of the pound or bushel to suit their private interest and convenience, under pretext of their being better able to compete in prices with European dealers, they must be allowed to buy 36 inches for a yard, and sell at any smaller number of inches for a yard, that they might find it to their interest to use. So a United States bank and branches may expand the currency when and where she wishes to sell exchanges, and contract it at such times and places as she wishes to purchase bills of exchange again.

This was loudly and bitterly complained of in the old United States bank ; but the situation of our foreign commerce and domestic credits is such, that the commercial evils would be quadrupled by such a system at this time. Our domestic commerce is greatly increased, and the amount of remittances from one part of the country to another, through bills of exchange, is proportionately enlarged ; while our remittances to foreign countries have become immense, both on account of the greatly increased amount of importations of British merchandise, and on account of the immense national or states debts that must be paid. Alas ! how much of all this evil is to be attributed to the accumulation of bank credit, owing to their *limited responsibility, private interest* and *political* ambition.

The advantages of chartered bank paper have been dearly bought, by bank expansions, contractions and suspensions, and consequent fluctuations in prices and business ; although chartered banks, by the laws of their own situation, (being chartered and established for the express purpose of making as much money upon a small capital, with a fictitious legal credit, out of the government and out of the people, as they lawfully can,) must either secretly combine to aid each other, as they thereby most positively assist themselves, or, having a similarity of interests act similarly in their contractions and expansions, and in the prices they pay for bills of exchange, and in their charges for remittances, a similarity of constitution, an identity of interest, with equal legal powers to exercise, must produce naturally the same results.

Yet, even the combined action of a great number of banks, is not so much to be feared as the immediate, direct and concentrated action of one large bank with branches throughout the Union. This concentration of the monied interests of the country, in one large bank; its monopoly of the finances of the country; its aristocratic tendency and influence over society ; with its power to control the currency, should be avoided by every lover of liberty and equality.

The influence of such an institution must be greater than that of all the other elementary principles of the government combined ; whether it be considered in a commercial, political, religious, social or financial point of view.

That portion of our commercial community that now want an increase of foreign credit, and seek it through the agency of a United States bank, would be the very first to suffer from its influence ; for being the first among its debtors, as soon as the business of the bank had become general, and the state institutions had been swallowed up by that leviathan, and the needy supplicant for loans, or for bank credit had been accommodated until nothing more could be made from his business, until he had paid up his previous loans, other " fatter clients" will offer, and the " lean kine" will be turned away as hungry as they came.

The merchant, who wants one great bank for the greater convenience of foreign or domestic remittances, forgets that as he increases the credit of one institution he lessens the credit of others, and that, while he more effectually secures the prompt punctual payment of the drafts of this bank in London and extends its credits abroad, that this is only temporary relief, and that the greater the expansion the more severe the contraction will be, that must inevitably follow it.

And that as soon as such an institution shall be once in complete operation, it would have the power to regulate the rate of interest on money, the price of remittances, and the amount of currency that should circulate, for the precious metals would all be in its vaults. The laws make the coins of several other countries besides our own lawful tender, some of which pass by tale and some of them by weight. And when the prices asked by the bank for bills the merchant thought too high, and he should ask specie to remit himself, instead of buying a bill of exchange, the banker if he gave him specie, could pay him in such foreign coin, as would only pass as bullion at a loss in the market to which he might desire to send it ; or he might give him light American coins, that, not having been called in by the mint, are still lawful tender—small pieces that are very inconvenient to the remitter—so that although the bank may promptly meet the demand for specie, yet the receiver would find that the additional half per cent. that the bank asked him for the draft more than he thought it worth, was still cheaper and better for him to pay, than to receive the specie which he must take, if he drawed the specie from the bank for remittances against the pleasure of the banker. And the bank now having the whole, sole, and entire control of the exchanges, as well as the currency, it would be in vain to remonstrate against the imposition. The only avenue to the good graces of a bank is always through their interest : when they have power they invariably exercise it.

Besides this, men in business, dependant upon bank credit, find that they are required silently to submit to many inconveniences and impositions, by the directors, or loose the benefits of their bank credit ; and having extended their business upon that credit, it would be nearly fatal to the credit merchant, to be deprived of a credit at the bank, when there is no other institution in the country from which one dollar can be borrowed. Hence they may better quietly pay the bank a higher price for a bill, a premium that would twice cover the expense of exporting specie, than loose their credit at the bank. These, however, are but a tythe of the financial evils that must inevitably flow from the creation of a national bank ; not to allude to it as the positive foundation of a national debt.

The tendency of the precious metals to go abroad, is the only permanent and absolute check upon over-trading ; for prudent men will not import more than they can sell, nor more than they can pay for ; and where exchange is not in-interfered with, by artificial means, this of itself will regulate the amount of our importations, and the amount of our domestic sales.

The charge against my proposition, of issuing more paper to circulate as money than the amount of specie in the vaults of the bank, giving the proposed bank paper a credit character, and thereby overthrowing the arguments used in its favor, have been, I trust, satisfactorily answered so far as the exchange is concerned, in rendering bank notes always perfectly convertible.

I hope I have made it clear to the understanding of every disinterested, well-constituted mind, that the natural tendency of coin to leave the country, when not artificially interfered with, will control importations and check over-trading ; that if the directors of the banks had no interest in the dividends or discounts of the banks, they would not depart from the legal, regular, sound, healthy business of banking (that of lending money, by discounting regular business paper, having but a short time to run,) to interfere with exchanges; and that, consequently, the exchanges being left to private competition, would always indicate the balance of trade, while private bills could be bought cheaper by remitters from competing individual venders in the bill market, than they would be likely to be purchased from banks.

It has been suggested, that the old practice of the Canada banks, of endorsing or guaranteeing bills, was preferable to the present practice of banks dealing in bills.

The endorsement undoubtedly benefitted the bill-holder where strict convertibility was desired; but it is a departure from the duties of the bank of very doubtful expediency.

According to the system of banking here recommended, the whole, sole and entire business of the bank should be to lend money by discounting actual business paper, having but a short time to run, and thereby furnishing a convenient, perfectly convertible money-currency, to make up the deficiency of the precious metals, and nothing more.

The invariable, perfectly uniform convertibility of bank paper is all that is desired in a circulating medium to give it a metalic character; and our system of currency should never admit of the issue of one dollar more of paper than possessed the metalic character perfectly, as could be proved on all occasions by being freely exchanged for silver or gold, at sight at the counter where it was issued.

But, if we succeed in showing, that the currency employed in foreign trade, bears no greater proportion to the whole amount of " medial commodity " circulating in the country, than the amount of capital engaged in foreign trade bears to the whole amount of capital employed in agriculture, manufactures, and in domestic commerce in the country, we shall have a data by which, in some measure, we shall be able to judge of what amount of paper and what amount of specie must always be freely exchanged for each other, to render the currency of the country easy, and yet, not to inflate it so as to lead to its exportation, perfectly to supply the demand for currency, but not to surcharge the channels of circulation. Although this may not be doubted, the data upon which this hypothesis is predicated may not be uninteresting by and bye.

That bank paper, intended to circulate as money, may not acquire a credit character, and ultimately become inconvertible; prevent any artificial interference with the precious metals, by which their free circulation and exportation should be restrained.

Circulate bills of no smaller denomination than is convenient for all classes of society.

Circulate no bills of smaller denominations than those which circulate freely, as money, in the countries with which our commerce is principally carried on; that balances of trade, may always be correctly indicated by the rate of exchange, and the excessess checked, by the free circulation of the precious metals from one country to another.

Separate the banks of issue perfectly from the banks of discount, so that the discounts may be made automatically upon the specie actually in the vaults of the bank at the time of the discount, always fully supplying the actual demand, and never exceeding it.

Separate the currency from politics, by removing the congress and states' legislatures the necessity of incorporating banking companies, increasing their capitals, renewing their charters, or in any manner interfering with the bank paper portion of the circulating medium; and placing the control of the currency in the hands of the people, through financiers elected by themselves expressly for that purpose, thereby preventing the infamous contractions and expansions of bank issues to serve private or political party purposes.

Separate private interest from the creation or circulation of that part of the currency, that consists of bank paper, as perfectly, wholly, and entirely as it is separated from the operations of the mint, that coins the precious metals.

Render the currency republican, by authorising the people, by act of congress, to elect competent financiers to supervise and regulate the currency; who should be responsible to the public for the faithful discharge of their duties, as the directors of the political machinery of the government are elected and responsible through the ballot-box; making it the private interest of every director, desirous of popular favor, or of being re-elected, to study to promote the interest of the greatest number of his constituents—by rendering and preserving the stability and soundness of the currency unquestionable—by keeping the bank accounts and monthly statements, intended to be published, mathematically correct—and by zealously promoting the accommodation and convenience of the whole community.

The directors of the banks of discount, being subject to the advice and direction of the state directors, as the states directors are to the United States directors—each and every one of them giving good security for the faithful discharge of their trusts; and, to prevent the possibility of their becoming interested in the discounts, all directors should be precluded from the privilege of discounting paper, in which a director has any interest, either in the discount or in the re-payment of the money.

Banks of discount should publish monthly statements of their business, that the people, whose servants they are, and whose currency they are elected to regulate and direct, may well understand the state of the monetary affairs of the country.

When the directors of a bank of discount are interested in common with the inhabitants of the place in the convertibility of the currency, and in the general prosperity of the place, and when they can by no possibility have an opposite interest from that of the community, they will be likely to do their duties faithfully; being also restricted from dealing in exchanges for the profit of the business, or in making their notes payable at a distant place, with a view of profiting by the exchange.

The business of every local bank will be conveniently, principally confined to the discounting business notes of the regular traders and residents of the place where the bank is located; making the payments due and payable on the spot and not elsewhere, for the sake of an increase of dividends. Then and not until then, will the thinking class of citizens desire to confine the operations of the banks to their proper legitimate business—that of lending money, by discounting actual business paper, having but a short time to run.

The frequently publishing of statements of the banks, together with the reports of the state directors, upon their examination and supervision of the institutions, will enable the public to understand the business of the bank, and to approve or disapprove of the various measures of the directors.

The laws and regulations established for the guidance of the directors, should be very definite and explicit, leaving but slight discretionary power with them, except that of only discounting safe and secure paper, when the amount of specie in their vaults justify it.

The people would then become familiar with currency, and elect only such persons as would conduct banking upon the true principles of prudent and safe banking, making the bank paper issued only sufficient to meet the demand for currency, above the amount of metalic currency in cir_culation, for all the small business of the country.

This will more effectually prevent the expansions of the currency, and the danger of its imperfect convertibility, than could be expected from individual liability or the security of public debts or lands, pledged with the comptroller of the state for the security of the bill-holder, as under the general banking law of the state of New York.

The people are always right in their cool judgment, and they would soon learn that every slight expansion of bank issues must be followed by triplicate contractions; and that paper money, although when strictly convertible may serve as a convenient currency, while it is the actual representative of coin, but that it can not be used as wealth ; that however perfectly soever it may be rendered in specie, it still is not specie, nor is it any more wealth than it is specie, consequently its true and only business is as the representative of specie to supply the deficiency in the precious metals in this country, in the same manner as bank paper supplies the place of the precious metals abroad. Bank paper has truly been said to be like faith, " the substance of things hoped for, and the evidence of things not seen."

Circulate bills of no smaller denomination than is convenient for all classes of society, so that those who prefer the precious metals may always have them, not only from their preference to them, but from the preference for paper of those who have inland remittances to make, or who, from

the amount of the business they have to transact, find large
bills preferable to them for specie.

The money that each individual prefers will be retained
by him as long as he has other money that will circulate
freely, whether it be the precious metals or bank paper.
That the precious metals will not circulate indiscriminately
with bank paper, among the same class of citizens, at the
same time, is evident, from the fact, that every man retains
the money he prefers, and passes that which is the least
pleasing to him.

Those who handle but a small quantity of money generally prefer the precious metals, especially if they have ever
had a bill that they had received at par, and was compelled
to loose a discount on it upon passing it—(and who among
that class of citizens has not ?)

Men in large business prefer bank paper, equally current
in every part of the country, and always convertible into
specie, except those whose business in trade is mostly with
farmers, mechanics, and laborers. They prefer the precious metals as more convenient change. Farmers prefer
the precious metals to paper money, because they are more
secure against loss, and against fire ; because they will always pass, whatever may be the fluctuations of trade, or of
currency, and because they sometimes are above par, but
never below par. Besides, they, as well as mechanics,
spend less money for useless articles, when they have only
gold and silver by them, than they do when they have bank
paper of doubtful convertibility ; because the pleasure
they take in having the rich gold and silver coins securely
laid by them, is greater than the pleasures they would enjoy in the occasional extra bottle, or other useless luxury,
especially if the family are ill, or if business is dull. The
family too, acquire an almost instinctive attachment for spe-

cie, that is left in their care for some time—it becomes an almost household god with them, and they feel great reluctance at having it passed ; this feeling is never so strong for paper money.

Excessive fondness for shows and amusements are often induced by the expansions of the currency. Men with small means, from finding money plenty and business lively, for a length of time—fancying that such times will always continue, indulge in luxuries and amusements, that their business and ordinary circumstances would not have warranted. The youth are left without a knowledge of the useful and necessary business of life, and without a correct knowledge of the value of money, to read novels, dress, see company, and learn accomplishments—all of which may have their proper time and place, but which but illy fit the youth of our country for our western wilds, where those who understand business, and are honest, sober, temperate, economical and industrious, are certain of becoming wealthy, provided they keep out of debt and live annually within their income. But idleness and luxury will render our young men effeminate, and our young women vapid ; and when they are left to earn their own bread by industry, they will find that they are neither fit associates for laborers, nor men of sense, and that, having passed their time in fanciful amusements, they are altogether unqualified for the important duties of life, which, as men and women, must devolve upon them in a few days. They have lost their self-command, or rather they have never learned the severe art of self-government. They have been flattered—they became vain and imperious ; they are now neglected, and they become peevish, fretful, and morose,— being unhappy and disappointed with every thing and every body, they are thus left fit prey for the first coquette

In love, or black-leg in matrimony, that may put their dis-
tempered brains at work to ensnare them.

And this is the daily and hourly consequence of LIMITED
RESPONSIBILITY CHARTERED BANK PAPER! *Private interest*
inflates the currency. The unwary and unsuspecting fancy that the paper that they receive is real money—is real
wealth—but they wake to the painful reflection, that " ill-
luck still haunts a fairy grot,"—they are poorer than they
were before they went to the bank for credit, and less able
to pay their debts.

Republicanism is plain, honest, homely, healthy, and happy. Wealth is the product of honest industry ; it is substantial, it is accumulating, and always convenient to those
who have earned it, and know its value ; but to those who
do not know its value, it is always deficient, it is sqander-
ed, and is, briefly, nothing better than want, by which it
must and will assuredly be followed. A knowledge of the
value of money consists in a knowledge of the value of
pence. Ten dollars in one bank note inspires less love
of money, that is, it is spent with less care and less anxiety
at parting with it, than is often felt in parting with one silver dollar. Coins, like old friends, are often preserved as
companions, for something like a personal regard and attachment that we have for them, by which we retain them as
long as possible. Bank paper is like agreeable steam-boat
or stage passenger acquaintances—they pass current with
us for a time, but leave no lasting impressions on our minds.

The preventing the circulation of small bills, and leaving
specie to occupy their places, retains a much greater amount
of specie in the country, than will remain under bank contractions, when the banks have all the specie in their vaults,
and the power to dispose of it as they choose.

It is believed that currency may be rendered sound, and

preserved so in circulation, much more easily when the division between the specie and bank paper shall be so established, that every class of community may have the medium that he prefers, and at all times and under all commercial or financial circumstances, exchange the one freely for the other.

But to accomplish this, there must be no small bills ; that those who have the paying off of laborers, and the purchasing of produce from the farmers, cannot have a depreciated currency to press upon them, with the threat, that unless you receive this currency you cannot be employed, or that you cannot sell your produce.   While a depreciated small bill currency exists, we have seen that it will be circulated by those who are interested in the passage of it, and by those whose necessities compel them to receive it in business and pay it out again.

It is true that paper money is not lawful tender in the payment of debts, yet it is virtually so, as well as in the payment of laborer's wages, and in the purchase of the farmer's products.

If the laborer is told, you must take paper money or I cannot employ you, with him paper money is lawful tender to all intents and purposes.   So too with the farmer ; if, when he has brought his produce into market, and is told that he must take paper money or not sell, by every purchaser, (as every farmer would be told who should ask specie for his loading,) to him paper money is lawful tender—he must receive it or he cannot sell his load.

This must naturally be the situation of the currency, and of the business of the country, while small bills are allowed to be issued and circulated as money by incorporated banks.

Small bills drive the specie out of the market.   They, being less valuable than specie, and the bankers hav-

ing an interest in their circulation, increased by their frequent destruction and loss, they will, by them, be forced into the market, while specie will be withheld from circulation.

## CHAPTER XXXVIII.

ON THE CONVERTIBILITY OF BANK PAPER; AND ON BRITISH
POLITICS.

A summary of the means by which bank paper may be prevented from acquiring
a credit character, and becoming ultimately inconvertible.—The government of
Great Britain.

The currency of the country may be rendered sound by
the following means :

Firstly : By removing all artificial restrictions upon the
circulation of specie, and more especially upon its exportation; leaving the exchanges truly to indicate the balance of
trade, and the propriety of increasing or lessening importations.

Secondly : Circulate no bills of smaller denominations
than accommodate all classes of community ; providing
large bills for men engaged in extensive business, and specie for farmers, mechanics and laborers, and all that class of
society that prefer the specie to bank paper.

Thirdly : Circulate no bills smaller than the smallest
that circulate in foreign countries with which our commerce
is principally carried on, that the balances of trade may be
indicated by the exchanges, and duly checked by the exportation of coin when excessive.

Fourthly : Separate the banks of discount from the banks
of issue, so that discounts may be made automatically upon

the specie actually in the vaults of the banks at the time of the discount.

Fifthly : Separate the currency from politics, by removing the necessity for legislative interference with banks, or currency ; and organizing the people to regulate their banks and their issues to meet the actual demand for currency.

Sixthly : Separate private interest from the issues or circulation of bank paper, as fully and perfectly as it is separated from the operations of the mint.

Seventhly : Require monthly bank statements of the business of the banks, full and complete, to be published for public inspection, and for the supervision of state directors, that all the operations of the banks may be approved or disapproved by the people through the ballot-boxes.   And

Lastly : Render the currency of the country republican, like the other elementary principles of the government, by giving the people the election of the directors as they elect the most numerous branches of their legislatures.   That it shall be the interest of the directors to promote the general public good, and not the private interest of the stockholders alone, as it is at present.

A strict conformity to these regulations, with such other minor checks and balances as might be indicated by experience, it is thought would completely change the character of paper money, and render it always perfectly convertible at sight, and equally current in every part of the U. States.

Having, as I trust, answered the objections made to the proposed plan of a mixed currency, consisting of specie for the ordinary business of the country, and large bills for those who prefer them for commercial purposes, lest the circulation of more paper than there is specie in the vaults of the bank should give it a credit character, and ultimately render its convertibility doubtful ; and having illustrated the advantages that must arise to the whole nation collectively, as well as the citizens in their private capacities, I now proceed to the examination of the currency generally; but, perhaps, I ought firstly to remark, that I anticipate the introduction of specie into common circulation would be slow, and for some time retarded by the continuance in circulation of the small bills of the chartered banks until their charters shall have expired.

But when investments in one general United States bank stock shall have been found to be more profitable, to pay a larger dividend, and be less liable to change and depreciation, than the stocks of private banking companies, capitalists will readily and promptly change their investments from private fluctuating stocks, to permanent national funds; freed from the anxiety attendant upon the financial or political changes that are daily occurring, both in Europe and America, by which the dividends of banks and the value of stocks are rendered so uncertain and fluctuating, and as the small bills disappear one after another, under a healthy state of the currency, specie will appear simultaneously as if by magic. Small bills and specie, we have before seen, cannot circulate at the same time among the same community; because the poorer material is invariably first offered in the market. Hence credit bank bills perform all the duties of the currency, of which they are capable, to the extent to which they exist in community. If you would check their circulation, they must be withdrawn or called in altogether, as they will occupy the small channels of currency against the desire of the holder, as long as they are permitted to remain afloat.

The national debt of Great Britain, as I have elsewhere explained, contains the strength of the nation—securing the wealth of the kingdom in support of the government, by uniting the private interests of the fund-holders to the public interests of the empire.

Every fund-holder has a direct interest in the support of the government of Great Britain to the amount of the funds he holds : and hence the fact that the irredeemable national debt of £800,000,000 sterling, is become the CAPITAL of the kingdom, and the perpetual bond of union between the government and the governed. Self-love—private interest—is the ruling passion; at whose shrine all the nations of the earth bow—forgetting patriotism, philanthropy, and the love of offspring, in the enjoyment of present ease and luxury : they consign posterity to ruin, wretchedness and woe, sooner than deprive themselves of the gratifications of to-day.

The fund-holders have no voice, and exercise no influence or control over the management of the funds. They receive their dividends regularly; their stock is always perfectly convertible into specie at will : and therefore, the public confidence is kept secure by the punctual payment of the interest on quarter days.

I am desirous of interesting American capitalists in favor of the republican government of these United States, to the same extent through *private interest*, that capitalists in England are directly interested in support of the government of Great Britain ; but by not exactly the same means— not by a *national irredeemable debt*—not by making the government of my country insolvent, or independent of the people, who would then be compelled by standing armies to support it, whether it was satisfactorily administered or otherwise ; but by giving the whole people a sound currency entirely subject to their own regulation, and capitalists a safe, profitable convertible investment, constituting a source of real wealth, connected with the currency, and

as perpetual as the other elementary principles of the government.

The stocks of this institution, being always themselves as
convertible as the funded debt of Great Britain is, would
become so much convertible capital stock in the hands of the
stockholders—being productive wealth while in hand, and
money in the market whenever the exchange is desirable.
Capitalists would have greater confidence in the permanence and stability of funds based upon specie, connected
with a government the choice of a whole people, than can
be felt in a government, however strong in its fortresses, army and navy, in King, Lords and Commons, Church and
State Union, in bank and government connection, when the
wealth of the nation only constituted the bond of union,
and when the titled pensioner and the dignitied churchman,
who live upon the hard earnings of the masses, are but a
tythe of the population, where fixed bayonets enforce the
laws, and where moral obligations are of no force.

Besides this, every man acquainted with the political history of England, for the last twenty years, has seen the
House of Lords, with its bishops and other church dignitaries and dependants, as violent in their opposition to the
several whig administrations of modern times, although they
profess to be whigs of the Pitt school, as was Pitt to the
administrations of North and Bute. These several administrations, down to the present long Melborne administration, are evidently each more liberal and more enlightened
than its predecessors, yet evidently far behind the advance
of intelligence and the wants of the people.

If the term tory signifies one in office, who supports a
church and state union, the levying and collecting the revenues necessary for the support of the government from the
labor and industry of the producers, rather than from the

wealth of the country, then the present administration is as truly tory as its predecessors.

The political revolutions, as they have been termed, that have occured in England within the last twenty years, the catholic emancipation law, and the reform law, have only changed the classes of persons who exercise and enjoy political and civil privileges, and not the persons themselves. True, the boroughs owned by a few gentlemen have been disfranchised, and the representation given to a more extended district of country, and to a greater number of electors, yet the latter are as dependant upon the Lord of the Manor, as were the citizens of a borough upon its proprietor. The same men may be still elected, as well by the ten pound electors of a district, as they could formerly by the dependants upon a borough. The same leading principles prevail as formerly. The landlords nominate and cause to be elected whomsoever they please, to continue the same leading principles—the connection of the church and state—the raising the revenue upon the labor, and not upon the wealth of the kingdom—and the right of the few to govern the many, with the necessity of the many to obey the few. This may be now done with more liberality perhaps, in some respects than formerly ; yet with the same ultimate object, that of keeping the laboring classes poor and ignorant, that they may be easily governed ; and of increasing the power and wealth of the wealthy, that they may govern with certainty, security, and ease to themselves, without having any common feeling for, or interest with the governed.

By these changes (for they can be called nothing else,) the people have gained new masters, without gaining important principles. Wealth and not numbers still govern. The funded debt still continues the bond of indissoluble union between the wealth and wealthy of the kingdom and the government, while fully four-fifths of the producers and tax-payers exercise, in fact, no independent influence in the representation.

Had not the great aristocracy of wealth been secure, even the love of power and desire of office, would have been insufficient to have produced among the wealthy (the only truly powerful class after all,) its advocates and defenders. The aristocracy of wealth and the Lords contested the passage of these measures inch by inch, as they were being matured and passed into laws, and only finally consented to their passage after the amendments by the Lords had permanently secured wealth and not numbers to be the basis of representation.

Heretofore old tory families controlled the House of Commons, through their nominees from the boroughs. The whigs, finding their power over the manufacturing and some of the agricultural districts greater than that of the tories, determined to disfranchise the old boroughs, and give the members to districts over which they had influence. They secretly stimulated the people—they occasionally headed the populace—they afforded them protection from the influence of tory magistrates and police officers, and obtained the passage of these important laws, by which they secured their seats in the cabinet and their continuance in power, as they are very equally balanced between the radicals on the one hand, and the tories on the other.

THE NATIONAL DEBT OF GREAT BRITAIN.

The national irredeemable debt of England, as I have before observed, contains the strength of the nation, by uniting the private interest of the fund-holders to the general public interest of the kingdom.

Every fund-holder has a direct interest in the support of the government of Great Britain, equal to the amount of funds he holds ; and hence the easy solution of what appears problematical to Americans, and the clear illustration of the fact, that the English irredeemable national debt of £800,000,000 sterling, is become the capital of the kingdom. Private interest, being the governing passion of him who has but £100, as of him who holds £100,000, from the highest in office to the lowest in servitude, " self-love, the spring of action, rules the soul."

### FUND-HOLDERS EXERCISE NO INFLUENCE OVER THE MANAGEMENT OF THE FUNDS.

Another important fact connected with this fund is, that the fund-holders exercise no influence over these funds, either with regard to the management of the fund or the rate of interest to be allowed.

The government have issued bonds at various times, at such a rate of interest as they would be likely to sell at, at the time ; they specify the rate of interest, and the time of payment of that interest, but establish no time for the payment of the principal. These bonds are sold in the market for what they will bring. If the rate of interest is placed above the smallest rate at which these bonds would have sold, they sell at a premium ; if the rate of interest is fixed too low, they remain unsold, unless that contingency be provided for, when they sell for less than the face of the bond, when they are said to be below par.

The only claim the government has allowed the fund-holder, is that of demanding the interest when it becomes due, on the amount of any given fund that he holds. Whether it be what is called three per cent. stocks, or five per cent. stocks, the holder of the stock has the right to

demand the full amount due to him; but not to enquire any
further respecting its management on account of his being
a fund-holder, or exercise any influence over the fund on
that account.

How to give American citizens a similar interest in the
support of the American government, without the evils of
a national debt, to that which the English have in support of
the mixed monarchy of Great Britain, is a leading object of
the present work.

The wealth of every country, being the most powerful
engine that the country possesses, either in support of peace
or war—the promotion of religion, moral education, or civil harmony or discord—I am desirous of enlisting and securing the wealth of the United States, that is, the wealth
of the American capitalists, in favor of the republican government of the Union, to the same extent that capitalists in
England are directly interested in the support of the government of Great Britain. Not in the same way—not by
involving the government of the United States in an irredeemable debt, either to themselves, that is, to their own
citizens, or to a foreign people, which is immeasurably
worse; but offering capitalists stock, always convertible in
the stock market, precisely as the funded debt of Great Britain now is, or as the bank stock of our incorporated banks always are, at a shade higher or lower price, as the stock pays
a higher or lower rate of interest, as compared with other
investments, or as any other contingency may influence the
price of funds generally in the market, but always commanding its highest value.

Capitalists would have the same confidence in the stock
of a people's republican bank, established by a general free
banking law, that English capitalists have in the funds of
the government of Great Britain.

In this stock, investments would be permanent, safe, convenient and profitable; yielding the largest dividends of any funds, perhaps, in the world—possessing equal security, and punctuality of payment of dividends and of convertibility.

The wealth of the people of these United States would be added to the democracy of numbers—giving strength, stability, consistency, and permanency to republican institutions, and rendering the currency of the country equally republican with the other elementary principles of the government. It would thus become the key-stone of the arch of the republican edifice.

## CHAPTER XXXIX.

### FREE REPUBLICAN UNITED STATES BANK.

Some of the benefits of an United States bank stock, derived from the transferable character of the stock in the fund market.

The addition of such an immense capital, as the bank stock of all the paper currency would constitute, to be added to the credit and commodity-currency of the country, would immensely improve the capital of the country, it being marketable at a given nearly uniform price.

The specie thus invested in bank stock, would continue to be available funds in the hands of the stockholders, while it would be productive wealth to them, to the amount of the dividends, which being regularly paid quarterly or semi-annually, would confirm public confidence in the institution, while it furnished the bank fund-holder with money in his pocket and cash at interest.

While individuals were thus immensely benefitted by the establishment of such a fund, the public would gain an acquisition of credit, or commodity-capital and currency, to the whole amount of specie thus invested in bank stock, the value of which would be enhanced by the separation of currency from credit, and thus rendering the currency uniformly convertible at sight.

THE ARISTOCRACY OF INCORPORATED COMPANIES.

All incorporated companies are aristocratic bodies, because they have peculiar rights, powers and privileges, which are not enjoyed by the public, and which the public are not unfrequently expressly forbidden practicing or enjoying. But among chartered companies none of them possess such anti-republican principles as monied corporations.

Bank incorporations, by their controlling the currency of the country, not only exercise an immense monetary and political influence at home, but they give the financial character to the country in foreign lands.

Whatever defects are found in the monetary affairs of this country, are charged upon its political institutions by those who are unable to understand our form of government; and the secret workings of anti-republican incorporations upon it, with all their baneful effects, by foreigners are charged upon our republican principles and institutions.

Nations of the earth bowed down by arbitrary laws, oppressed and impoverished by taxes, tythes and poor rates, who are zealously, quietly struggling, peaceably to renovate their own governments, and to infuse into them the pure principles of democracy, of equal justice, and equal, civil and religious liberty to all, are met upon the threshold with the charge of American suspensions of specie payments by their banks, and the extravagance and idebtedness of our states to foreign countries; thus stopping their mouths with arguments, drawn from republican America. While all Europe is tending toward democracy, we are becoming daily more and more aristocratic.

This should enlist the energies of the philanthropist and the patriot, to come to the investigation of the cause of our retrogradation, and the defence and support of truth and justice, and of equal rights to all mankind, with the ultimate universal peaceful extension of equal, civil and religious liberty throughout the world.

Incorporated banking companies, by giving the country a credit paper currency, in lieu of a sound metalic currency, are forever tending to sever the bonds of republican union, founded upon liberty and equality. They are forever opposed to the universal extension of equality and human happiness to all mankind.

The learned professions are naturally aristocratic and exclusive in their religious, political or financial views ; partly from the laws of their situations, and perhaps from their exclusive possession of certain sciences and branches of useful and profitable knowledge, and from their mixing almost exclusively with men of letters, and men of their own or other learned professions.

The least defensible of all aristocracies are legalized credit aristocracies; they,to obtain their exclusive privileges, argue, reason, and administer to the *gullibility* of mankind, until their earnest and apparently sincere protestations in favor of bank paper, its convenience, its excellence, and its value to the community, captivates thousands of honest men, who are charmed into a belief that bank paper is money, and that such money is real capital. Hence the immense number of flatterers and courtiers that continually follow in the train of this credit aristocracy. They seldom, however, leave this flickering credit light, until like the miller fly that turns his giddy whirl around the lighted taper, their wings are touched with the flame, and they are unwittingly drawn into its vortex and lost in the blaze of their blind adoration.

## MANKIND LEARN SLOWLY EVEN BY EXPERIENCE ; THEREFORE THE NECESSITY OF " LINE UPON LINE AND PRECEPT UPON PRECEPT."

There is no instruction in the past. The explosion of one incorporated bank only gives place to another. That, too, in its turn, follows rapidly " in the footsteps of its pred-ecessor ;" and thus the circle of promises and belief, decep-tion and disappointment, distress and ruin is complete, and continued on " from generation to generation."

The public stock of gullibility is unexhausted, and oth-er artful intriguers practice the trade of deception upon the public again with like success.

Hence the importance of the Congress of the United States seriously taking up the subject of the currency, and providing some salutary remedy of guarding the public against these repeated impositions.

*Extracts from Governor Carlin's Message to both Houses of the Legislature of Illinois, on the 26th Nov. 1840.*

The Governor says:

" The pernicious consequences inflicted upon the country by the operations of banks within the last few years, is too indelibly stamp-ed upon every department of business to be misapprehended by the most sceptical.

" The fluctuations in the prices of labor, property, and trade of every description, have kept pace with the alternate expansions and contractions of their issues, and whether the injuries thus sustained are attributable to their guilt or innocence, the effect upon the pros-perity of the people is the same.

" So interwoven have the affairs of our citizens become with these institutions, that it cannot be denied that they control and direct the circulating medium, commerce and wealth of the country; and not only so, they frequently wring from legislative bodies an acknowledgment of their utility, and exercise an influence over the public mind which it is difficult to overcome.

" Thus have they fortified themselves behind an almost invulnerable rampart, erected by encroachment, and justified by the tyrant's plea, 'necessity.'

" Usurpations of whatever character, are usually preceded with the persuasion, that they are essential to the advancement of the people in the scale of prosperity and happiness; and in this way they are stripped of their rights, and bound in chains of political slavery, before they are aware of their danger.

" To guard against such startling power concentrated in banks, all the virtue and energy of the patriot must be called into action and constant requisition."

This warning voice should be re-echoed from Maine to Georgia. An insidious foe is lurking in the bosom of this republic. It is the offspring of private interest and credulity, nursed in the lap of luxurious idleness, and matured in the school of treachery and deceit.

Will not the people rise in their might ?—they are the sovereign power. Their representatives cannot, or will not act, until they hear the public voice bidding them do their duties or retire. They are the creatures of party; and a few designing, artful leaders give them the cue, which they as cunningly execute. And, unfortunately, these leaders are too often aristocrats themselves at heart, however loudly they may proclaim the excellence of democracy, and the beauties of republicanism; or they are indebted to some monetary power, or are feed and employed by some bank as agent, attorney or counsel, or they have some powerful friend whose interest favors credit power, and the party are carried against the people. Thus the whole weight and influence of one party is brought to silence just alarm, and, siren-like, to charm the watchful republican to repose.

CONGRESS SHOULD INTERPOSE THE AUTHORITY OF THE NA-
TION, TO PRESERVE THE PEOPLE FROM IMMINENT DANGER
AND IMPENDING RUIN.

The congress of the United States should take up the
subject of the monetary affairs of the country, and lend its
powerful aid to guard the public against the portentious
dangers that threaten every part of the Union, and protect
them against the repeated impositions of incorporated companies ; by organizing the people to control and regulate
the currency according as their own interests shall require,
to promote the greatest good of the greatest number, in the
best possible manner, at the least expense and labor.

The people are the best judges of their own wants, and
know best how to promote their own interests. All they
require is organization for the purpose.

The people are always right when they are not misled
by artful demagogues ; and they will always be found quite
competent to govern themselves, as well in matters of currency as in matters of politics, provided the question to be
decided by them be fairly and honestly stated when submitted to their consideration. A moral education and particular
instruction of the people upon matters to be referred to them
for their special consideration, is all that is necessary to secure their correct judgment and right decision, upon whatever questions may be necessarily submitted to their particular attention.

Much danger to the republic is to be apprehended from
the establishment of a national debt ; but that evil is greatly increased when that debt is to be due to foreigners.

Notwithstanding the wide difference between the public
debt of the United States and the irredeemable public debt
of England, still the dangers of a national debt are immense. The value of the funded debt of England *consists*

*in its being irredeemable,* and being held and owned by the wealthy portion of the people, whose interests are therefore identified with the funds, and through them, with the government of the kingdom. The continuance of the punctual payment of that interest, and the convertibility of the funds, through the instrumentality of the Bank of England, aided by the government and aristocracy, with the assistance of exchequer bills and public and private loans, renders the government secure, and the notes of the Bank of England equally safe.

There is something a little inconsistent (in this country where a national debt is looked upon with so much abhorrence,) in making this debt the basis for the issue of paper to circulate as money ; yet such is the case according to the provisions of the New York General Banking law.

There is far less objection to passing public debts as part of the credit-currency, than there is in making them the basis upon which to issue paper to circulate as money.

The national debt of Great Britain can in no way compare with the national debts of the individual states or of the United States. The former, although irredeemable, is and must be perfectly convertible at the will of the holder in the fund market ; that is, the government must always support the credit of the funds to such an extent as to render them desirable investments for capitalists, by the prompt punctual payment of the interest at stated periods, or the government itself must cease.

But in the United States, party influence usurps the power of right, and improvident loans and unwise and extravagant expenditures by one party, lessens the fancied responsibility of the other party, when they come into power, to fulfil faithfully to the letter, the improvident, unpopular expenditures of their political opponents ; and casualties may prevent the punctual payment of interest or principal due in a foreign country, by which the public faith may be materially impaired ; while in England no such an event can occur, and the government of the kingdom continue. A change of ministers is the natural consequence of the government being unable to carry any measure of the administration.

A large proportion of the productive wealth of the nation consists in this fund, if that can be called productive which only transfers the earnings of one man who has no funds, to him who holds the government debts.

Yet, such is the fact, that the interest of the national debt of England, collected upon imposts and taxes from the industrious laboring and consuming classes, is equal to half the produce of England. And this constitutes the productive wealth of a large proportion of the influential men of the nation.

While the government continues to preserve the credit of the funded debt, the credit of the bank of England must continue. For, with a loss of credit, there must be a loss of confidence, and a loss of support by the wealthy, and with the withdrawal of their support must terminate the government.

Money possesses a powerful influence in governments, a potency and undeniable charm in making things agreeable, that would not be pleasing without it, and in making a government popular that would have otherwise been obnoxious to the people.

Hence the importance of interesting the private feelings and pecuniary situation of every American in support of the institutions of this country, to the same extent that the English are personally individually interested in the support of the government of England ; otherwise the greater zeal occasioned by the greater interest of the English, must, since the almost daily intercourse between the two nations is established, by degrees, imbue the American people with a love of foreign institutions, and a distaste for their own plain, simple, republican government of equality, which has so far less power to dazzle and blind the people, than the splendid brilliancy of show and parade that attends "the churchman's pomp and statesman's pride."

---

## CHAPTER XL.

INDIRECT TAXATION BY COLLECTIONS OF CUSTOMS, DUTIES, AND IMPOSTS, ARE MORE OPPRESSIVE, BUT GENERALLY LESS OFFENSIVE TO THE PEOPLE THAN DIRECT TAXATION.

In England a large proportion of the revenues of the Crown are derived from duties, imposts, excises, various licenses, and other indirect taxes, which are paid by importers, manufacturers, wholesale dealers, and merchants from foreign countries, and in such a variety of ways, that few individuals in the nation know the extent to which they are taxed.

Indirect taxes, as they are paid by the consumer, fall more heavily upon the labor of the producing classes than upon the legitimate objects of taxation, (wealth and luxuries.)

The retailing merchant pays the wholesale dealer the price of his commodities, with the duties, to which is added his profit upon the whole. The retailer, too, must have the same per centage of profit upon the outlay, as well upon that part of the amount paid for duties, as upon the charge for the articles; hence the consumer not only pays the duty chargeable upon the articles, but he also pays profits

to some two or three, and often perhaps, to twice as many
dealers in the article, in addition to the cost of the article
and duty.

### AN ILLUSTRATION OF THE DIFFERENCE BETWEEN INDIRECT AND DIRECT TAXATION.

Suppose a yard of cloth costs, or is entered at the custom house at $4 a yard, and that twenty five per cent. *ad-
valorem* duties are charged upon the article, the wholesale
dealer has the cloth at $5 a yard. Suppose he charges
twenty five per cent. profit, this brings the cloth to cost the
retailer $6,25 a yard. He charges a retail profit of 33⅓
per cent. on his outlay; enhancing the price of the yard of
cloth to $8,33 to the consumer—provided it be not sold
more than twice after the duties are paid ; but should the
profits have exceeded the above statement, the advance
upon the amount paid for duties would keep pace with
the profit charged upon the amount paid for the cloth, so
that the consumer pays $1,66 for duty and profit on duty,
instead of one dollar duty, being all that was charged at the
customs, and in fact more than was actually paid into the
treasury, since the per centage, or portion of the collector's
salary must be deducted. Hence it is easy to see, that $100
raised for public purposes by impost duties, costs the consumers some $200.

This would certainly appear excessively, and uselessly
oppressive, were it not that when this duty is levied only
on such articles as can be grown, manufactured or produced in the United States in sufficient quantities for domestic
consumption, it may and does encourage Americans to compete with foreigners in the produce of these articles—thereby rendering the United States independent of foreign
manufactories, as well as lessening their imports, and pre-

venting (as is the natural consequence,) the exportation of specie.

The people are least oppressed by a high tariff, when the duties are levied upon articles that may be grown, manufactured or produced in sufficient quantities in the United States for domestic consumption; while such necessaries of life as cannot be produced in America ought not to be heavily taxed, except it be for the special purpose of raising a revenue.

The tariff would not require raising so high to prevent foreign importations, if the people were allowed to regulate the paper portion of their currency as congress does the coining and value of the precious metals.

From these remarks, we can collect some idea of the difference between credit bank paper in England and in America.

In England, the whole united strength of Crown, Lords and Commons, army and navy, agriculture and commerce, manufactories, internal improvements, and public and private prosperity of the nation, with the very existence of the government, all depend upon one word, CREDIT : let that fail—let the interest cease to be paid—let the funds cease to be saleable—and let the wealthy of the native become dissatisfied—and revolution *must* instantly follow. Consequently the credit of England has the positive absolute necessity, and actual subsistence of the individuals owning the money of the nation, united to the government in the strongest possible manner.

Credit cannot fail, and the government continue. Happily for America, no such bond of desperate and dangerous necessity exists here. But it would be wise to secure the pleasing, profitable, private interest that the English have in support of their government, in support of that of the

American. This may be successfully and profitably done by the plan proposed of a people's currency—a United States Republican Free Bank of Issue, with a divided administration of the Banks of Discount.

A marketable national debt due to the citizens of a country, though the taxes necessary to pay the interest would be a galling chain, is nevertheless an indissoluble bond of union between the people and the government, especially in a sub-military government.

In England, a large proportion of the revenues of the government is derived from duties, imposts, and indirect taxes, that are paid by the merchants, importers and manufacturers : the existence of which is hardly known to the consumer, who pays them all ultimately, with a large per centage of profit on the duty, as we trust we have satisfactorily explained.

But from this we can easily understand, that in England the non-payment of the interest of the national debt, would destroy the interest of the wealthy, and turn them against the administration. The non-payment of the sailors and soldier, would arouse the Lion of old England in its full strength, and teach Kings and nobles, churchmen and statesmen, that " the voice of the people is the voice of God." With England, credit is every thing.

The national debt of Great Britain is, therefore, a permanent fund, that must continue and remain coeval with the government ; always marketable, and therefore convertible at the will of the holder into bank of England paper and exchangeable for other commodities. But should the bank again suspend specie payment, and the assistance of the Chancellor of the Exchequer and the ministry, by loans, or otherwise, be unable to prevent the notes of the bank from becoming materially depreciated, while the gov-

ernment remained popular their bills would be far preferable to the notes of suspended American banks, even although exchequer bills which are receivable in all dues to
the government, would no longer circulate freely, and although the rate of interest per day be greatly increased,
they must pay debts while the government continues more
desirable for capitalists to the extent of the duties they had
to pay than other funds, or than hoarding up of their specie.
This must, however, soon overturn the government, as
they will be returned upon it in payment of taxes, and
leave them without the means of supporting themselves or
paying the army or navy, or the civil list.

Still, however, the suspension of specie payments by the
bank of England, differs widely in its effects upon commerce and business, from that of suspension by American
banks in the United States. The bank of England has the
credit of the British government for its support, while
American banks have not even the stockholders liable.

### REMARKS UPON THE SUSPENSION OF THE BANK OF ENGLAND.

When the bank of England suspends specie payment,
she does not do so because she has paid out her capital, for
that remains the same and as secure as the government itself, with which its credit is so intimately blended.

Suspensions of the bank of England can only occur
when the receipts of the government have not been
paid in specie ; or when the amount received from the Exchequer, and the amount of specie received from the ordinary commercial transactions of its own business, have been
less than the demand for specie upon the bank, for the redemption of their own notes in the ordinary business of the
bank ; while the suspension of specie payment by American
banks, is not rendered quite unavoidable until the whole of

the paid up capital of the bank and its specie deposites have
been drawn from its vaults, and its available funds have all
been disposed of. The prospect of the ultimate redemption of the notes of an United States bank having suspended specie pa ment, depends wholly upon the solvency of
its debtors, and the prudence and economy of its directors.
The government of the United States has nothing involved—and ought never to have, in the solvency of an incorporated banking company, any more than it has in the
solvency of any canal or rail road company, or in the liabilities of any private individual.

Banks claim precedence in their claims upon the estates
of insolvent debtors—with how much justice let other
creditors enquire.

Although the English nation have the most unlimited
confidence, both in the strength of the government and the
credit of the bank of England ; yet even with this powerful and decided advantage in point of credit enjoyed by
the bank of England over the credit of chartered banks in
America, after both of them have suspended specie payment, I am not prepared to say that the Queen, Lords
and Commons, Church and State union, with the army and
navy, would be able to keep the people silent, should the
funds of the nation become unsaleable, and the notes of the
bank of England inconvertible, or even greatly below par.

But should the market price of specie remain but a shade
higher than at present, and the capital of the nation, that is,
the funded debt, remain marketable, with but a slight depreciation, the suspension of specie payment by the bank
of England would have far less influence on the commercial prosperity of England, than a general suspension by
American banks has upon the American money market ;
since the notes of the bank of England are a lawful tender
in the payment of all debts except its own.

But if the value of specie should not materially vary from its present value, or former rate, and the balance of trade should not be substantially against the kingdom, and the crops should be plentiful, and the foreign demand for manufactures should increase, the business of the large manufacturing districts would continue; or should some foreign expedition furnish employment and pay for the surplus population of the kingdom, the bank of England might suspend without material injury to trade or manufacturers : the administration might not be even changed by the suspension, the government might continue firm, and the business of the country continue as though nothing had happened, and the bank might ultimately resume specie payment.

The notes of the bank of England are money, receivable by the goverment in the payment of all rates, taxes and dues accruing to the government; and in the payment of all private debts, and commercial transactions within the kingdom. And while the balance of trade was not against England, her bills on America and other countries where she had funds, stocks or moneys lent upon interest, would enable her to continue her foreign commerce, (as her bank paper would support her domestic business,) as perfectly as she could do with the precious metals in abundance.

But reverse the wheel of fortune. Let the crops be light and insufficient for domestic consumption, the demand for manufactures for exportation be checked or removed altogether, and discontent accompany distress and hunger at home, in the agricultural districts, as well as in the manufacturing towns ; and for the want of capital, labor should cease, an advance in the price of bread-stuffs must immediately follow, without an increase of the means of payment, if they must be imported ; the corn laws must be re-

pealed, or the people must starve, and with their repeal under such circumstances, the landed interest must suffer.

England mighl then rejoice in her American investments.
It may be safer and better for the government, as well as
for individuals, to have more resources than one ; for, in
times of difficulty and danger, it may not be the safest way
to have all one's effects in one boat : and American funds
are valuable commodities to exchange for English stocks
with those who are desirous of removing to America. If
times should become harder and more intolerable, and property inconvertible, a small investment in American stocks
will be comfortable, besides American stocks, to persons
living in America, pay a higher interest than English stocks.

But from all this we see, that in England the notes of the
bank of England must remain nearly convertible as long
as the government preserves its present form. The notes
of the bank of England would be as convertible into most
kinds of property, and be nearly as current under a suspension of specie payment as they are at present. The
brokers would probably advance a shade on the price of
specie upon the first suspension of specie payment; but
should a wide difference exist between bank of England
notes and specie, the convertibility of the funded debt would
be proportionably diminished—the bills of the chancellor
of exchequer would be returned in the payment of taxes—
the monied men of the nation would waver in their uniform support of the administration—business men would
fear to extend their operations—the laboring classes would
find lessened employment and lessened wages, with increased
demands for prompt payments, which accompany diminished credit. The government would be driven to rely upon
physical aid for support. This would be unpopular among
the producers. Combinations would be formed against the

administration : minister after minister would be defeated—parliament must be dissolved.  Money would be liberally advanced to secure seats in parliament.  Candidates would make innumerable promises of cheap bread, better wages, and more employment, which each in turn would find himself unable to perform.  Discontent would increase; the poor would accumulate ; the producers would diminish; the strength of the tax-payers would become increased, while the powers of the collectors would be diminished. The demand for work, for wages, and for bread, would in crease, until the strong arm of hunger and necessity would seize whatever came within its reach.  The civil authority would be disregarded ; " might not right" would rule.  A military despotism or anarchy would govern the country. An equality of conditions would be sought by many; agrarian principles would become popular among the people.  The army and navy could no longer be paid by collections from the people ; the mutiny act could no longer be enforced ; and an equality of conditions would produce an equality of feelings, and a concentration of designs and uniformity of operations.

The great secret of governing a nation, through fear, with a standing army, consists in keeping the people *poor* and *ignorant* : in this, then, consists the certain safety of the government of Great Britain.  When the landlords and fund-holders complain, their voices are heard.  They possess the sinews of war—the strength of the government—and they have the means of being felt, if they are not heard, when they complain.  In England, all the reforms have been brought about by the Barons, the landed aristocracy, or the fund-holders : the voice of the democracy of numbers is never heard, except through the wealthy of the nation.

The common laborers may not offend their masters, unless they would risk perishing in the streets. Their home, the subsistence of their families, and even their very existence, depends upon the will of their landlords. Therefore, while the landlord is contented the government is safe. When the wealthy rise, the government must fall. Hence a government debt there, is the bond of union between the people and government, that cannot be dissolved, until the government are unable to meet the payment of the interest on the debt, and support their civil, military and naval armaments.

But a government debt in the United States is a very different thing. Its credit depends upon entirely different principles. The people are the sovereign power. They could never make money by taking out of one hand to pay the other, while liberty and equality exists among them. Suppose one administration to involve the country by their extravagance, improvidence or ambition, they would assuredly be expelled from office very soon; and their successors in office would hardly feel themselves bound to tax themselves and friends to support the extravagance of their predecessors—their political opponents. They would hardly incur the odium attendant upon direct taxation to meet promptly demands for debts contracted against their votes and in opposition to their opinions.

Suppose, under such circumstances, the balances of trade for some time should continue against the United States ; and that remittances could only be made in specie. The collection of taxes in specie for exportation, under a heavy depression of trade, could not long continue to be popular. Importing merchants would find much inconvenience in making remittances to meet their importations, and would unwillingly become defaulters in a foreign country.

There is, to say the least of it, some uncertainty in the convertibility of paper to circulate as money, based upon *any thing* but the precious metals, but more especially upon government debts, where the payment of that debt depends upon a vote of a popular legislature. Republics should always avoid the contraction of debts, that circumstances may render extremely difficult for them to pay. Direct taxation is uniformly obnoxious to the people. Imposts and duties on imported articles are slowly collected, and subject to many contingencies and circumstances liable to its defeat. Direct taxation, although generally the most obnoxious, is uniformly the most certain and expeditious mode of raising a revenue. When the trade of a country has been free for any length of time, the imposition of heavy duties checks importations, and changes the investment of capital from mercantile to manufacturing business.

The tariff ought not to be lightly changed, unless under circumstances of absolute necessity, except upon a scale for years, that capitalists may make their changes of capital with safety and permanence.

Hasty and ill-advised changes in the tariff, unsettles trade and deranges commerce. When the balance of trade is largely against a country, duties may lessen importations; and unless it is attended with a corresponding diminution of exports, it may aid in restoring the balance of trade.

Until I can believe that chartered bank *credit* paper is money, and that such money may continue to circulate as specie in any unlimited quantity, and be used as capital, I shall have my doubts of the wisdom of extending credit by heaping credit upon credit, beyond the actual demand for business purposes, and the limits laid down permanently for the issue of not more than three times the amount of specie actually in the vaults of the bank at the time of the discount. The currency should be permanently uniform, that it may not constitute an unequal measure of values, and that it may safely pass currently from hand to hand, without surcharging the channels of circulation. For, whenever the channels of currency are surcharged, there will be an immediate tendency of the currency to be exported; the specie only being exportable, that of course constitutes the whole exportation. The pressure upon the channels of circulation will be relieved immediately upon the exportation of but a very small amount of specie. The precious metals will not be exported so long as stocks of any kind can be sold in the foreign market at par, or bills of exchange be purchased to meet foreign demand. American stocks have been sold in England, until the interest due on them from the different states amounts to several millions annually.

Thus the United States of America, with a fertile soil, salubrious, inviting, healthful climate, pure purling streams of water, and immense variety of superior timber—inhabited by a hardy industrious race of economical and ingenious inhabitants, have become tributary to a nation whose capital is an irredeemable debt of £800,000,000 sterling; and all through extravagance, induced and encouraged by the facilities of borrowing, produced by the great number of credit paper machines, and the amount of paper that their private interest induces them to palm upon the public as money. The use of which, like the use of distilled liquors, has been so long continued in the U. States, that business men almost fancy they cannot live without it. Bank credit is useful when properly used and not abused ; but, as dis-tilled spirits should not be relied on as food, although it prevents hunger, neither should bank credit be used as capital. Many of our citizens, from witnessing the evils of excessive expansions and contractions of the currency, have honestly come to the conclusion, that paper money of any description ought never to be used, or allowed to circulate. We aim at the medium course. We would no sooner use bank credit as capital, than we would use distilled spirits for food; and yet, we would use either the one or the other when necessary—that is, we would use distilled spirits only as a remedy when other better remedies could not be found, and we would use only so much bank paper as would barely supply the deficiency of the precious metals, and to meet the actual demand for currency to transfer the commodities of the country from hand to hand.

I am not prepared to say, that it would not have been better for sober, honest, republican Americans, if neither distilled spirits nor bank paper had been known among them; but having been known and used, and habits having been formed upon their use, they can hardly be wholly dispensed with, without violence to society. Unfortunately some men have been so completely consumed by distilled spirits, that by instantly withholding it from them altogether, they must sink under the deprivation; so there are some men who have so completely allowed the banks to absorb their whole substance in bank discounts, and interest on notes to the bank, that without bank credit they would hardly be able to continue their business.

I would not do injustice to any, or subject them to inconveniences from the restriction of their credits. In short, the plan proposed would rather encourage than diminish *sound* bank credit, and afford those who have used fictitious paper and bank credit for capital, time to wind up their business in the best manner possible; while it will furnish them with a better currency, and a more certain and safe

mode of transacting business, using such paper only as is
equal to specie wherever it is required to be used.

The establishment of one general free system of banking throughout the United States, with a centralized government and divided administration, would give the people
the regulation of the monetary affairs of the country, as
they have of their political, religious or literary institutions ;
while it affords them a mixed currency, with gold and silver for those who prefer hard money, and large bills for
those to whom paper money, perfectly convertible and uniformly current, is preferable.

This at first appears rather hypothetical; but before we
despair, let us examine the subject and see what reason we
have for believing that giving the people the direction of
the currency, and the election of the directors of the banks
of discount, would not restrict the discounts and direct them
into their proper channels, domestic circulation, and thereby lessen our imports.

## ON THE CURRENCY TO BE PRODUCED BY FREE BANKING.

The United States bank bills, upon the system of free
banking, should be issued to each state in proportion to the
amount of currency required for the business of the state,
aided by the specie reserved for small change. These
bills, and the specie upon which they are to be issued,
should be apportioned by the state directors between the
banks of discount, in each county or city, where banks of
discount are located. The election of the directors of the
banks of discount by the people, will change the business
of the banks, improve the state of the currency, and benefit the exchanges. The directors of the banks of discount,
having given good security for the faithful discharge of
their duties ; they should execute the bills apportioned to

them for circulation, and commence business, by discounting only actual business paper, having but short periods to run, to an amount *not exceeding three times the amount of specie actually in the vaults of the bank at the time of the discount.* The directors should be prohibited from discounting any note or acceptance in which the director of any bank had any interest; and the receipt of any bonus, private fee or perquisite for such bank accommodation, should be made an indictable offence, and punishable by fine or imprisonment.

If " self-love be the spring of action that moves the soul," when we have secured the private interest of the directors of the banks in favor of the accommodation of the fair trader, he will be most likely to be accommodated to the lessening of the business of speculators.

The directors will be selected for their skill, ability and integrity as financiers; their securities being ample, they will have no perquisites or " stealings " to induce corrupt conduct.

The directors being removed from *temptation to fraud,* and receiving such salaries as would be sufficient to command the *best and ablest financiers,* without making it an object worthy of great sacrifice to obtain at an election, will also aid in rendering bank notes sound and convenient.

The business of the directors should be clearly defined, and comport with the public interest. They would then soon learn that if they discount a speculator's note for $50,-000, although that might have been made more profitable to the stockholders, by having the sum paid in some distant market, yet as this would deprive them of the power of lending five hundred dollars each to one hundred men, it would be more to the interest of the directors to secure the votes of the 100 fair traders, than of the one speculator,

They will, therefore, be most likely to accommodate the many, and let the speculator have only an equal share with them, making their notes payable at the office of discount.

Their duties and interests coinciding with the wishes of the inhabitants, they will do good to the greatest numbers, at the least danger of loss or expense, and preserve the paper portion of the currency convertible, sound, and current throughout the Union. Their monthly published statements would give the people, as well as the state directors, the means of witnessing their whole proceedings, and dictating or preventing any improvidence, peculation or fraud, of any bank of discount, before the evil could become extended and dangerous to the institution.

The prices of all commodities would be advanced as money became easy ; and as importations of foreign merchandize ceased to control the money of the country, that would become invested in domestic manufactures.

Thus all classes of American citizens would be benefitted, financially and politically, by having the control and regulation of the currency as they have of the affairs of the townships.

The prosperity of a place, like the prosperity of individuals, depends more upon the uniform healthy growth and increase of the business of the place, than upon any temporary expansion of the business of the place. For, after expansions there will assuredly follow contractions. An increase of expenses are usual during expansions, with diminished means of meeting the contractions firmly. For instance : the man whose business was worth to him $1,000 annually, by excessive temporary expansions of credit and business may have his profits increased to $1,500 a year. This causes him to relax in his diligent and unremitted exertions in acquiring wealth, by which he looses some profits upon his business, while his expenses keep pace with his increased income, as nearly as they did when his income was but $1,000. He rents more expensive buildings for his accommodations, and most of his former savings are invested in the improvement of these rented premises, the fixtures of which cannot be sold, should he at once wish to retrench his expenses, by being released from his higher rent, which his lessened profits may require. Besides this, his family may have just received and returned the visits of a class of citizens of more leisure, and of a style of living above what his former prudence had justified.

When the contractions of the currency reduces his income to far less than his former $1,000 a year, he begins to regret his increased expenses, and would fain return to his former habits of industry and economy. He sees that his only safe course is prompt and immediate retrenchment : yet this is opposed by his own vanity, the feelings and new fledged hopes of his family. He sees, if he returns to his former lodgings, he must positively loose largely in the relinquishing the house he has but recently had fitted to his taste and convenience, and in his new furniture, adapted to the place and situation of the house. If he continues in the house, his other expenses must keep pace with the appearances he has commenced, or be subject to the unfavorable remarks of his former associates.

What is to be done ? Disgrace must attend him, sooner or later, whatever course he may take. While he debates in his own mind, and hesitates what to do, his daily increased expenses still continue, until he is compelled to use some part of his business capital to support his style of living, or what is worse, to contract debts for luxuries which he feels he cannot long maintain. He now sees, and to his sorrow, feels, that, but for the inflation of the currency by the char-

tered banks, he would not have been led to these expenses,
and the unnecessary debts he has incurred, but he would
have quietly pursued his former safe and profitable way;
and had that been his good fortune, he would not now be
met at every turn with the taunts and sneers that encounter
him wherever he goes.

His domestic peace and felicity have fled with the failure
of bank credit; its discounts have been checked, and ruin
has followed. The family have lost confidence in each other's good, and honest intentions. The house is divided
against itself: the wife against the husband—the children
against the father, and the father against the children. Business becomes neglected—the family become disorgani-
zed—division exposes their follies or weaknesses, and envy
gives new fangs to scandal; social intercourse is interrup-
ted—domestic happiness, and all the warm, generous feelings of the heart, are destroyed. For all these evils, he
may thank bank expansions and unlimited bank credit.—
Property falls in price—wages fall—money rises—and the
banks refuse to discount paper for any but the directors or
stockholders themselves.

The directors have but one duty to perform, and but one
interest to regulate all their operations; and that is, the
amount of the dividends of the bank. Their business is to
make as much money for the stockholders as they lawfully
can. Consequently, if speculators will pay them in a distant market, where the price of bills is above the value of
money at the place of the discount, they will accommodate
these speculators, although they must restrict their discounts
to their regular customers to the same amount. The only
question for the directors to settle is, which will be the most
profitable, and this can always be settled by mathematical
calculations. When dealing in exchanges will pay better

than discounting the business paper of the place, buying and selling bills of exchange becomes the order of the day with the banks.

The loan of $50,000 and the payment of that sum in a market where the profit upon the sale of bills is from 5 to 10 per cent. every ninety days, gives a clear gain to that amount, which the fair traders of the place cannot expect to compete with. The only avenues to the favors of banks are through their direct interest, as shown by the dividends.

Another mode of increasing the profits of the bank is, by discounting notes for a much larger amount than is to be drawn—one half of the amount, or such a proportion as can be agreed upon, being left in the bank as a deposite ; increasing the profits of the bank fifty per cent. and showing, upon inspection by commissioners from the legislature, a fair exhibit.

Well, we have before seen, that in the people's republican free bank, the directors would be governed by directly the opposite principles. They would not have loaned so large a sum to foreign speculators, for, with directors elected by the people, their ability to aid them in their election would be trifling, when compared with the votes of fifty or one hundred regular dealers of the place, who must have been disappointed in their discounts, and consequently in their business, by the accommodation of these speculators, because they could or would pay the bank in a dis_ tant place, where bills drawn by the banker for the amount would be worth ten times the profits on the loan of the same amount of money to regular dealers. Besides this, the directors of the people's bank would be liable to be reprimanded for departing from the regulations of the bank in accommodating the few to the exclusion of the many.

These regulations should be clear and definite ; simply requiring the directors to discount only safe *actual business paper*, having but short periods to run, in which no director has any interest.

One of the decided advantages of separating currency from *private interest* is, the direction of currency into its legitimate channels, that whatever profit is made upon the business of supplying the public with a circulating medium should go into the right pockets.

The pervertion of the business of banking to that of brokerage, would be such an infringement of their regulations as to subject them to an investigation before the state directors, and leave themselves and their bail accountable for their malversation.

Bankers should never lend money with the view of aiding speculators ; as they firstly borrow all the money that the banks have to lend, then, having monopolized the money of the place, they monopolize the business of the place, injure the fair trader, the producer, and the business of the country, for the benefit of themselves and the banker. For he who gets large loans can regulate the price of the commodities he is purchasing. The farmer, therefore, really often receives less money for his beef, pork, wheat or flour, than he would have received from the regular business men of the place, had the speculators not been interfered with. One speculator, with fifty thousand dollars, will be less likely to raise the price of commodities, than fifty speculators, with the same amount of money divided between them. Prices may, however, be temporarily advanced by speculators ; but suppose they pay ten per cent. advance upon the regular prices for the articles they purchase ; suppose they purchase wheat, and that, in consequence of their monopolizing the money of the place, the price of wheat should be advanced ten per cent., this would appear at first sight to be so much actually in the pockets of the farmers, but when it is recollected that so much of the money as is monopolized by the wheat speculator is abstracted from the purchase of other commodities, it will appear plain that the price of other articles must be depreciated in just the same proportion that the price of wheat is advanced. Hence we see again, that loaning large sums to speculators, if they do advance the prices of some articles, they diminish the prices of other articles in a still greater proportion.

We have before stated, that regular prices, in good money, in hand paid, even although the price be somewhat lower, is far better than the same amount of money, expended in high prices for some articles and lessened prices for other articles, accompanied with uncertainty. This may be thus illustrated : The farmer, finding that wheat pays a profit of ten per cent. more than any other commodity this year, very probably makes the growth of wheat his principal article of farming for exportation for the next year, when, to his surprise, he finds the price of wheat very low, that there are no speculators in the wheat market this year. The price of wheat the preceding year having been advanced above its real value, did not pay as well as many other articles of produce to its dealers ; and hence fewer persons engage in the speculation of wheat the ensuing years. The farmer has not the usual quantity of other commodities for sale, and the price of wheat is as much below par this year as it was last year above par, while his expenses have been increased to keep pace with his expected large crop, and high price of wheat : he finds himself involved in debt and ruin. He may charge the whole of his misfortunes to interested temporary expansions of the currency by chartered banks.

Private interest, unlimited credit, and *limited individual responsibility*, connected with the issue of paper to circulate as money, as they exist in chartered banks, must produce expansions of the currency in times of prosperity, to be followed by consecutive contractions in times of adversity.

The directors, being only responsible to the stockholders, whose interest is not the same as that of the other inhabitants of the place, the stockholders must be profited, although the inhabitants should be ruined. The laws of their situation compel them to make as large dividends as they legally can.

But change the interest of the bank directors, by changing their electors—let them be elected by the people instead of the stockholders—will not the same men use the same zeal and diligence in serving their new electors faithfully, that they formerly have in serving their old electors ? If they are as well paid they undoubtedly will. The new electors will have one common interest with the directors, that of doing the most good to the greatest number, at the least expense ; and this interest and these principles must govern the business of the banks that furnish a sound currency, and plenty of it.

The *sole business* of bankers is to make money for themselves, upon the investment of their capital in bank stock. This has been repeated and may be repeated, " line upon line and precept upon precept," and yet not appear to be sensibly brought to the full knowledge of mankind. Bankers are blamed for not doing more business. They are blamed for not lending more credit. Then they are blamed for not redeeming what they have loaned. If the directors were chosen by the people, and accountable to them for their conduct, the public could hardly be more

censorious upon bank directors than they frequently are
now. I do not complain of the bankers, the stockholders,
or the directors. They are perfectly consistent in their business. They are governed in all their operations by the
laws of their situations. Their *love of money* is not exclusively or peculiarly the weakness or property of bankers—
it is common to human nature ; and if the government
gives them exclusive privileges for their private interest
and aggrandizement, is it at all remarkable that they should
exercise their privileges during the short time they are
likely to be allowed to enjoy them to the best advantage ?
Credit ever has its ebbings and flowings ; and like the tides
that follow closely behind the moon, so does American
credit follow foreign exchanges, with this very material
difference, however, that the full and neap tides occur at
regular periods, and may be anticipated, and their dangerous effects guarded against, while credit bank paper is
equally fluctuating, but far less regular and certain in its
fluctuations.

To have a sound currency in a republican country, the
people must elect the directors of their banks from among
themselves. They must be persons whose interests are
identical with the people, and who can by no possibility
have any private interest in the discounts of the bank. A
careful supervision of the banks of discount by the state
banks, with full monthly published statements of the business of the banks, would soon correct the defects of the
paper currency, that are so loudly complained of by all parties not interested in the abuses of public confidence, daily
experienced by holders of bank notes and dependants
upon bank credits for their business.

The United States, to remain independent, must establish a sound currency. They must be released from debt.

They must reduce their imports to the par exchange of their exports. They must establish a standard measure of all values, as immutable and uniform as our weights and measures. They must provide for the election of the directors of the banks by the political electors of the country, as freely and independently as the election of township officers are provided for by the laws of the states. The currency must be based exclusively upon the precious metals, and rendered uniformly perfectly interchangeable. The discounts must be restricted to actual business paper, having but short periods to run. In short, the issue of bank paper intended to circulate as money, should be so conducted, as to render it equally current with gold and silver in every part of the Union, and as easily to be obtained as any other commodity; and such a system is intended to be the one proposed. Enquiry is important to the thorough knowledge of the currency, and to its necessary and perfect reform. Let those who have leisure and ability engage in the important task, and it will, it must be accomplished.

## CHAPTER XLI.

### SAFETY FUND.

#### THE SAFETY FUND PRINCIPLE ADAPTED TO FREE BANKING.

In the plan herein proposed, the safety fund principle is well adapted to the preservation of that equilibrium and uniformity of circulation so eminently desirable in the circulating medium.

The dividends to be made to the stockholders, being made from the whole profit of all the banks of discount collected and summed up, firstly by the state directors of each state, and finally by the United States directors, from the returns made to each state by the banks of discount, and transmitted to them through the state directors, there will be no jealousy of the prosperity of the institutions of one state over those of another, nor of the success of one bank of discount of a state over the other banks of the same state. Thus the United States directors might order, that the safety fund principle be applied to all the banks; that a given sum be preserved for a safety fund, and profitably disposed of, as the safety funds of the safety fund banks of the state of New York are at this time employed, or in such other profitable manner as they may deem proper.

To the stockholders, this fund would only be a reserved profit, ultimately to be enjoyed as a bonus and not a loss to the public. It would still be so much capital for general business purposes, whether used as any portion of the currency, or otherwise. The stock, being all bought and paid for in specie, delivered to the directors of each state, subject to the apportionment by the United States directors between the several states, to be by the state directors apportioned between the banks of discount in each state (the coin would not all require to be moved from place to place, the balances only would require actual transportation.) This would enable one or more banks, upon this plan, to go into immediate operation, that the stockholders might not loose their dividends from the time of the first payment, until the whole business of the country would ultimately be conducted upon this general free banking system.

That capitalists, desirous only of increasing their capital profitably, safely and honorably, would prefer stock in this general United States bank, there can be but little doubt. But that speculators, who have long made money by shaving and passing uncurrent money upon the public at par, and by buying it again below par, through the agency of their brokers, will be violent against this system, there can be as little reason to hope. Their craft is in danger. Sharks in the business of brokers, and black-legs in the gambling of the currency, succeed best with the most defective systems of currency, and plunder the public with most facility during times of fluctuations of the currency, suspensions of specie payments by the banks, and oppressive contractions. As the proposed plan is intended to obviate and prevent these evils of the currency, this class of citizens may be expected to withhold their funds from the institution.

The habits of the American people of " going ahead " with whatever they undertake to do, renders a sound currency more indispensably necessary in the United States, than in most other countries ; for they earn money with all their might, and with all their powers of body or mind, and when they have earned it, no people ever spend it more freely, or enjoy it better while they have it to spend ; no object of charity but what receives their kindest private blessing and public munificence. To lessen this diffusive habit, and to restrict the exhuberance of their passions for amusements, and for show and parade, the precious metals are far preferable to credit bank paper money. But there is a force and energy of character peculiar to Americans, that should never be repressed or crushed. All the elementary principles of the government, except that of currency, promote and encourage it. Currency, on the contrary, is aristocratic, illiberal, exclusive, partial and uncertain.

The second sober thought of Americans is always correct. As soon as they can find leisure, from the hurry of passing their doubtful chartered bank notes, lest the banks should fail while the notes are in hand, they will see that

there is some radical defects in the present paper portion of
the currency, and in good earnest set about discovering
and remedying them.

## CHAPTER XLII.

### ON THE NEW-YORK GENERAL BANKING LAW.

The law—12¼ cents in the dollar in specie—87½ cents in credit—Advantages—Disadvantages.

This law has established a new era in banking in the United States. It has substituted public debts, and mortgages
on lands, in part, for a basis upon which to issue paper to
circulate as money; twelve and a half per cent. only of the
amount of notes in circulation, being by this law required
to be kept in the business of the bank in specie.

It is true, that from the tenor of the law, one would be
led to view the government bonds and mortgages, pledged
to the Comptroller of the state in security to the bill-holder
for the redemption of the bills as collateral security, and be
led to infer, that the ordinary security of incorporated banks
to the bill-holder remained unchanged, and that, therefore,
the bills of the New York General Banking Law system
were doubly secure. But here is the fallacy : incorporated
banks are only allowed to issue three times the amount of
paper money that they have specie, or paid up capital, while
the New York General Banking Law allows the directors
of banks established under it, to issue eight times as much
bank paper to circulate as money, as they are required to
have of specie in their vaults ; and upon their failing to redeem their notes in specie, the twelve and a half per cent.

is no part of the security to the bill-holder, as the associations are *expressly* released from all responsibility for the redemption of their notes, or for costs. The property of the
association, and the security pledged with the Comptroller
for the redemption of the bills of the bank, are the whole
of the security to the bill-holder.

The security for the bill-holder, given to the Comptroller of the state, may consist of any portion of the public
debt of the United States, or of any individual state, equal
to New York state five per cent. stocks; for which the
Comptroller shall deliver to the person, or association of
persons, an equal amount of bills in blank, which he shall
have procured in the best form, to prevent counterfeiting,
countersigned, numbered, and registered in proper books,
bearing the uniform signature of such registerer. Or the
person, or association of persons, may,in part, pledge lands in
the state of New York, by transferring to the Comptroller
bonds and mortgages upon real estate, bearing at least six
per cent. interest, to double the amount of bills received
for circulation upon this security; and after the person or association shall have executed the bills, making them payable in specie at sight, at the place where they are to be put
in circulation, they may be passed and circulated as money.
The depositor may receive interest on the debts or mortgages pledged, so long as he redeems the notes for which the
security is held, and no longer.

The provisions of the New York General Banking Law,
will be better comprehended from the following synopsis of
the law.

The law authorises the Comptroller to cause to be engraved and
printed, in the best manner, to guard against counterfeiting, such
quantity of circulating notes, in the similitude of bank notes, in
blank, of the different denominations authorised by law, as he may

deem necessary; and he shall cause the same to be countersigned, numbered and registered, in proper books provided for that purpose; and each note shall bear the uniform signature of a registerer.

Whenever any person, or association of persons, formed for the purpose of banking under the provisions of this act, shall legally transfer to the Comptroller any portion of the public debt of the state of New York, or of any other state, or of the United States, equal to five per cent. stocks of the state of New York,

The person or association transferring the same, shall be entitled to receive from the Comptroller, an equal amount of such circulating notes, of different denominations, countersigned, numbered and registered as aforesaid.

Such person or association of persons are authorised, after having executed such notes, so as to make them payable on demand at the place where they are issued, within the state of New York, to loan and circulate the same as money.

In case such person or association of persons, shall fail or refuse to redeem such notes in the lawful money of the United States, when demanded, according to law, the holder of such notes may cause them to be protested for non-payment by a Notary Public; and the Comptroller, upon receiving and filing such protest, after notifying the maker of the same, if the maker shall omit to pay the same for ten days after the notice, the Comptroller shall give notice in the state paper, that all the circulating notes of such person or association will be redeemed out of the trust funds in his hands for that purpose; which he shall do, together with costs of suit.

The depositor may receive the interest, or dividends of the stock, unless they shall fail to redeem their notes, or unless the stocks deposited shall not be deemed by the Comptroller sufficient security for the circulating bills.

The Comptroller may change the bonds to make the bill-holder more secure.

Or in lieu of receiving such stocks, the Comptroller may receive security for one-half of the amount of bills so to be issued, by having mortgages on productive improved lands, yielding not less than six per cent. per annum, assigned to him for twice the amount of bills issued upon such security.

The persons assigning such mortgages to the Comptroller, may receive the interest on the same, unless upon default to redeem their notes or secure the bill-holder as aforesaid.

The plates, dies, and materials procured by the Comptroller for the printing of such notes, shall remain with him and be paid for out of the St; te Treasury, and be reimbursed by a per centage on such notes sufficient for that purpose.

The aggregate amount of such association shall not be less than $100,000.

Any association may provide for an increase of their capital and the number of their associates.

The association shall be capable of sueing and being sued, BUT THEIR JOINT PROPERTY ONLY SHALL BE HELD LIABLE FOR THE DEBTS OF THE ASSOCIATION, unless their articles of association shall declare otherwise.

Such association shall make out and verify, under oath, to the Comptroller, a full statement of the affairs of the association in January and July annually.

Which statement shall contain

The amount of capital stock paid or secured to be paid;

The value of the real estate of the association, specifying what portion is occupied as necessary to the transaction of the business of the association;

The shares of stock held by the association, whether absolutely or as collateral security ; specifying the number and value of each kind and description of stock, and the number and value of the shares of each ;

The amount of debts due the association, particularizing from whom due, and how secured, and the amount that ought to be included in the computation of losses;

The amount of debts due by such association, specifying such as are payable on demand, and such as are due to monied or other corporations or associations;

The amount of claims against the association not acknowledged by its debts;

The amount of notes, bills, or other evidences of debt, issued by such association;

The amount of its losses, and statement of its dividends, during the same period ;

The average amount in each month, during the preceding six months, of the debts due and specie possessed during each month; the amount of notes put in circulation as money, and outstanding on the first day of each of the six months ;

The amount due the association from the share-holders;

The names of all the parties that may have been added, or may have withdrawn, and the amount of increased capital during the last six months.

The Comptroller shall publish monthly statements of the association.

The officers shall keep a list of the names of the share-holders, and shall file a copy of such list in the office of the clerk of the county, and in the office of the Comptroller, on the first Mondays of January and July, in every year.

The association shall not make notes of a less denomination than one thousand dollars, payable at any other place than at the office where the business of the association is carried on and conducted.

They shall not have less than twelve and a half per cent. in specie in their vaults for more than twenty days at any one time.

This synopsis of the New York General Banking law, evinces a desire on the part of the legislature to secure the bill-holder. How well they have succeeded we will con. sider hereafter, and time will show.

This system however has its advantages. It gives less immediate power of expansion of the currency to the banks of discount. It separates the private interest of the banks of discount from the bank of issue, (as the Comptroller's office may not inappropriately be styled.) It furnishes a uniformity of currency throughout the state, and a uniformity of bills for circulation, in their engravings, and printings, and in certain parts of their execution, bearing the uniform signature of the registrar, numbering, and countersigning. And the system furnishes a better representative of property than the incorporated bank system does, but whether its bills more nearly resemble the precious metals than the bills of incorporated banks remain to be tested.

The proposed plan provides for a still greater uniformity of the bills, especially in their execution, and for their uni-

form general current circulation throughout the several
states of the Union. Hence, if there are advantages in the
uniformity of circulation throughout one state, the proposed
plan extends these benefits, with superior force, throughout
the Union; and provides for a still more perfect similarity
of all the bills of circulation throughout the Union.

The bills of the same denomination should be precisely
similar throughout their engraving and printing, and have
the uniform signatures of the United States directors; and
possessing the advantage in each state of being countersigned
by the State directors; after which, the directors of each
bank of discount should execute them, making them redeemable in specie at sight at the bank of discount where
they were put in circulation.

This similarity of the bills of circulation throughout the
Union, would enable commercial men to judge of the truth
or forgery of any bill from any bank of discount, in any
state of the Union, almost as well as they could judge of the
bills of his own state. This would facilitate the extension
of the circulation, and equalize it throughout the Union, and
thereby give the paper portion of the money-currency a
more perfectly metalic character.

Whenever a paper currency can once assume, throughout the Union, a perfectly metalic character for convertibility, (and the proposed plan, well conducted, must give the
currency that character,) the bills of these banks will be
equal to specie in the amounts in which they are issued for
domestic circulation and business, and preferable to specie
for making remittances. The immense saving that a uniform currency throughout the Union would be to the public,
is quite incredible, and can only be estimated by observing
the great number of brokers, who amass large fortunes rapidly in every part of the Union by "shaving" the public,

that is, by exchanging the money of one place for that of
another, or by selling current bankable money to those who
have payments to make in the banks, or to some public office, or to some particular individual, where the currency of
the place, for barter, for produce, or for merchandize, will
not be received, and by charging a per centage on the exchange for the accommodation.

An important feature of the New York General Banking
law, is the separation of the power of issuing paper to circulate as money, from the power of discounting notes and
putting them in circulation; or, in other words, in separating
the bank of issue from the banks of discount. Thus removing the power of increasing the issues, upon any temporary excitement or prosperity, or upon the occasion of great
demand, or of great temporarily increased ability, as upon
the receipt of a large public or private deposite, from the
control of the directors of the banks of discount to officers
of issue, altogether free from the private interest of the association of discount, or sympathy with the borrower, whose
situations may safely be considered by the credit dealers of
the country, but who should never influence, in the slightest
degree, the money-currency of the country. This sympathy, together with the hope of gain by stockholders of incorporated banks, induces an increase of circulation to
meet any emergency or chance for gain; thereby inflating
the currency of the place to the amount of the increased issues, to be followed by an equal or greater excess of contraction, and extended ruin. The greatest habitual evil of
incorporated banks is, their excessive expansions of the
currency and consequent ruinous contractions, with their occasional suspensions and inconvertibility of their paper.

The continued free and uniform convertibility of paper,
to circulate as money, is never to be lost sight of while
speaking of currency.

Suppose that the New York General Banking law should, from its apparent better security to the bill-holder, obtain the entire control of the currency of the state, and its bills be extended and circulated through every ramification and channel of business in the state of New York, and in the adjoining states; and that the interest of the different associations should become such as to induce a mutual forbearance in the demand of specie to redeem balances in each other's hands, and thus the currency of the state should be inflated until there would be in circulation eight times as much paper money as there would be specie in the state, their provision for the redemption of their notes in the cities of New York or Albany, which at first required only a small portion of the twelve and a half per cent., by law required to be kept as a specie basis to bank upon, would soon require to be greatly increased, and daily remittances for that purpose would become often necessary to meet the fluctuations in trade in a large city like New York, intimately connected with foreign commerce, and transacting daily an immense business upon credit. This must be followed by corresponding contractions of the discounts of the several banks; and some of them, failing to meet their city redemptions, would find themselves shortly after in the hands of the Comptroller of the state, and their liabilities in the hands of the Sheriff.

Suppose, at the same time, any casualty unfavorable to the trade of the Union, or to the sale of American stocks in England, should produce such a reversion in trade, and such an advance in the rate of exchange, that specie should be demanded for exportation to meet the interest on the large debt already contracted in England, what would be its effects on a currency consisting of only 12½ cents in the dollar in specie, and 87½ cents in the dollar of inconvertible credit? For here, let me remark, that the balance of trade between two countries, is a balance between the individual merchants of the two countries, and may be said never to be settled. Thus if all the imports and exports were entered at the Customs, which probably is not the case, there would be no great difficulty in ascertaining the state of the trade between the two countries; but as money is frequently conveyed in trunks, and about the persons of individuals, and as drafts, checks, bills of exchange, and various evidences of debt are transmitted from one country to another, without any entry of them being made either upon the clearance or entry of the vessel, the only feasible mode of judging of the balance of trade between two countries is by the rate of exchange between those countries; and this is not by any means a very definite method, as there are numerous causes that induce a rise or fall in the rate of exchange between two countries, independent of the immediate commerce between them; there are also causes that give the rate of exchange, as reported, to differ widely from what the actual exchange between the two countries is; thus the rate of exchange between the United States and England, when quoted a 9½ per cent. in favor of England, is really at par, owing to causes quite unconnected with the actual amount of exports or imports of the two countries.

## THE RATE OF EXCHANGE AND DESCRIPTION OF BARTER.

The rate of exchange may be varied by the sale of the public bonds of one country in the money market of the other; and where the balance of trade has been created by such a sale, it is against the country making the purchase.

This has been the situation of the trade between England and the United States, during the sale of American stocks in the English market.

Yet, as the rate of exchange between the two countries, independent of the sale of public stocks, was so largely against the United States, from the immense importations of British manufactures, that the sale of public stocks in England, within the last few years, even to the amount of two or three millions of dollars, did not raise the rate of exchange, or produce a balance of trade against England with the United States, at any one time to such an extent as to render the importation of specie to any considerable amount profitable. This is evident from the fact, that there are at this moment but small sums of British coin to be met with in the United States, which, if the avails of the sales of the public stocks now owned in England had been received here in money, the country would have been filled with British coin.

True, the payment for those public stocks may have been made in money; yet, since American merchants and bankers were indebted in England, bills of exchange upon some American merchant at New York or New Orleans, was better than specie, so they were received and specie was not imported into America. The rate of exchange always indicates the balance of trade between two countries, when not interfered with by banks or other artificial causes. The free exportation of specie is the only sure check upon over-trading and over-importing. When the exchanges are at par, bills are preferred to specie; the saving in each remittance being about one per cent. to cover insurance, freight, cartage, counting, and wear and tear of the precious metals. But where a remittance is to be made in the coin of one country, not receivable as coin in the other country—but as bullion—then the expense of coining or seigniorage, is still to be added to the other charges; making the exportation of specie so much more expensive, and the value of a bill of exchange so much the greater. Thus the price of bills of exchange, like the barometer of the weather, indicates the state of trade between two countries. The exportation of specie, or any other commodity, will be resorted to to equalize the trade between the two countries: this is the situation of the trade between the United States and England at this moment.

American coins pass as bullion in England, while English coins pass in the United States at or above their par value in England. The sovereign is worth a shade more by law in the United States, than it would be if it was coined into American gold coin. At the first appearance, one is led to consider the conduct of the English nation, in not receiving American coins of the same fineness with their own as coin, but only as bullion, as a great want of reciprocity; and so it undoubtedly is, yet the effects upon the American currency and American commerce, are not so injurious as it at first appears to be.

True, when the rate of exchange is so high against the United States as to render the exportation of specie necessary, the American merchant has to pay more for a bill, that is, he must pay, in addition to the ordinary expense of exporting specie, the price of the seigniorage or coinage, of the specie that must be sold as bullion.

By the purchase of British coin, for remittances in coin, the saving of a seigniorage is accomplished when British coin is to be bought in the American market; but the quantity of British coin being small in the United States, the remitter purchases some other commodity, as cotton, which, perhaps, he would not do but to save the small loss in a remittance that he must sustain if he remits American coin. This advances the price of cotton, or other articles of exportation, a shade higher than it would otherwise have

been. So this seeming want of courtesy and commercial
or financial reciprocity, on the part of the English, is not
so injurious to American prosperity as it appears to be.

It is not material where the exports of the remitter are
directed to be made, for the payment of a debt in France,
England, or the East Indies, or West Indies, the magic
power of bills of exchange, transfers the payer and receiver
both to London—the great seat and centre of British, European, Indian, and in fact of American commercial operations. The London Exchange is the focus, around which
the business, the commerce, the wealth, the credit, and the
exchanges of all these nations and countries revolve again
and again until they find their level, that is, their proper value. The exporters and importers from any country are
not uniformly the same individuals. If they were, much of
the necessities for bills of exchange could be dispensed
with ; because the exporter, selling his goods of one description (as of cotton,) to the house, or in the city from
which his outward bound cargo was to be taken, he could
barter the one commodity for another; as is often the case
in new countries, where goods are bought and sold for
other goods—cattle are exchanged for horses, for grain, or
for merchandise, called " store pay,"—and for the balances
notes are given, to be paid in so much produce, according
to the market price, or according to the current value at
such future period—or notes are given for so many bushels
of wheat of such and such a quality, to be delivered at such
a place, without any mention of price, or with a proviso,
that if the said note is not paid by such a particular time,
that the same shall be paid in so much money at some day
later; or what is not unfrequent in lumber countries or in
iron manufacturing countries, where the principal business
of the place is the producing one or two staple articles of

exportation, pot and pearl ashes, any and all of these commodities have often been used as the medium of exchange; and the owners of the large mills, furnaces, asheries or distilleries, become the banks of deposite to the people. The man who has lumber, iron, ashes, or whiskey, at one of these establishments, draws on the proprietor for the amount he owes, in the exchange of farms, horses, or oxen, or for the amount of his bill, for whatever he may have bought at the store; and the merchant charges such price for his goods as makes the article he receives equal to him in value to money. These bills are received and accepted by the banker, that is, the manufacturer, &c. The boards are not counted—the iron is not weighed—the ashes or whiskey are left in his possession, until the owner chooses to remove or transfer them to some other purchaser. Notes are often given for trade or for property, and no particular kind of property specified. In that case, the drawer of the note must deliver horses, hogs, cattle, sheep, lumber, iron, pot or pearl ashes, whiskey or merchandise, to the person to whom it was made payable at the time it was due, or the value would be expected in money. At times, this amount is described as being due in such an article as wheat or whiskey, at the price it will command at the time in some other place, where there are uniformly some buyers of the article, who will pay the money for the article; and the receiver of the article agrees to receive it at the residence of the man who pays the material, either in the expectation that the article will be worth as much there, as it will be at the place named, by which the price is to be governed : or he has added such a profit on his article of sale as will make his receipts equal to the expense of transporting the commodity to be received, to the nearest or best market.

In all these transactions, some of the leading principles

that govern the London exchanges are prominent features;
and, although from the bad roads and want of communica-
tions with other parts of the world, there is but little foreign trade or foreign commerce involved in the transaction,
yet they measure their property in dollars and cents, or in
pounds, shillings and pence, of a sound good currency, although their medium is every thing but money. Whenever the drawer or the acceptor of a bill fails to pay his note
bill or acceptance, the payee recovers in money, by law, a
judgement for the amount of the note. And it often requires much more of the promised material to meet the
payment in money, than it would have required had it been
met promptly in the commodity. This seems to be necessary, in order to induce punctuality in payments, and to
compensate the creditor for the delay in the receipt of his
property, or money, as it has now become. Where no sum
has been mentioned in the note or draft, as for so many
bushels of good merchantable wheat, or so many hundred
weight of black salts, or pot or pearl ashes, the jury will
give judgement against the defendant for so many dollars
as the quantity of the material would have been worth at
the time when due, and at the place mentioned.

CHAPTER XLIII.

THE BALANCE OF TRADE AND UNCURRENT MONEY.

The balance of trade between two countries, as was before observed, is the balance between the individual merchants of the two countries.

When the balance of trade is occasioned by the commercial transactions of the individual merchants of two countries, and entries have been made of the imports and exports

in the Custom Houses, some estimate of the state of trade may be had from these sources; but when the balance of trade has been created by the sale of state stocks of the one country, in the money market of the other country, the balance of trade is estimated from the rate of exchange, and the whole value of exports of one country, including stocks, specie, and merchandise, is compared with the whole amount of like imports. And hence, although the state of New York may have more wisely avoided running in debt, or have borrowed money from her own citizens, or from capitalists in the United States; for, even although it costs her even a shade more than to borrow money in a foreign country, there is still an advantage in borrowing money in the United States, for in making remittances to a foreign country, when the balance of trade is uniformly against the country, that amount, whether great or small, is to be added to the remittance by the remitter. Yet, when the avenues of the state are completely surcharged with paper money, and the specie has been exported, the demand for specie will be just as great from the state of New York, and from the banks supplying the currency to that state, as it is from the states that have sold stocks abroad, and have the remittances to make. Here the principle of the equalization of the currency, so happily illustrated by Adam Smith, in his comparison of currency with water, is exemplified.

The demand for specie, to make remittances from any one part of the country is extended over the Union, and becomes general; affecting such portions most as have most inflated their currency. Hence, if the whole amount of irredeemable credit paper in the state of New York, was equal to the whole amount of credit paper issued by all the banks in the other states of the Union, it is very clear that

the money pressure in the state of New York, during a
panic, would be far greater than in other states of the Union. This has been, unfortunately, repeatedly practically
illustrated during the last few years, particularly at the
south.

The following, from the New Orleans Price Current of
1840, will serve to illustrate the fact.

RATES OF SPECIE, BANK NOTES, &c.

| | | | | |
|---|---|---|---|---|
| Specie - - - - | 5 | to | 6 | per cent. prem. |
| Alabama State Bank and Branches - | 3½ | " | 4½ | " discount. |
| Tennessee Banks - - - | 4 | " | 6 | "        " |
| Arkansas Banks - - - | 30 | " | 35 | "        " |
| Pensacola, Florida, - - - | 20 | " | 25 | "        " |
| Life and Trust, Florida - - | 20 | " | 25 | "        " |
| Planters', Agricultural and Commercial, | | | | |
| on demand, (fives) - - | 5 | " | 10 | "        " |
| Do.   do.   branches, on demand - | 10 | " | 20 | "        " |
| Natchez Rail-Road - - - | 75 | " | 80 | "        " |
| West Felicana, at Woodville - | 16 | " | 20 | "        " |
| Bank of Port Gibson, (fives) - | 10 | " | 15 | "        " |
| Commercial Bank of Manchester - | 10 | " | 15 | "        " |
| Do.   do.   Rodney - | 35 | " | 45 | "        " |
| Union Bank of Mississippi - - | 55 | " | 60 | "        " |
| Commercial Bank of Columbus - | 30 | " | 40 | "        " |
| Grand Gulf Rail-Road Co. - - | 50 | " | 55 | "        " |
| Lake Washington and Dover Creek | 55 | " | 60 | "        " |
| Com. and Rail-Road Bank, Vicksburg | 55 | " | 60 | "        " |

POST NOTES.

| | | | | |
|---|---|---|---|---|
| Commercial, Agricultural and Planter's, | | | | |
| 12 months, spring of 1839, bearing in- | | | | |
| terest, - - - - - | 30 | " | 40 | "        " |
| Union Bank of Mississippi, bearing in- | | | | |
| terest, - - - - | 55 | " | 60 | "        " |
| Woodville, Manchester and Port Gibson | 30 | " | 40 | "        " |
| Rodney - - - - | 35 | " | 45 | "        " |
| Natchez Rail-Road - - - | 75 | " | 80 | "        " |
| Com. and Rail-Road Bank, Vicksburg | 60 | " | 70 | "        " |
| Water Works Bank        do· | 60 | " | 70 | "        " |
| Bank of Vicksburg - - - | 60 | " | 70 | "        " |
| Citizens' Bank of Madison County | 80 | " | 85 | "        " |
| Tombigbee Rail-Road Co. - - | 78 | " | 84 | "        " |
| Brandon Bank - - - | 93 | " | 95 | "        " |

And this is the currency for the south ! We will hereafter see what the currency of the North West is : see " currency of Michigan."

This is truly a beautiful comment upon the palatable doctrine, that credit bank paper is money : that incorporated banks enrich a country—that they add to the capital of a country—and that any thing that will pass as money, is equal to money, and is money !

Now let me ask, what principle is there in the New York General Banking law, that will prevent like results, from similar management of their banks ? Is there less *private interest ?*—is there less *credit ?* Private interest may be less directly temporarily exercised, but it is not the less powerful in its operation. And *credit is extended,* rather than being lessened ; yet, the apparently better security of the bill-holder may, by the increased liabilities of the company in the deposites with the Comptroller, more than balance this evil: time alone can tell ; to me it appears doubtful.

Next let me ask, what has caused the depreciation of the currency at the south and west ? Whatever the cause may have been, their returns to their respective legislatures show a previously inflated currency, and an intimate dependance upon *credit*, under the direction of *private interest*. Their discounts had been liberal ; had been made upon various evidences of debt instead of confining their discounts to the specie actually in their vaults at the time of their discounts. If " like causes produce like effects," although the pressure upon the money market in the state of New York, under the General Banking law, may be longer delayed, partly from the counterbalancing influences of the safety fund banks, and partly from the increased credit that these bills will be likely to enjoy at home, from a belief that the bill-holder is better secured than chartered banks secure their bill-holders, they having the properties of so many individuals pledged for their redemption. Besides, their personal exertions to favor each other, to collect safe-

ty fund notes, to raise specie for their own private uses, or
for exportation, may give the banks established under the
General Banking law important advantages, while it will
very materially lessen the safety of the " safety fund "
banks, or lessen their discounts, and, consequently, their
dividends.

The safety fund banks can have but little support from
each other, in giving a preference to their own bills over
the bills of the banks established under the General Banking law, because as *self-interest is the motive power*, the
banks under the General Banking Law have, to a certain
extent, one common interest—one bond of union—that of
extended credit, and like persons living in " glass houses," they are each of them unwilling to commence
throwing stones at the other. They even would, if occasion should require, aid each other, and collect the safety
fund bank notes to supply their demands for specie, while
the safety fund banks, from their limited responsibility,
have less to loose. Besides, the stockholders of incorporated companies have generally been able to secure
themselves in, and by their business of banking, whether
their notes were at par, or very far below par. Hence,
one real advantage of the banks of the General Banking
Law is, private responsibility and the vigilance of direct
interest to sharpen their attention to their business. From
all these causes they may be able to do business longer,
with the same amount of specie in their vaults, than the incorporated banks could. But, since the amount of specie
required to be kept in their vaults is less, (and few banks
for any length of time keep more specie on hand than the
law requires them to, unless they have some direct interest in so doing,) their issues are more dependant upon
credit than the issues of incorporated banks.

The banks under the General Banking Law, may issue eight times the amount of paper that they are required to have of specie in their vaults. But to make a paper dollar, having but one eighth part of its value in money in deposite—the remaining deposite being credit—pass current for any length of time, would be like making *bogus money* of twelve and a half per cent. of one of the precious metals and seven parts alloy, pass current as standard gold or silver coin : it would only pass so long as the public stock of gullibility lasted. This base coin might serve the public as well as credit paper money ; but take the spurious coin to an assayer, and it vanishes into smoke. So attempt to make foreign remittances in credit bank paper, and it evaporates like the base coin in the chaldron of the assayer : the chemical touch of the foreign specie exporter melts it to dross, and every body wonders how that could not have been foreseen.

True, the securities pledged with the Comptroller of state may ultimately redeem the notes. But this could not be done under a suspension of specie payments by the banks, as there could be no buyers ; nor until some favorable state of the money market enabled the Comptroller to sell debts and lands, the only security deposited with him for the redemption of the bills, could they be redeemed. But, supposing the securities could be sold, and the money be raised to redeem the bills at any time, and that the institutions, one after another, could be wound up, as some of them already have been, without loss to the bill-holder, the effects of the previous enormous expansions, owing to the evils of a credit currency, regulated by private interest, would be precisely the same. True, the bill-holder would not be the only loosers ; yet, the whole business of the country would be checked, and the contraction of the curreney (the certain consequence of previous expansion,) would lessen prices, retard improvements, throw thousands out of employment, and produce all the afflicting scenes that uniformly accompany collections and sales made by the sheriffs. It is probable, that the sales of bonds and lands by the Comptroller, might not proceed farther than would satisfy the actual demands for specie for remittances abroad, yet this would not afford any relief to the domestic business of the country. The other institutions would find the price of specie too high for them to purchase it, and attempt to extend their business upon the purchase. The rate of exchange would be too high for the purchase of bills to meet the demand for specie for remittances; and the only remedy for these credit paper-machines would be to contract their circulation, and thus relieve themselves from the universal pressure with which they are surrounded. Perhaps the first defaulters would be the only institutions forcibly disposed of at a sacrifice; for, it might happen for once, that men might learn wisdom from the past. But the pressure of the times would be severe indeed, when the banks shall actually *feel* the pressure. The expansions of the currency, and its fluctuations, are the great causes of complaint against credit paper being allowed to pass and circulate as money. The losses by bill-holders are to be avoided when that is possible; but I fear that the revulsion in business, and trade of the state of New York, produced by such a paper currency as shall substitute credit for capital, and securities for money, will be quite as great an injury to the state of New York, and last longer in that state, than the ruinous expansions of the currency of the state of Michigan by their " safety fund," " real estate pledged," and " private property holden" "wild cat" bank system has been to them. The shock will not be so sudden, nor violent, perhaps, in the state of New York, as it was in Michigan; but, if the currency is inflated upon credit to the same extent as it was in Michigan, the same discredit, fluctuation, depreciation, and contraction of the currency must follow : and it is yet to be seen whether the derangement of business, occasioned by an expansion of the currency is overcome, and the community enabled to commence a healthy business sooner, where the business passes through several changes before it is ultimately withdrawn from the public, or where it fails at once, and the bill-holders suffer the loss direct.   They are both of them loosing, gambling speculations to the public, and ought to be discountenanced by every honest man.

No farro bank, wheel of fortune, or roulette, is more certain to loose, or show a more plausible face, or greater probability to win, than does credit bank paper, when authorised to circulate as money.

Lotteries are now very generally wisely prohibited throughout the northern states of the Union; but when will the great and grand lottery of incorporated bank credit, with *limited responsibility*, *in chartered bank paper*, be dealt with after the same manner ?   Gambling vitiates the morals, destroys the mental and physical faculties, enervates the constitution, lessens the love of virtue, and of correct moral principles, and establishes artificial and desperate notions of honor, not founded in the moral law, but inconsistent with the doctrines of divine inspiration and revelation.

Virtue and intelligence are as indispensable to the peace, prosperity, perpetuity, and good government of a republic, as fire and water are to domestic comfort.

The moral education of the whole people of these United States, is not only wisely, but indispensably necessarily encouraged by every legislature in the Union.

Temperance societies, through the blessing of heaven, have checked, in a great measure, the fatal career in which the American public were madly wildly driving to destruction. Although intemperance be not entirely removed from the whole land, yet it has the mark of infamy and the stain of disgrace upon it in every form; and in every shape in which it makes its appearance, whether it be seen in the palaces of the rich, or in the hovels of the poor, at the private dinner or at the public festival of our national jubilee, the finger of scorn is pointed openly, honorably and publicly at it; and when thought shall have been tortured to find an epithet opprobrious enough to blast it with a breath, it will call it *intemperance.*

Vice will sooner hide its frightful head from shame than for legal enactments. Public sentiment should be directed to the pursuit of virtue and morality. Legislatures should carefully avoid encouraging an immoral spirit, by authorising an immoral practice. Far more can be done by removing the temptation to vice, than by penal enactments and severe punishments for crimes committed. In this opinion, I am supported by the history of the temperance reform; which proceeded with more uniform success, and accomplished more salutary and permanent benefits, under the mild guidance of *female* precept and *example,* than when legislatures have attempted to force this good upon the public, *nolens volens.*

Thus with regard to the circulating medium; I am more desirous to show the proposed plan to the public, than to compel them to adopt it. Reforms should always commence in the domestic circle, and proceed from thence to every channel of commerce, and every avenue of society. I would not attempt to reform by a rigid legislation, that should forcibly drive all credit paper from the business of

the country at once. That would be unjust, if not impracticable. Nor would I interfere with vested rights, or meddle with existing bank charters. But I would offer to
capitalists a better investment than private bank charters or
public debts would furnish ; freer from anxiety and care,
more readily convertible into specie at a moment's notice,
and more permanently secure in the regularity of its dividends, than other American investments.

It is true, the plan I propose precludes the stockholders
from that immense, improper, and powerful influence they
exercise in society, in the credit they possess in the legal
privilege and right to issue, lend, and circulate bank paper.

To those who desire an usurious, unjust profit for the use
of their money, my system of currency will be any thing
but palatable. I am ready to meet their demurrers, and
plead to them specially. But to convince them may be a
very different thing; for, " convince a man against his will,
and he is of the same mind still." But the honest money-
lender, who is desirous to receive only the highest fair rate
of interest, in the form of dividends, that can be safely and
honorable made, will see that this system possesses and
offers numerous decided advantages to the money-lender ;
in the lessened expense of the business of banking, and in
the increased amount of the dividends—in their being more
uniform, more permanent, and safer than any other funds
or stocks in America.

The expense of conducting an institution of this sort,
with five millions of dollars to lend, where the smallest
notes used were not less than the smallest Bank of England notes used in England, might not be more, perhaps
not as much, as the expenses usually attendant upon the
conduct of a chartered bank with a capital of one hundred
thousand dollars.

The sole business of the local banks being that of banks of discount, simply discounting only safe actual business paper, having but a short time to run, and collecting the discounted notes. The other complex and incompatible duties of the chartered banks, being conducted by the directors of the United States and states banks of issue.

These facts will hardly be doubted by any one at all familiar with the ordinary business of our chartered banks.

They will admit the following facts in favor of this free system of banking. That it will be more permanent, and that its paper will enjoy a much more extended circulation. It will be safer, because the failure of one local bank (which can hardly by possibility happen if the directors have given good security, and if the state officers do their duties faithfully as supervisors,) cannot effect the stability of the whole institution; besides, a safety fund should be provided from the bonuses or profits of the stockholders, to meet any casualty or defalcation of any bank of discount.

The currency of the country ought never to be subjected to the direction of private interest, or left for its stability to the chances of commercial transactions, political party policy or passions, or to the management of interested speculators, who give no further security for the soundness or convertibility of the currency, than just as far as the continuance of the business makes it their interest to pay or withhold their specie, or as their own use of it renders it convenient or profitable to themselves.

I know, that at this time to compare any system of banking to the " wild cat" banks of Michigan, is to endanger one's character for similies; and more especially, when the comparison is made between the " wild cat" banks and the most popular system of banking that has of late years made its appearance,—and, in fact, a system that does possess lessened evils and increased advantages over chartered banks in several respects, if these advantages are not found to be counterbalanced by the increased credit that is incorporated in the very essence of the system, and, consequently, containing a dangerous power of expansion. Yet, I am inclined to believe, that the defects and failures of the late safety fund banks of Michigan, was not so much an error in the system of credit upon which they were based, as upon the credit itself; and I fear that there will be found nearly the same tendency to expansion, to depreciation, and consequent contraction, in the currency issued under the N. York General Banking law, that so rapidly overturned the Michigan banks.

In Michigan, a mania for banking prevailed throughout the community, The facility for gratifying that propensity was afforded by their general banking law. They indulged to their entire satisfaction and conviction that credit is not capital, and that paper is not money. The shock was severe, and much money was lost to the state, as well as to private individuals, by this speculation. But the buoyancy of spirit, industry and economy of its inhabitants, will enable them to recover their former flourishing condition and prosperity, and, perhaps, to profit by their past experience; and a few years hence the currency of Michigan may be as sound as the currency of any other state of the Union.

Ohio is now laboring under a severe pressure from credit paper, and diminished specie for circulation. The southern states are no better situated respecting their currency. And from former statements, I fear that brokers, bankers, and stock-jobbers, will make more money by the western banks, than all the merchants, farmers and mechanics collectively. Instead of the banks having benefitted mechanics and laborers, mechanics and laborers may often trace their *ruin* to the influence of the banks.

318 DUNCOMBE'S FREE BANKING.

Banks have an appearance of aiding enterprise, and of promoting industry. But this, too, is a fallacy. They are, in fact, a check to industry, and destroy public confidence. They encourage a spirit of *legal gambling*, bribery and corruption, to induce legislatures to favor private interest at the public expense. In fact, legislatures should never interfere with the currency.

Legislators, in the incorporation of banking companies, have often appeared to have had more the interest of the banking company in view, than the public good ; and hence the evil effects of partial and local legislation upon subjects of general interest and importance.

But the New York General Banking law evinces a more extended and enlightened legislation; for, while it amply provides for the profit, interest, and advantages of the associations intended to be formed, it takes special care to secure the bill-holder by deposites pledged with the Comptroller of state. Yet, as far preferable as this system of banking may appear to be (on account of the better security of the bill-holder,) than the present system of chartered banks, I am apprehensive this system, too, has its incurable defects.

*Credit cannot be used as capital* for any length of time. And, although the bill-holders may feel themselves secure, receive the notes, and even lay them by them as they would receive and lay up specie ; yet, the continuance, for any length of time, of an inflated currency, must advance prices and increase foreign importations, which, being often purchased upon credit in a foreign market, must be met and promptly paid in specie, bills, drafts, or other remittances. Besides, the expansions of the currency induces habits of indolence and extravagance. The temporary rise of prices lessens the exertions of all classes of producers ; while the consumptions are increased instead of being lessened.

The balance of trade will continue to increase against the country, the rate of exchange will also increase, the expense of remittances will increase, and the exportation of specie must follow as a matter of course.

The natural tendency of credit to expand, and the facility with which bills may be obtained for circulation under the New York General Banking law, will be liable to inflate the currency beyond measure, and increase importations; this will be positively followed by the exportation of specie and a drain of the banks.

The payment of the annually accruing interest upon the enormous loans already made, can only be met by direct taxation, or a resort to additional loans. In this state of our accounts with European nations, or with England alone, domestic afflictions will exceed any thing that has ever before been witnessed in America. Formerly, the wealthy, the bankers, the importing merchants, and the speculators, were the persons who really suffered most from contractions; but when a contraction of the currency under the General Banking law takes place, the lengthened credit which their bills have had, their having involved securities upon which minors, orphans, lunatics, and insane persons could have been supported; and also the mortgages of lands in which two families have an interest, and upon which perhaps both of these families, with their respective dependants, relied solely for their support; these bonds, and these farms, must be sold, and at an enormous sacrifice, if the bill-holder is to be saved harmless. But alas, for him! when there has been more consumed in the community than has been produced, public works are necessarily delayed or suspended for want of capital. From the day laborer to the highest officer of state, one general ruin awaits them. For when *credit* has been too long, and too freely employed as *capital*, there must come sooner or later a pay-day ; and the longer the payment is deferred, the greater will be the amount to be paid, and the more extended the ruin necessary to meet the payment. The sacrifice must be greatest, where the urgency is greatest, and the means to accomplish it the most disproportionate. But the rules which regulate currency, are as immutably established " as the laws of the Medes and Persians, which altereth not."

But how defective and imperfect will be found the se-curities that will not sell for the money that they have been pledged to secure. The Comptroller may rigidly adhere to the law ; offer for sale, and perhaps sell at a great sacri-fice, lands and public bonds. But here is the secret: when the securities, from the extreme pressure of the times, can-not be made available to half the amount of bills in circu-lation, the legislature must again intervene, and these banks must have relief afforded them by law. The bill-holders, finding they are not secure if they press the sales of their securities at a sacrifice—and the ruin becomes general. The sacrifice necessary to be made by the most prudent or these institutions, would only allay, not cure the complaint. This sacrifice by so many, and by such influential and res-pectable persons, cannot be expected to be made even by those unconnected with, and hostile to these institutions. The influence of the bankers and fund-holders may be suf-ficient to procure the passage of a law, shewing them as great lenity and indulgence as has heretofore been extend-ed to incorporated banks, under far less urgent occasions and circumstances. What has once been done may be done again; and, after having been frequently repeated, it be-comes a matter of right, which it would be the highest in-justice to refuse : and this will be the natural course, and the probable history of the currency produced by the General Banking law. We may have a credit inconvertible currency for years, perhaps, before one dollar out of the eight that circulates will be specie. True, if an inconvertible paper must be used by the public in lieu of money, this may as well be used as any other; and the General Banking law may be so amended as to give perfect security to the bill-holders. Perhaps time would secure the bill-holder under the present law; but not until after a sufficient length of time shall have elapsed for the whole country to emerge from the chaos and ruin of the shock of suspensions and contractions. But every shock the currency receives, and every expansion and contraction of the currency, retards the healthy growth and prosperity of the country—weakens the government, by lessening public confidence in republican institutions, and gives the enemies of democracy new cause of triumph and rejoicing.

The bonds of the free and independent states of this Union, will be hawked about the market of our rivals, as valueless as the notes or bonds of any insolvent debtor; and to increase their value in a foreign market, the General Government will be required to endorse for the several insolvent states. A majority of the states being involved in debt, will agree to give this additional security to our foreign creditors in order to delay the payment of the interest for a short period, or to obtain additional loans, out of which to meet the interest. And thus we will have once more commenced a national debt, which, when once established upon such broad principles, and for such universal, yet local purposes, of internal improvement, will be likely to be continued.

The General Government, once involved for the amount already expended, the completion of these works will be

strenuously urged; and policy will be thought to dictate
that they should be completed. New loans must be made
to effect this object. And the same majority that would
pledge the revenues of the general government in a foreign
market, for the debts of the different states, will extend
their credit to complete the works that have been thus be-
gun; and with much more plausibility than before : as, by
completing them, they may, perhaps, pay something more
than sufficient to keep them in repair, and thus save at least
part of the money thus invested. Hence, a foreign national debt, the worst of all public or national debts, will pro-
gress, until the General Government will be obliged to
have recouse to direct taxation (for local purposes,) to meet
the annually accruing interests on public bonds. Or what
is even worse than taxation, they must submit to pursue
such a commercial policy towards England, as her Majesty's Ministers may dictate, and her credit system require.
And all these evils are the natural effects of the connection of currency with credit, with politics, and with private
interest.

Credit should never be allowed to usurp the place, execute the office, or perform the functions of real capital, as a
basis for the issue of paper to circulate as money. Its
natural tendency and power of expansion, will fill all the
channels of business and commerce ; which, when once
filled, flow into foreign channels as instantly as they are
surcharged. And here, since only the precious metals are the
exportable materials, every dollar exported lessens the
circulation eight dollars ! Do not stare—it lessens the positive power of circulation in that proportion. But that is
not all ; the panic induces many, who before had kept these
bills by them and felt quite secure, to exchange them for
specie. Here the effect is the same as before. Every one

hundred dollars thus drawn from the banks, lessens their power of circulation eight hundred dollars; specie is required, by the high price of bills of exchange, for exportation, and the banks must be again and again brought back to their first starting point.

From the returns made to the legislature of the state of New York, it appears that, while the safety fund banks have wisely contracted their discounts and lessened their circulation, the banks under the General Banking law have expanded to more than enough to supply their place. The high rate of exchange, and the demand for remittances, should forewarn every banker and every large dealer, of the danger of extending credit under the present indebtedness of so many of the states.

One of the most valuable features of the New York General Banking law is, the separation of the power of issuing bills from the power of discounting notes, and of putting them into circulation. Besides, the delay necessary to the issuing of notes, gives the depositors of real property time for reflection and consideration, and even for present emergencies to subside, before they hypothecate their debts or lands for bank paper; which time will prove is not money, nor wealth, and only the representative of either, while it is convertible at sight—beyond this all is fallacy and delusion.

"Knowledge is power"—but few reflect upon the importance of a correct knowledge of currency, of finance, of banking, and of exchanges. We grope on in the dark,—find no instruction in the past. We treat the subject of finance, as one of chance, of expediency, of circumstance, and of fluctuations; while we neglect the enquiry into its elementary principles and into the laws by which it is governed. Instead of commencing our investigations, by thoroughly

comprehending the first principles into which every question of currency resolves itself, we direct our attention to
the easiest and most rapid means of acquiring something
that will circulate for a time as money, or, when one credit system has exploded, to the creation of a new one that
will explode as certainly, sooner or later, as the preceding
system has done.

## OF THE IMPORTANCE OF A KNOWLEDGE OF CURRENCY TO LEGISLATURES.

A knowledge of the workings of the machinery of an
ordinary chartered bank, with all its fiscal agents and leger-
demain, constitutes but a very superficial knowledge of
finance and of currency: the first principles of which
are never changed or varied by the ingenuity of man, or
the "collective wisdom" of legislatures. It may be dammed up in one direction, but it will flow back, and through
other channels find its level. The currency of the country,
as has ben remarked, consists of the precious metals, coined
into various shapes and forms, and stamped in mills with
the heads of the rulers of the nations, or with their national honors, or some emblem or device adapted to their
country.

In order to obtain a thorough knowledge of currency,
we must understand what currency is, and what wealth is,
and what capital is. Wealth is riches, money, or precious goods, whether productive or unproductive, whether
convertible or inconvertible, whether moveable or fixed,
or whether unchangeable and uniform, or of an unknown
and ideal value. But in all this where is the representative of value? The wealth of any person must
possess substance; it must be tangible—it must be composed of that which costs labor and care, and thought; it

must be that which can be enjoyed, possessed and known, either as a comfort or luxury of life, or it must be something that will produce or can be exchanged for that which adorns, beautifies or gives support or comfort to man.

To a correct knowledge of any art or science, two things are necessary; firstly, an acquaintance with the elementary principles of the art or science; and secondly, a distinct knowledge of the technicalities or language of the art or science. As this work is designed principally for the benefit of the youth of these United States, it may not be amiss to define the terms most frequently used, while speaking upon this subject.

CURRENCY may be defined to be circulation; passing from hand to hand; generally received; the rate at which any thing is vulgarly valued; the papers stamped in the English Colonies by authority, and passing for money.— WALKER.

MONEY—Metal coined for the purposes of commerce.—WALKER.

MONEY is applied to every thing which serves as a circulating medium.—GEORGE CRABBE'S ENGLISH SYNONYMES.

WEALTH is that positive and substantial share in the goods of fortune which distinguish an individual from his neighbors, by putting him in the possession of all that is commonly desired and sought after by man.

> His best companions, innocence and health,
> And his best riches, ignorance of WEALTH.

He who has money has great WEALTH.

> Along the lawn, where scattered hamlets rose,
> Unwieldy WEALTH and ponderous pomp arose.
>                                    GOLDSMITH.

The WEALTH of a nation must be procured by the industry of its inhabitants. We speak of WEALTH as it raises a man in the scale of society. The WEALTHY merchant is an important member of society.
                                    CRABBE'S SYNONYMES.

The capital of the young American frequently consists exclusively of a sound constitution, a clear conscience, with habits of industry and economy : his money is his time, and his currency is his labor.

The capital of the North American Indian is his hunting

ground, which he possesses in common with his tribe; his bow and arrows and his skins, with a few trophies of the field or of the chase—and the latter of these comprise his wealth.

The capital of the merchant consists of ships, cargoes of agricultural produce, merchandise, and provisions for his crew.

The capital of the farmer consists of lands, houses, cattle, horses, hogs, sheep, poultry, waggons, harnesses, ploughs, harrows, spades, shovels, hoes, axes, and the whole long list of farming utensils, with provisions for man and for beast, and seed, manure, clothing and implements of husbandry and gardening.

The capital of the mechanic consists of his tools and machinery of his trade, his shop or factory, and the necessary grounds for yard, out-houses for storing materials, and raw materials, together with his stock in the factory, and the manufactured articles.

The capital of a state consists of the productive labor and industry, as well as the property of all the inhabitants; rail roads, canals, ferries, wild lands, duties on importations, on licenses, patents, &c.; duties collected on sales at auction, on tavern licenses, and on all other taxable or dutiable articles.

Yet, from the government of the state by the monarch on his throne, to the Indian who roams the forest wild, and free as the wind that warns him of the necessity of his buffalo, bear, or beaver skin, none take promises for capital— none consider promises wealth—and none consider promises productive industry. All prefer the substance to the shadow. The only use of cash is as a measure of the value of other materials, and as a medium of exchange; as being more convenient for circulation than grosser or more per-

ishable articles ; as possessing the greatest and most perma‑
nent intrinsic value within the smallest weight and bulk of
any commodity known to all nations.

The amount of capital that the state, the merchant, the
farmer, or the mechanic possesses, indicates the number of
men that can be employed and paid, and the quantity of ma‑
terial, and the amount of business that can be performed, in
all these operations. Money, cash, coin, is only the instru‑
ment, the medium of circulation, between persons not re‑
quiring the interchange of their own products. That is, A,
an iron manufacturer, requires flour, pork, beef, and veget‑
ables, for the support of his laborers, from the farmer, who
does not require iron in full for his products, as he requires
the necessaries for his family, and something to pay his
workmen. The instrument that both can use, is money ;
that is, therefore, used as the medium with which the far‑
mer can buy merchandise, clothing and groceries, from
stores or hawkers, who would not take iron in exchange
for their commodities. Money is the instrument, the medium
that each class of society can use ; and hence its true title of
currency and of medial commodity. Money, then, is the
measure of value of all the different commodities that com‑
prise the whole capital of the community—the whole ag‑
gregate mass of things possessing exchangeable value,
which are destined to supply the necessities, the comforts,
and the luxuries of life, or which is intended to be employ‑
ed in the production of other things with such ultimate
view.

As a measure of value, paper issued and intended to
pass and circulate as money, can only be used so long as the
measure is correct, that is, so long only as the value of the
note, from its perfect convertibility, is of the exact value
with the coin it represents. But as neither the medium

when coin, nor when the representative of coin, is among
the conveniences, necessaries, or luxuries of life, as food or
clothing, let us examine the difference between them, in
order the better to understand their respective values. The
precious metals have cost much labor, and other convertible commodities, to produce them, as rent of ground, cost
of provisions and labor in smelting and assaying, and in
transportation to market, or to the mint to be coined. In the
United States there is no seigniorage or charge for coining.
Besides, the precious metals possess a value independent of
the value given to them by the common consent of the
commercial world : they are the most valuable metals of
which to form certain materials for use and ornament,
which give them an intrinsic value greater than that of most
other materials ; so that, should the nations of the whole
earth agree to substitute some other commodity in lieu of
gold and silver as the measure of value and circulating medium, it would not probably materially lessen the value of
the precious metals as bullion. Some nations, at this moment, circulate other materials than gold and silver for their
currency ; as shells among the Africans—bags of valueless
materials among the Arabs—and furs among the Northern
Indians. The Chinese use for their currency, and circulate
as their only money, square bits of metal, with a hole in the
centre, by which they are strung on a string. In Mexico, copper, coined for the purpose, passes as money at far above its
value—and great injustice is stated to have been done by that
government to the commercial and monied portion of their
community recently by the lessening the legal value of the
copper coin.

The same method of alloying the coins of different countries, to increase the revenue, or lessen the claims against
the government, and for other purposes, have been frequent-

ly adopted in the old world. The coins retain the same denomination, but are diminished in weight, or in purity, or in both—so as to contain less of the precious metals in them than before—whilst they are declared to be legal tenders for the discharge of debts, for an equal number of former coins, contracted long before the alteration took place.

In England, the pound of silver, which was originally coined into twenty equal parts, called shillings, by successive diminutions and real alterations, both by lessening the fineness and diminishing the weight, has been coined into sixty-six pieces—each of which retain the name or denomination of shilling; and by law, twenty of these shillings are made legal tender for the payment of a debt contracted when twenty shillings contained a pound of silver. And the fraud thus practiced, has been greatly increased by the introduction into circulation of large quantities of credit paper intended to circulate as money.

In France, the *livre*, or pound of silver, has been reduced by a similar succession of legal frauds to the present livre or franc, equivalent to less than one-fifth part of a Spanish milled dollar.

The recent reduction and deterioration of the gold coins of the United States, had precisely the same effect upon creditors, where the contract was to be paid in gold coin, (if any such contracts existed.) But no great injustice could have been done by the passage of this law in the U. States, as the gold coins were previously valued by tale below their market price, when compared with silver, or with most foreign gold coins. It was also thought to be expedient to prevent its exportation. This latter reason is a sad apology for injustice, however slight the wrong. But when the greater evil of limited responsibility chartered bank notes is compared with it, we are led to say that congress chose the lesser of the two evils; besides, while the eagle contained 247½ grains of pure gold, as it did until the passage of the "gold bill" in 1834, and as amended in 1837, by which the quantity of pure gold in the eagle was reduced to 232½ grains, whenever the rate of exchange was against the U. States, the high price of American eagles in England, made them desirable articles of exportation, both on that account and on account of their being less weighty or bulky than silver, and equal to foreign coin in England, as compared with their mint value in the United States.

Now let us examine the intrinsic value of paper money, and compare that with the intrinsic value of gold and silver. The paper, intended to circulate as money, is comparatively of no value, except what is given it by law. Previous to stamping, engraving and printing, very little labor or cost had been expended upon it, and its value, having been made of old rags, (even although they be silk rags,) was almost nothing. This fact any one may easily prove by offering an unexecuted bill in the market.

The value of paper money is purely a *credit value*, given to it by its execution under a special law, authorising its issue and circulation as money. And when perfectly convertible, its increased value consists in its affording facilities of transportation greater than that possessed by the precious metals—provided the paper be current throughout the Union. The saving, of what would otherwise be lost by the wear and tear of the precious metals when they are constantly in circulation, by their abrasion, gives paper money another advantage over the precious metals. But, if statements that I have seen be correct, as to the injury of gold and silver coins by use, by which large silver coin are estimated not to become defaced, or have their weight lessened so much as to require a new coinage necessary oftener than

once in every hundred years, and large gold coins not oftener than once in two hundred years, the saving of the precious metals, by the use of paper to circulate as money,
would be but a small per centage upon the commercial
world, unworthy of comparison, or even mention, in opposition to the annual loss sustained by the people upon uncurrent chartered bank paper. There is no equal comparison between the cost of producing a given large amount of
the precious metals, and an equal nominal amount of paper
money, whereby the profits upon the precious metals employed in commerce, or converted into capital, is in favor of
the use of paper for a circulating medium. Yet, long and
sad experience has proved, that the loss sustained by the
public from the depreciation of chartered bank paper, is
uniformly far greater than the profits made upon the exportation of specie, or its employment as capital.

The question then stands thus : if there be no intrinsic
value in the paper used as money, and if the cost of producing gold and silver coin be nearly equal to its value when
coined for circulation—if there be not a sufficient quantity
of the precious metals to serve as an instrument, with
which every class of citizens may labor equally profitably,
or, to use the ordinary phrase, if there be not a sufficient
medial commodity of the precious metals for the business
circulation of the country—who then ought to give an additional nominal value to the material that is to supply its
place, and make up the deficiency of the precious metals ?
And if any seigniorage or other profit is to be made upon
the currency that is to supply the place of the precious
metals, ought it to be received and enjoyed by the people,
who are the sovereign power ? or ought these profits, with
this immense power and privilege, to be given to a few individuals, for their private interest and aggrandizement, to
the exclusion of the whole people ?

Whether these men have made themselves favorites by merit, or by bribery and corruption, or by sycophancy, it matters not, so far as the solution of this question is concerned.

The question is, who shall supply the deficiency of the precious metals—give an artificial value to some commodity to supply their place, and enjoy the benefits derivable from this substitution ? To answer this question correctly, let us enquire what was the opinion of the founders of this republic, and what the practice of European financiers upon similar subjects.

The framers of the constitution say, " Congress shall have power to coin money, and regulate the value thereof, and of foreign coins."

Clearly to comprehend this sentence, let us observe the signification of the verb to " regulate," as established by the best English writers.

*To regulate,* in its most familiar acceptation, signifies to direct, to dispose, to govern, to rule.

We direct for the instruction of individuals ; we regulate for the good order or convenience of many ; we dispose for the benefit of one or many. To direct (to conduct,) is personal, it supposes authority. To regulate, from the latin *regula,* to rule, signifies to settle according to a rule ; is general, it supposes superior information. An officer, directs the movements of his men in military operations.

> Canst thou, with all a monarch's cares opprest !
> Oh Atreus son ! canst thou indulge thy rest ?
> Ill fits a chief who mighty nations guides,
> Directs in council or in war presides.          Pope.

The steward or master of ceremonies, regulates the whole concerns of an entertainment.

> Ev'n Goddesses are women ; and no wife
> Has power to regulate her husband's life.     Dryden.

The constitution declares, that "Congress shall have power to coin money, and *regulate* the value thereof, and of foreign coin."

We have been thus particular in settling the definition of the word "regulate," to show what the framers of the constitution meant by the regulation of the value of money. Observe, it is "money" that congress "shall have power to regulate the value thereof." Congress shall regulate the value of money. Had the framers of the constitution said congress shall have power to coin money, and fix the value of the coin, there could have been no construction, other than the one expressed, by fixing the value from time to time of the coins, whether domestic or foreign. But the term to regulate, we have seen is the only single word in the English language that would have given congress the whole and entire regulation and control of all the circulating medium. And to regulate the value of money, we have seen is the most comprehensive term, and almost the only one in the English language that would have given congress the same full, free, perfect, unlimited, discretionary power, evidently hereby intended to have been given by this clause, of doing all and every act and thing, that can ever be found necessary or expedient, or that can ever be deemed right, just, or proper, relating to the value of money for the promotion of the peace, prosperity, and good government of the United States.

Had a limited power have been intended to have been conferred on congress by that clause, and had the acts of congress relating thereto have been intended to have been restricted to the regulation of the coins, that should circulate in the United States, that would have been expressed in words that would clearly have conveyed such a meaning; as from time to time fixing the value of the coins, &c.

But to *regulate* the value of money embraces the whole subject matter under consideration.

As the steward or master of ceremonies *regulates* the whole concerns of an entertainment, so has congress the power to regulate the whole concerns of the money-currency of the country. Besides, the evident intent of the framers of the constitution, in using the word regulate, was to confer the most extensive powers upon congress. The whole spirit of the constitution goes to confer the power of the legislation of the country upon that legislature that will be the most likely to comprehend the subject, and do it the best justice. Whenever the states can better promote the peace, prosperity and good government of the whole community, by legislating upon any subject than the congress of the United States would be likely to do, the power to legislate upon that subject is given to the states; but where the interests of this vast republic can be better promoted by a uniformity of the law, and by its being passed by congress, than by state legislatures, then congress has been empowered to act.

Few persons, if any, who have travelled throughout the United States, but have felt the inconvenience and additional expense and trouble they have sustained from local, partial, state legislation upon a subject of such great national importance and general public interest as currency. But lest I should be misunderstood, I do not mean to say, that, although the old United States bank removed this inconvenience to a very great extent, that there were not greater inconveniences and dangers attendant upon such an incorporation, than even the lessened expense and trouble of the present exchanges. That involved the liberties of the whole people—this only robs the few who travel, and taxes the many who have remittances to make; and, in short, taxes the whole community. But more of an United States bank by and bye.

The reader should be again advised, that money-currency is one thing and credit or commodity-currency is another thing; and that I have never recommended the legislature of any state, nor the congress of the United States, to interefere with the credit-currency of the country. I have long believed and taught, that the whole business of legislation was comprised in the protection of persons and property ; that we have far too much legislation, and that the freer the currency of the country is, the simpler and more easily will the subject of finance be to be comprehended ; and the more certain will the monetary affairs of the country be well conducted, as they are easily and well understood by the whole people.

One of not the least important benefits anticipated to be derived from the proposed system of currency is, that it closes all future legislation upon the subject of the currency, as effectually as is the legislation upon our politics or form of government closed. The whole subject being referred to the people—who are the sovereign power—will be thoroughly comprehended by them, and there not being volumes to be read over and over again to be comprehended, like the present unwritten constitution of the United States upon the subject of money-currency, which must be collected from bank acts, from bank reports, from reports from the different legislatures upon the subject of finance, currency and banks, and reports from the Secretaries of the Treasuries of the several States, and from the Secretary of the Treasury of the United States, from the different Prices Current, and reports of exchanges, in newspapers ; in short, at this moment, to comprehend the subject of currency thoroughly, would require whole years of faithful reading and study for a man of ordinary acquirements and abilities.

The question of the currency in the United States, is like the unwritten constitution of Great Britain, to be found and comprehended only after great research, and even then left to be confirmed or not, as it may be expedient or inexpedient, with the party in power.

The Constitution of England may be collected from Blackstone's Commentaries on the laws of England, and from other books, reports, and decisions; provided the doctrines or principles thus collected, when compared, accord with, or promote the interests and views of the dominant party ; so it is with the currency of the Union. After all the opinions, from that of the learned and able American Commentator, Kent, down to the humblest editor of any periodical newspaper, have been read and carefully studied, if the result is not favorable to the dominant party, the opinion is unconstitutional and liable to rejection.

I am desirous of simplifying the science of money—and of making it the business of every American to comprehend it; of indicating the means by which the American people can exercise their inalienable and inherent rights as American freemen, with regard to the subject of the currency, as freely and fully as they now do their political rights. They would then learn economy in public, as well as in private matters; and that the man, whose expenses exceeds his income, and for the balance lives upon credit, must find himself annually more and more in debt, not only to the additional amount of the annual excesses of his expenses over his income, but by the addition of the interest of his former excesses of expenses, and the diminished credit which he possesses, which compells him to pay annually higher and higher prices for his purchases, as his prospects of punctual payments diminish. He may continue to live in part upon credit in this manner, so long as money is so plenty that his creditors prefer the chance of getting a great profit by and bye from him, to that of receiving small profits from punctual payers; but the moment money rises in the market, this man is called upon, and if he cannot pay, his means of subsistence is taken from him, and his situation is rendered proportionately worse and worse, as he has exceeded his actual means of payment.

The United States, in a financial light, is the same as an individual. So are the several states. And our present indebtedness abroad is a stain upon the American character, that can only be obliterated by the extinction of that disgraceful transaction and debt. A national debt has ever been held in abhorrence by every lover of liberty and eqality—of independence, peace and plenty; but the sale of American stocks, and the receipt in payment of old rags, firstly, in the shape of imports, and, secondly, in the form of limited responsibility bank paper, from the monopolizers of our currency, has established a national debt abroad of greater evil, and of more portentious danger, to this republic, than a debt of ten times the same magnitude would be if due to our own citizens. " The borrower is the slave of the lender;" and the creditor in England will exercise more influence over the future destinies of this republic, than a standing army of American soldiers; for American soldiers still are Americans; they are men, possessed of a love of American institutions, and of liberty and equality; but the foreign monied aristocrat, who must and will hereafter, if not checked, decide the fate of this republic, but who might, if not directly interested in the political and financial economy of this country, have remained silent, or only given a disregarded sneer to Americans and American institutions,

must now, for his own safety and the protection of his private interest, intermeddle with the political economy of
such states as are indebted to him, and even with the domestic economy of its inhabitants ; and all our extravagance
and indebtedness and humiliation is to be attributed to our
form of government, a mobocracy, as they sneeringly term
this republic. The foreign money-lender is not to be blamed for his inquisitiveness respecting our national or domestic policy, when we apply to him to lend us money. And
having once lent us money, it is not at all surprising that he
should feel that he too has a right here to protect, and ought
at least to be allowed to express his opinions freely of our
institutions, of public policy and economy, as well as of the
men and measures of the government generally. This,
however, must annually lead to greater and more dangerous interference of aristocrats with republican institutions.
And so long as the currency of the country is anti-republican, and so long as foreign aristocrats, through their connection with our credit-currency, exercise an influence over
our money-currency ; that is, so long as incorporated banks
make up the deficiency between the precious metals and
the amount of currency required for the circulating medium
of the country, so long must the republican institutions of
the country be constantly opposed in principle and in practice by the money power of the country, and so long must
credit serve to amuse the people, enrich the few, and im-
poverish the many. Money has a natural tendency to accumulate in amount, and in its influence ; and whenever
the money power (perhaps I ought to have called it the
credit power) of the banks, shall be greater and stronger
than the democracy of the country, the democracy of the
country will yield to the aristocracy of money and credit,
the money of foreigners and the credit of banks, will pro-

duce annual changes in the administrations of this republic, until the democracy of numbers will be sneered at, as much by the native American as it is now despised by the foreign aristocrat, who holds that wealth only, or at least principally, should be represented. This is the first step in a policy, by which the many are made to serve the few ; and which can only end in a strong splendid government, with a weak impoverished people.

If these portentious evils are the natural effects of the existence of incorporated banks, and the consequent extension of the credit system, are we not instinctively led to enquire after a remedy ?

To judge correctly of the necessary remedy, we must clearly understand the nature of the complaint. And as incorporated banks, with limited responsibility, are charged with being the first stepping stone in the road to ruin, and in the march of excesses, by which the free citizens of this American Republic are being bound out to English task-masters, as "hewers of wood and drawers of water," to pamper the pride and flatter the vanity of the very nation from whom they boast of having gained their independence—vain boast ! delusive glory ! fallacious flattery ! If an English heartless monied aristocracy are again to claim us as tributaries, let no American lay the flattering unction to his soul, that our forefathers resisted their encroachments upon our liberties : they fought and conquered, and so can, and so will we. But remember that then we were unwilling slaves—we had never consented to the terms of our humiliation; now we forge the gilded chains that bind us, and entail to our posterity a national *foreign* debt, and habits of excess in expenses exceeding our incomes, that could not be enjoyed except by the *abuse* of sound and healthful credit.

To see the justice of the charge, made against chartered

banks, with limited responsibility, let us refer to our former
description of banks, and briefly recapitulate the different
kinds of banks, and the use of each, necessary to the illustration of our subject.

Banks we have divided into three great classes, banks of
deposite, banks of discount, and banks of issue. The latter
frequently embracing all the duties, and performing all the
functions, of the three classes. And whether these be established by joint stock companies, or by private individuals, by special local legislation, or by some general banking
law, or by common consent without any legislation upon
the subject, these three kinds of banks embrace all that is
necessary for us to examine to the comprehension of our
subject.

Banks of deposite and banks of discount were the only
banks known to the ancients.

The introduction of banks of issue, has produced a new
era in banking and in currency. Formerly, currency was
uniform, or nearly so ; it may now be divided into money-
currency, and credit or commodity-currency, as connected
with the different kinds of banks.

And here allow me to digress from the description of
banks, to show the nature and character of the different
currencies, or of the money-currency and the credit or commodity-currency.

Money-currency comprises only the precious metals, and
such paper passing for money as is always perfectly convertible into specie at sight, under every situation and state of
trade, such as the notes, bills, and other transfers and evidences of debt in banks of deposite.

Credit or commodity-currency, consists of such bank
notes, drafts, bills of exchange, and mercantile remittances,
as are convertible under ordinary circumstances into specie

at sight, or at fixed periods of time, as at the maturity of a
bill, or at a time nearly fixed, as at the arrival of a cargo,
or on the arrival of some other probable event, but yet dependant upon the possibility of defeat from the casual happening or not happening of some circumstance or contingency.

This will be better comprehended, by bearing constantly
in mind the difference in the business of the different kinds
of banks.

In banks of deposite, specie is only kept; the credits on
the books of the bank represent certain quantities of bullion, ascertained by weight and placed there for safe keeping, without any power or authority on the part of the directors of the bank to lend it, or use it, until it is called for
by its owners, or transferred by bills or drafts, or by entries
upon the books of the bank to other persons. This bank
greatly facilities mercantile transactions, by safely keeping
large sums of money that would otherwise require to be
kept in iron chests; by saving the labor of repeated countings, and of removal from house to house, as well as diminishing the risk by fire and other casualties, and the wear
and tear of the precious metals by friction. This bank paper is perfectly convertible on all occasions, as the amount
of bullion is actually in the vaults of the bank, and may be
weighed to any person who should desire to remove his
amount. Hence, the impression upon the mind of every
person originally is, that bank paper is money, and is perfectly convertible into specie, as are the notes of banks of
deposite, where there can be no doubt of the bills, notes,
checks, or drafts of the depositors, being positively and *bona
fide* paid at sight.

Banks of discount, too, were used long before the introduction of banks of credit circulation. They are generally

companies of monied men, associated together to maintain a
survivorship, and for the purpose of lending their money to
the best advantage, and to prevent an unnecessary competition among themselves in the business of money lending.
They become a monopoly, and regulate the price of the
loan of money as suits themselves.

Banks of discount lend money, by discounting promissory notes and acceptances, originating in the sale of property, having but short periods to run. They also receive money on deposite at a small rate of interest, or only for the value of its safe keeping, for an indefinite period or for fixed
periods. This money they lend, with their own capital, in
discounting business paper.

In some respects, the banks established under the authority of the New York General Banking law, resembles banks
of discount. As one company may furnish the funds deposited with the Comptroller of State, in security for the
blank bank notes intended to be executed and circulate as
money, and another company may (if the depositors choose
to employ them,) take the management of the discounts.

I can easily conceive a case, in which a bank established
under this law, would nearly resemble a bank of discount.
Suppose the farmers of a neighborhood to mortgage their
farms, and pledge their government debts with the Comptroller of State, to the value of $100,000, in the hope of ma-
king their own money, and keeping their property besides;
and then lending their money at six per cent., having only
twelve and a half per cent. of their circulation necessarily
to be kept in their vaults : it will pay them the interest of a
dollar for each shilling in their vaults ; so that the interest of
the $100,000 thus loaned will be six thousand dollars a
year—while the deposite would only bring in interest of
$750, leaving a balance of $5,250. The extra profits of the

business of banking—loss of notes by accidents to note-holders, &c.—is nearly or quite equal to the increased expenses of loaning, by banking, the $100,000 in paper, above the expenses of loaning the amount of the deposite in specie. Upon this calculation, it would not be surprising if farmers, with a little money, and a great love of money, pride and ambition, should attempt to multiply their interests by eight, since they would receive their interests on their mortgages if they were real, and upon their government debts, just the same in the hands of the Comptroller, as if they were in their own drawers.

Then, suppose these farmers to employ bankers and financiers to transact their banking business: their bank would become a bank of discount. The farmers are not holden for one shilling beyond the amount of their deposites with the Comptroller, and that security is not a personal security, but a property security, and the directors of the bank of discount are not bound for one shilling, either in their private or associated capacity ; for, although they may sue and be sued, the funds of the bank only are held for the judgement that may be obtained against them.

The only banks in the United States that more perfectly are banks of discount, than the banks established under the General Banking Law, are the offices where money is loaned by brokers in New York, and perhaps some other cities. The great evil of these offices is, that the brokers are in no way responsible for the redemption of the paper they put in circulation. They often lend the poorest credit paper money, as they can borrow or buy that money at a very cheap rate and lend it at par, or often even at an advance while money is scarce and the rate of interest on money high.

These brokers' offices, or banks of discount, are suppo-

sed to loan only their own money, which they have bought
or borrowed. Perhaps, at times, they become the secret
agents of banks, and lend their money for a commission
when money is scarce and the rate of interest high, or
when the banks from any cause do not discount publicly—
as when the rate of interest should be three, four, or five
per cent. a month, and the charter of the bank would not
allow them to receive more than lawful interest, they could
double or treble their profits by changing their business and
not discounting paper for the public, but by engaging a broker to loan it for them at as high a rate as he can get. Or
they may sometimes employ a broker during suspensions,
when the banks are not supposed to be in funds.

In the large cities on the continent of Europe, they do
not issue notes ; and in England, many of the banks, except the bank of England, are banks of discount, strictly
speaking. They loan only bank of England paper—
which, by the bye, is lawful tender in the payment of all
debts except those of the bank of England. The notes of
the bank of England are truly the lawful currency of the
kingdom. In England, and on the continent, discounts are
paid only in money : an important distinction between discounts there, and discounts here, where you receive only
promises to pay, in which there is very great uncertainty—
for the limited responsibility-principle has made the notes
of the banks frequently less secure than the private notes
of individuals they receive in exchange. The latter is
upon interest, or pays interest in advance ; yet that is not
equivalent to the name of money, and the fine figured silk
paper, upon which the bank promise-to-pay is printed, are
given with limited responsibility in exchange.

The separation of the bank of issue (the Comptroller's
office,) from the bank of discount, under the provisions of

the New York General Banking law, evidently lessens the temporary facility of expansion ; yet, so long as credit is used as capital, and private interested individuals are allowed to interfere with the currency of the country, there will be, there must naturally be, by the laws of self-love, and power uncontrolled, excessive expansions of the currency and ruinous contractions, with occasional suspensions and frequent total failures of banks and bank notes.

Admitting that this law provides perfect security for the bill-holder, (which, by the bye, is **very** doubtful,) and removes the office of issue from the office of discount, and from all sympathy and interest with the borrower, yet still the bills are issued upon credit, the kind of security for the payment of the bills only is changed, and instead of personal security, this law provides funded debts or landed security. It is still credit, and credit still connected with private interest ; and it must be subject to those immutable laws by which credit, trade and commerce are governed.

The *uniformity* of the currency, that would soon be established throughout the state by the adoption of this system of banking generally, is highly desirable ; but uniformity is not all that is necessary to a perfectly sound currency. The principles of responsibility and convertibility are also highly necessary. But this will not be likely to be obtained, until the directors of the currency are a part and parcel of the people, elected and chosen by themselves and accountable to themselves for the faithful discharge of their duties. Until that time, there can be no safety, no reliance upon paper intended to circulate as money. It is the highest injustice, and a most disgraceful reflection upon the intelligence and integrity of the people, to refuse to give them the election of the directors of the currency upon the ground, that, although they may govern themselves in

political matters, yet that they are incompetent to govern
the currency. That they would not elect proper persons
for the management of money : as though the people would
be more liable to err upon a matter of the deepest interest
and daily business with themselves, than they would upon
the subject of religion or literature and of politics. When
will the free born sons of America show to the world, that
they are *free and independent* of both the money power and
the " statesman's pomp, and churchman's " pride of England ? There is no standing still in currency any more
than in politics. We must be running deeper and deeper
in debt, or we must, by retrenching our expenses and lessening our imports, be regularly lessening that debt. If
we firmly, zealously and faithfully adhere to principles of
economy and punctuality in all our commercial transactions,
we may lessen our imports to the par exchange of our exports, and finally release ourselves from the baneful effects
of a foreign monetary domination, but if, on the contrary,
every succeeding year is to bring its additional hundred of
millions of dollars of debt, we may rest assured that if we
have not a Queen to reign over us, we shall bow with great
respect and deference to the London Exchange. The only
difference between the regal and monetary domination,
will be, that we may quote the authority of Thread-Needle
Lane in London, instead of Downing street and the Royal
Palace, for the justification of our financial or political conduct.

The reader may begin to tire of my repeated intimation
of fatal consequences from this unlimited extension of credit, but rest assured, the rising generation will not sneer at
its effects when they are groaning under its weight.

There is an old adage, " that any thing is worth what it
will fetch." Whatever a thing will sell for is certainly the

price of it; but it does not prove that the sale price is the value of it.

The bills of the banks, established under the New York General Banking law, may pass current among the people, and be received as gold and silver for a time throughout the state of New York; yet, to render them quite like gold and silver, they should be separated from credit, have their issues based exclusively upon the precious metals, and like them, be free from the influence of private interest, and the power of individuals to increase the circulation from sympathy with the borrower or personal interest as stockholders. What we are desirous of, is recommending a system which, if adopted, will exclude the possibility of notes being discredited. This we think can only be done by separating the issuing power from all interest in the issues made ; and from all sympathy with the borrower, by separating the offices of issue and discount. By requiring the directors of the bank of discount to give security for the performance of certain well defined duties, and for the prompt and punctual payment over to their successors in office, of all money and property of the bank at the time in their possession; punctuality in business will be best promoted, by giving good security for the strict compliance with promises and undertakings.

We have seen the wildness of speculations, and the extravagance of living induced by excessive issues of the chartered banks, under their limited responsibility. Can we desire its continuance or its repetition.

The great difficulty attendant upon an incorporated bank paper-currency is, the uncertainty of effectually preventing their notes from being discredited. And this we maintain, can only be done by restricting bank issues to the proportionate amount of specie actually in their vaults *at the time*

*of issue.* By removing temptation to excessive issues from
the directors, of either banks of issue or the banks of discount. The business of the banks of discount should be
conducted automatically, by well established and clearly
defined laws and regulations. The directors should have
their operations clearly defined and explained in their published monthly reports, (not mystified) for the public inspection, and for the examination of state directors or commissioners, whose re-election should depend upon the manner
in which they discharge their duties as state directors, to be
approved or rejected at the ballot-box.

Neither the directors, nor the institutions themselves,
should be in any way dependant upon the legislature for
any grant, privilege, right, interest, or matter or thing connected with the legislature or executive government. The
currency should be as independent of party as the issues of
the mint.

The passage, by congress, of a general free banking law,
upon republican principles, would, with a little experience,
accomplish this desirable object. The people, having the
control of the money, would elect directors who would accommodate the fair trader, and expend the money they borrow in the improvement of their private fortunes, and in
their accommodation in business, or in necessary profitable
public works; while the foreign gambling speculator would
be precluded from bank credit, or only share equally with
the fair businesss men of the place.

Let me once more repeat, that the circulating medium
should be equally current in every part of the Union;
separated from politics and from credit and from private interest, and always perfectly and indisputably convertible
at sight, at the counter where it was put in circulation;
free from any connection or influence of the foreign or domestic money market, or of the exchanges.

So much of the currency, as is not composed of the precious metals, should be so perfectly based upon them, that any contingency or circumstance of trade or of credit, at home or abroad, should not inflate the currency beyond the limits of the actual demand, and the precious metals in their vaults justify, so that the bank credit currency of the country may not be made a substitute for capital. Currency should only be issued in such quantity that it can constantly pass freely from hand to hand ; it is only the instrument by which all other commodities are measured in value, and which answers the purpose of the receiver for a measure of value for him, and the medium of exchange. When bank notes, based upon credit, are used as capital, the effect upon currency is the same as if a smith put up his own tools and investments for sale, or manufactured them into marketable articles.

Unlimited individual liability of the stockholders would do much towards securing the bill-holders, were it not that there are innumerable ways by which this responsibility would be liable to be avoided, by the nominal or actual transfer of the bank stock to minors and men of straw, by which the actual security of the bill-holder would be rendered merely nominal.

The giving *bona fide* security to the public for the benefit of the bill-holder, is certainly better security than the limited responsibility of incorporated stockholders.

I have said nothing of the General Banking law not providing security for depositors or other creditors ; for, by a legal fiction, incorporated companies are considered artificial bodies. And although strictly speaking, banking associations are not incorporated companies ; yet, they are capable of suing and being sued, and of maintaining perpetual succession, and, consequently, under the same respon-

sibilities as other bodies, firms or houses. Hence, depositors, and other creditors, have the same means of investiga-
ting the solvency and liabilities of the banks, before making
the deposite or entering into any contract with them, as
they would have of learning the responsibility of any private individual with whom they may deal. The case,
however, is materially different with the bill-holder. He
receives the bank note as money; and from the very nature bills are designed to perform, the rapidity with which
they are required to pass from hand to hand in the ordinary
transaction of business, precludes the receiver from the
possibility of enquiring into the responsibility of the drawers. Besides this, the great number of banks in the United
States, being not less than nine hundred banks and branches, and the great number of unauthorised banking houses,
precludes even men of the most extensive business from a
knowledge of the character of the bills they occasionally
receive.

If the legislature have a right to pass laws for the punishment of crimes, how much more commendable the passage of laws to prevent crimes, by removing the temptation to crime.

The coining or circulating base coin, and forging or passing counterfeit bank notes, is capitally punished in some
countries, and severely punished in all christian or commercial countries. If the committal of this crime is so severely
punished by law throughout christendom, ought not legislatures to remove the temptation to the commital of the
crime by such salutary laws as they have it in their power
to pass? The cause of humanity is much better promoted
by the prevention than by the punishment of crime.

The New York General Banking law commences by authorising the Comptroller of the State " to cause to be

engraved and printed, *in the best manner, to guard against counterfeiting,* such quantity of circulating notes, in the similitude of bank notes, in blank," &c.

The legislature of the state of New York have very wisely considered the preventing the crime of counterfeiting as one of so much importance as to place it first in the provisions of the New York General Banking law, not only because it prevents the commital of a most flagrant crime, but because it protects the confiding public from the loss and injury occasioned by the passage of forged or counterfeit bank paper.

If, then, the legislature so zealously and wisely protect the public from the ruinous effects of counterfeit money, ought they not, with equal care, to protect them from a still more dangerous, because a more insidious, foe, that of the passage and circulation of uncurrent money? Notes wholly counterfeit, that is, notes no part of which will be paid, are not defended by any body, because there is none who will receive them in change, knowing them to be wholly inconvertible ; yet, notes partly counterfeit and partly genuine, have their defenders and receivers in trade, that is, in exchange for articles at such an advanced price, that the exchanger ultimately receives but a small part of the nominal amount of his bills. So far as the prosperity of the individuals or of the public are concerned, notes uncurrent, as they are politely termed, are as effectually counterfeits in such part as they are uncurrent, as the notes that are wholly uncurrent, whether the notes of broken banks, notes of fictitious banks, or counterfeit notes of solvent banks.

If a crime against a statute law, such as that of passing counterfeit bank notes, varies in its magnitude and turpitude, the evil is in proportion to the injury done to society. And he who defrauds his fellow man of one dollar is not as culpable, so far as the protection of the public from loss and injury in their property is concerned, as him who defrauds thousands of persons of hundreds of dollars. The moral guilt, perhaps, of the offender may be measured by the moral punishment that the laws of God and man award to the crime; yet, the duty of the legislature, as we have seen, is as necessary to prevent crime, by removing the temptation to the commital of it, as to punish criminals after the crime has been committed with a view of deterring others from the commital of similar offences.

Hence, we infer, that he who passes only a few bills of a bank that he knows has failed, or a few notes of a fictitious bank, or a few notes that are counterfeit, knowing them to be such, upon innocent persons who believe them to be current money, is only culpable to the amount of injury he does society, although the crime may involve him in a punishment for life. And we maintain, that he who utters promises-to-pay as money, and circulates them among unsuspecting persons as convertible current money, knowing them to be at the time inconvertible, or that, from their funds or business they are likely soon to become inconvertible, or that they are convertible at five or ten per cent. below par, is worse than him who passes wholly uncurrent money, because he adds his public character to the currency of the note to make it pass, while he who passes wholly uncurrent money, knowing it to be such, carefully avoids being known, and the receiver takes it upon his own responsibility ; while he who passes notes to the amount of $100, only ten per cent. counterfeited, and ninety per cent. genuine, puts in circulation ten dollars of counterfeit money, that is, of money that is not what it purports to be, that is, ten dollars that is not worth more than blank paper, and that produces the same injury and loss to the receiver, as if he had passed him ten ten dollar notes, one of which was counterfeit. The evil is worse on another account. The country people cannot separate the counterfeit part of the money, notes or bills, from the genuine part; and hence the broker, or exchanger, must have his profit on the business of exchanging. And this, together with the trouble and expense of sending or taking it to a broker or exchanger, is all to be added to the loss of the innocent receiver, so that he must loose perhaps fifteen dollars instead of ten dollars on the one hundred received. But this species of counterfeiting extends the evil still farther. The man who has received the hundred dollars, with only ten per cent. counterfeited, that is, ten per cent. in promises-to-pay above the actual pay ever to he received, feels that this has cost him honestly and fairly $100, and that he ought not to loose ten per cent. discount, as it is politely called, so he silently passes one bill here, and another bill there, upon the unsuspecting and unwary for their full value; or if he does not get really the value himself, as he not unfrequently buys what he does not want for part of the value of the bill to get it changed into more current money, he thus extends the loss and divides it perhaps among ten persons, who are all interested in passing the uncurrent notes at par, and consequently their characters are added to the reputation of the bills to impose upon many more; and hence the greatest of all the evils, (even far greater than the loss of the ten or fifteen dollars that must ultimately be sustained by somebody, before the $100 of uncurrent notes can be made to pass current as specie,) is its immoral effects upon society. The great evil is, the loss of moral principle—the overturning that moral character, that correct and honorable feeling, that gives virtue to human nature, stability to society, and strength to a nation. The man who would not steal ten dollars from his confiding neighbor, and who respects his neighbors property as he does his own, thus, by degrees, becomes familiarized to crime. His conscience may at first have asked him whether it was strictly honest for him to pass an uncurrent note upon a traveller for its full value, who never could receive but nine dollars for the ten, and he must have felt that he would much rather the money would pass current with the traveller, as though the passage of it from him as current money, would relieve himself from the guilt or crime of passing it. But the evil may be increased instead of being lessened by its repeated passage ; for, as many as pass the notes at par, knowing them to be uncurrent, become involved in a moral crime— a crime against the laws of God, only, to be sure, but one that destroys that firm moral bulwark of all virtuous and moral peoples. They may continue to pass uncurrent money until they will boast of having passed it, knowing it to be uncurrent upon the unwary. Alas! " when all shame is lost all virtue is lost."

CHAPTER XLIV.

ON ANNUAL LEGISLATION UPON FORMS OF GOVERNMENT, OR UPON CURRENCY.

Annual legislation upon forms of government compared with annual legislation upon currency.

What would be the situation of the United States, or in short of any other country, were they to legislate annually upon their forms of government ?

Whatever be the forms of government adopted by any country, whether republican or monarchical, the frequent discussion of their elementary principles has been sedulously avoided. And when discussed upon occasions of indispensable necessity, it should be entered upon with reserve, caution, prudence and judgement, not rashly, passionately or unadvisedly. The venerable founders of our form of government carefully provided, by our present constitution, that it should not be altered or amended, until such alterations and amendments had been discussed in Congress, and afterwards considered and acted upon by the people, and carefully reviewed and debated by Congress again, before it becomes part of the constitution of these United States. The constitution is thus preserved from the influence of great party political excitements and dangerous hasty changes ; our diplomacy with foreign countries is thus preserved respectable and uniform in its character, commanding the respect of other nations, and the esteem of our own citizens.

The same rule is applicable to currency, so far as permanence and stability in both are required, and so far as the frequent discussions of the subject produces useless and dangerous excitements.

Frequent legislation upon the subject of currency is liable to render it the instrument of party success or party policy, and thereby as fluctuating as is the ebbings and flowings of party excitements. This renders it unfit for a measure of all values.

A sound currency is as indispensably necessary to the permanent prosperity of a country, as a sound government is to its peace and happiness.

Governor Throop, in his message to the legislature of the state of New York, in 1832, says : " Here national prosperity is the prosperity of every individual. Not a cent is contributed by way of tax—not a dollar is expended from the public coffers, which is not assented to by the people, and employed to enlarge their means of enjoyment." In a country thus free and independent in their politics, is it not very unfortunate that their currency forms an exception—that the frequent discussions upon the subject keeps it constantly fluctuating and unstable? While the chartered companies tax the public in sums more than equal to all the annual expenses of the government for the use of their credit to circulate as money, we have taxation without representation. But this system will not always continue. The spirit of enquiry is abroad, and people begin to ask why paper money is so uncurrent, and why they are incompetent to elect directors of the currency as well as directors of their political machinery? When the answer is heard, it will be, we are able and will elect the directors of our banks.

THE END.